Children's London

GW00370514

Evening Standard

Children's London

Lydia Conway

ESB

To Jake and Benja without whom this book would not have been possible, and to Sasha and Tara with whom it nearly wasn't

First published in Great Britain in 1996 by
EVENING STANDARD BOOKS
Northcliffe House, 2 Derry Street, London W8 5EE

ISBN 1 900625 00 8

Text copyright © Lydia Conway 1996
Illustration copyright © Ross Collins 1996
Design copyright © Evening Standard 1996

The moral right of the author has been asserted.

Publishing Manager Joanne Bowlby
Editorial Manager Charlotte Coleman-Smith
Production Manager Roger Hall
With thanks to Sally Blackmore

Designed by Nick Cave

All rights reserved. No part of this publication may be reproduced, stored in
a retrieval system, or transmitted, in any form or by any means, electronic,
mechanical, photocopying, recording or otherwise, without the prior permission
of the copyright holder.

A CIP catalogue record for this book is available from the British Library

Printed and bound in Great Britain by BPC Hazell Books Ltd, Aylesbury, Bucks.

This book may be ordered by post direct from the publisher,
but please try your bookshop first.

Corporate editions and personal subscriptions of any of the Evening
Standard Guides are available. Call us for details. Tel 0171 938 6774

Also published in the series:
The Good Food Shop Guide (ESB)
Best Of... London (ESB)
London Restaurant Guide (Pavilion Books)
London Wine Guide (Pavilion Books)
London Pub Guide (Pavilion Books)

Contents

Introduction

If you think children and London mix like oil and water, you might be in for a surprise. There are, in fact, few better playgrounds than the capital. In recent years, London has become a much more child-friendly city; museums and art galleries are no longer places in which you have to whisper or behave as if you are at Great Aunt Ethel's funeral; there are buttons to push, trails to follow, prizes to win, costumes to wear, old-fashioned games and workshops galore.

What stops most people from enjoying London with children is not knowing what to expect before they arrive. For this reason, I have emphasised things that will be specifically relevant to children. For example, is there anywhere to picnic? How long are the queues? How can I avoid hidden expenses? What do we do if it rains?

I visited most of the places suitable for a family outing accompanied by twin babies, a toddler, and a selection of older children (see opposite). Each entry offers enough information to take into account the age, interests and physical abilities of the children when you plan your trip. Going on a five-mile nature trial with a baby in a pushchair or a toddler might be rather taxing as would taking a diminutive five-year-old to a theme park where there might be height restrictions. On the other hand, older children might enjoy places that relate to a school project – and so on.

Attention span can also vary with age, so I have tried to give an indication of how long to spend at each venue. The weather can, of course, ruin a day out – entertainments that are particularly suitable for rainy days are clearly indicated and, where possible, there are suggestions on what to do and where to go if you are caught out in the rain.

Children's London is a very emotive subject – there will be things left out from choice, others from ignorance. There are always new venues opening and old ones being revamped, so if you have any suggestions based on your experiences – pleasant or unpleasant – please do write in about them.

LYDIA CONWAY

AUTHOR'S ACKNOWLEDGMENTS

The real 'authors' of this book have been all the children listed below, whose fads and foibles, views and voices can be heard throughout the book. The babies have been breast-fed on benches and put to sleep in dark corners; the toddlers have thrown tantrums up towers, fallen in ponds and climbed on exhibits; the older children have been variously loud, stubborn, quiet, cynical, enchanted, bemused and, above all, honest, as only children know how!

Alice (nine); Benja (three); Felix (five); Jake (five); James (eight); Jared (six); Kitty (six); Lucy (eleven); Oscar (three); Sally (ten); the twins, Tara and Sasha (six months) and Tom (eight).

KEYS

😊 **Suitable for under–fives**

F **Free admission**

☼ **Suitable for fine weather**

Suitable for rainy days

Suitable both for fine and rainy days

◔ **Suitable for less than two hours**

◑ **Suitable for half a day**

● **Suitable for a whole day**

⇌ **Railway**

⊖ **London Underground**

Eros Awards

Getting Around

Children often enjoy the novelty of using different forms of public transport, so try to travel by one means of transport and return by another. Whether you go by bus, tube, train, Docklands Light Railway, car or taxi, this chapter deals with all aspects of transport in London. For information on bus, underground or Docklands Light Railway services in Greater London, call London Travel 24-hour Information on 0171 222 1234. For information on trains throughout the South-East region, call 0171 928 5100.

Travelcard: a daily, weekly or monthly Travelcard allows unlimited travel in Greater London on the rail network, buses, Underground, and the Docklands Light Railway. You can then travel on any combination of tube, train, bus and DLR within your selected zone/s as many times as you wish, for as long as your ticket is valid (weekdays only after 9.30am; not night buses).

Buses: under-14s travel at a reduced flat fare (until 10pm). Under-5s travel free (up to two under-5s per fare-paying adult). It is advisable to have the correct fare in change.

London Underground: tube and bus fares are based on a five-zone system and the most economical way of getting around is to buy a Travelcard (see above). Under-14s travel at a reduced-rate fare (15 and 16 year-olds need to carry a Child Rate Photocard available free from all tube stations and London Post Offices). Under-5s travel free. If you are with young children try to avoid rush hour (Monday–Friday 7–10am and 5–7pm). *Access to the Underground* is a booklet for disabled people which details lifts and ramps at each station and is useful for buggy users (£1 at any Travel Information Centre or from London Regional Transport, Unit for Disabled Passengers, 55 Broadway, SW1H OBD). Most tube stations do not have public toilets. For recorded information, telephone 0171 222 1200.

Docklands Light Railway: the DLR runs on raised tracks from Tower Gateway (near Tower Hill) and Bank station to the Isle of Dogs. This is a good way to see the Docklands but service is limited in the evenings and at weekends.

Railways of London and the South East: Rail Travel Enquiries 24hr information on 0171 928 5100 or British Travel Centre, 0171 730 3488 for information on fares, maps, timetables, etc. Toilets and mother-and-baby rooms can be found at: Euston, King's Cross, Liverpool Street, Paddington, St Pancras, Victoria and Waterloo.

Taxis: black cab drivers know central London very well. They can be booked by phone (0171 286 0286, 0171 253 5000 or 0171 272 0272) or hailed in the street when the yellow Taxi sign is lit. Tipping is not obligatory but a 10-15 per cent tip is common. When hailing a taxi in the street black cabs are not obliged to accept a hiring of over six miles, but if they do and the journey is wholly within the London area the fare payable is shown on the meter. If a driver accepts a hiring to a destination outside the London area of over 6 miles the fare becomes negotiable (with the exception of journeys to Heathrow Airport that are less than 20 miles). Minicabs are unlicensed, often do not know even the local area well, do not have to be good drivers and cannot be hailed in the street (either phone for one or go in person to the cab office). However, they usually work out cheaper than black cabs especially for longer journeys. Negotiate a fare when you phone. There is usually a £3 minimum charge. There are several companies in London which offer women drivers for women and children (see local phone directory). The Six 2 16 Car Club, 32a Goldney Road, W9 (0171 286 6216). Open 24 hours daily. London's first taxi service exclusively for children with fully trained, predominantly female drivers. Prices are comparable to mini-cabs.

Car: on-street parking in central London can be expensive and difficult. Gone are the days when traffic wardens didn't work in the rain (their excuse used to be that their pens didn't write). Illegally parked cars may also be clamped or removed. Restrictions are shown by yellow lines on the road and kerb and an accompanying yellow plate on lamp posts. Parking restrictions are usually between 8.30am and 6.30pm Monday–Friday and 8.30am-1.30pm on Saturday; meters cost anything from £2 per hour and the stay is often limited to two hours (check details on individual meters). Watch out for Parking Permit Holders Only signs – wardens are very strict about illegally parked non-permit holders. Charges for off-street parking vary enormously from the expensive to the exorbitant. For a free map of National Car Parks in London send a 35p stamped addressed envelope to Map Offer, NCP Ltd, 21 Bryanston Street, W1 (0171 499 7050; Marble

Arch). Listed below are a selection of central London 24-hour car parks:

Arlington Street, W1 (0171 499 3312); £9.30 for three hours.
Audley Square, W1 (0171 499 3265); £9 for three hours.
Brewer Street, W1 (0171 734 9497); £5.50 for two hours.
Park Lane, W1 (0171 262 1814); £3 for two hours.
Young Street, W8 (0171 937 7420); £3.60 for two hours.

Lost Property:
property left on trains is held for one week at the station at which it was handed in before being forwarded to Central Lost Property, Marylebone Station, Marylebone Road, NW1 (0171 387 9400). Southern Region lost property is held at local railway stations only.

Charing Cross Station (0171 922 6061)
Euston Station (0171 922 6477)
King's Cross (0171 922 90181)
Liverpool Street Station (0171 922 9189)
Paddington Station (0171 922 6773)
St Pancras Station (0171 922 6478)
Victoria Station (0171 922 6216)
Waterloo Station (0171 922 6135)

London Transport: London Transport Lost Property, 200 Baker Street W1 (Baker Street tube). Open Monday–Friday 9.30am–5.30pm. Go in person or write with as much detail about the items as possible.

Taxis: If you leave anything in a black cab phone the Metropolitan Police Lost Property Office (0171 833 0996) Monday–Friday 9am–4pm.

Left Luggage:
you can leave your luggage at the following places while you see the sights (costs vary from £1–£2.40 per item per day):

Heathrow Airport (0181 759 4321); daily 6.45am–10pm.
Euston Station (0171 928 6482); 24 hours.
Paddington Station (0171 922 6793); daily 7am–midnight.
Victoria Station (0171 928 6216); daily 7.15am–10.15pm.
Waterloo Station (0171 928 6135); Monday–Saturday 6.15am–11pm.

From Trooping the Colour to burning the Guy, from teddy bear, dolls' house and model train fairs to Christmas lights and Santa's grotto, there is something for children every week of the year. Whether you want to join a pancake race, watch an Easter parade, attend a clown service, or sing carols in Trafalgar Square, this quick-reference section will guide you in the right direction.

London by Season

DAILY CEREMONIES

Changing of the Guard

Hours
Daily,
April–August,
11.30am (Bucking-
ham Palace);
Mon–Sat, 11am or
Sun, 10am (Horse
Guards Parade);
Mon–Sat, 10.30am
(Windsor Castle)

Travel
✪ Hyde Park
Corner (Bucking-
ham Palace);
✪ St James' Park
(Horse Guards
Parade);
≥ Windsor
(Windsor Castle)

Buckingham Palace, SW1 (recorded information 0839 123411)

Every child reading A.A. Milne should see this event at least once, if not with Alice. If you can't face the crowds outside Buckingham Palace, other good vantage points can be found outside St James's Palace, at Wellington Barracks in Birdcage Walk, or by walking behind the Old Guard to Buckingham Palace. The ceremony lasts half an hour and takes place inside the Palace railings. The procession, usually accompa-nied by a military band, leaves Wellington Barracks at 11.27am and marches to the Palace via Birdcage Walk. It also takes place at **Horse Guards Parade**, Whitehall, SW1 and **Windsor Castle**, Windsor, Berks. May be cancelled in rain.

Ceremony of the Keys

Hours
Daily, 9.40pm
Travel
✪ Tower Hill

Tower of London, Tower Hill, EC3 (0171 709 0765)

The Chief Warder of the Yeomen Warders of the Tower, with an escort of the Brigade of Guards, locks the West Gates, the Middle Tower and Byward Tower in one of the oldest contin-uous military ceremonies in the world. For free tickets write, with a stamped addressed envelope, to The Resident Gover-nor, Queen's House, HM The Tower of London, EC3N 4AB. State number of people (not more than seven) and dates.

JANUARY

Chinese New Year Festival

Hours
11am–6.30pm
(Jan or Feb)
Travel
✪ Leicester
Square

The area of Soho around Newport Place and Gerrard and Lisle Streets comes to life with firecrackers, papier-maché dragons and colourful paper lanterns adorning windows and balconies. Along with the famous lion dances in the streets there is usually a stage in Leicester Square on which per-formers depict scenes from Chinese history to passers-by.

International Boat Show

Earl's Court Exhibition Centre, Warwick Road, SW5 (0171 385 1200)

The largest sailing and power boat show in Europe with a colourful Central Harbour scene where you can see boats of all shapes and sizes and equipment from complex radar to simple yachting shoes.

Hours
One week in early Jan

Travel
Earl's Court ⊖

Lord Mayor of Westminster's New Year's Day Parade

A massive parade with over 5,000 performers – marching bands, cheerleaders, colourful floats, clowns, horse-drawn carriages and veteran vehicles. Starts at noon from Parliament Square, then proceeds along Whitehall to Trafalgar Square, then Lower Regent Street to Piccadilly and ends at Berkeley Square (best views are from Whitehall or Piccadilly).

Hours
Noon, Jan 1

Travel
Westminster, Embankment or Green Park ⊖

Toy and Train Collectors' Fair

Alexandra Palace, Alexandra Park, N22 (0181 365 2121)

Large sale of collectors' toys and model trains. A fair is also held in June.

Hours
Mid–late Jan

Travel
Wood Green ⊖ then Bus W3

FEBRUARY

Clowns' Service 😊 ◑ 🇫

Holy Trinity Church, Dalston, E8

A popular church service in memory of Grimaldi, attended by clowns in full costume and make-up. Arrive early.

Hours
First Sun in Feb

Travel
Dalston Kingsland ⇌

Great Spitalfields Pancake Day Race 😊 🇫 ☼

Old Spitalfields Market, Brushfield Street, E1 (Alternative Arts 0171 287 0907)

Watch the teams run with their frying pans, tossing pancakes, or join in the bizarre ritual (phone the week before).

Hours
Shrove Tuesday, 12.30pm

Travel
Liverpool Street ⊖⇌

Holiday on Ice

Prices
From £7.50–£16
(children and OAPs
half price)

Travel
≥ Wembley Park
⊖ ≥ Wembley
Central
Bus N18

Wembley Arena, Wembley, Middx (0181 900 1234)

This annual ice-skating family extravaganza has been touring for half a century and is, according to the Guinness Book of Records, the world's most costly entertainment to stage. Ring for times.

Queen's Accession Gun Salutes

Hours
Feb 6, April 21,
June 2; noon
(Hyde Park), 1pm
(Tower of London)

Travel
⊖ Green Park (for
Hyde Park) or
Tower Hill (for
Tower of London)

The anniversary of the Queen's accession is heralded by a 41-gun salute in Hyde Park, and a 62-gun salute at the Tower of London. Also on April 21 (the Queen's birthday) and June 2 (Coronation Day). See also page 112.

Road Racing and Superbike Show

Hours
Jan 30–Feb 2

Travel
⊖ Wood Green or
≥ Alexandra
Palace

Alexandra Palace, Muswell Hill, N22 (0181 365 2121)

Display of racing motorbikes. Adults £7, children £3.

MARCH

Daily Mail Ideal Home Exhibition

Hours
Daily, mid- to late
March for three
weeks

Prices
Adults £9,
children £5
(under-5s free)

Travel
⊖ Earl's Court

Earl's Court Exhibition Centre, Warwick Road, SW5 (0171 385 1200; box office 0895 677677)

Europe's greatest consumer show. Kids love browsing around the show houses while adults can hunt about for the latest labour-saving gadgets and gizmos.

Head of the River Race

Hours
March 22 '97 at
3.45pm

Travel
⊖ Putney Bridge

(0181 940 2219)

This takes place on the last Saturday in March and runs from Mortlake to Putney. The Oxford and Cambridge boat race (see below) may be more famous but for children this race is more colourful and easier to see. The procession of eight-man boats, which set off 10 seconds apart, takes over an hour and it's fun guessing which boat has won (the race is timed so the results aren't known until the end).

Ideal Electronic Games Show

Earl's Court Exhibition Centre, Warwick Road, SW5 (0171 385 1200)

Hands-on displays of the latest electronic games.

Hours
Late March

Travel
Earl's Court ⊖

Oranges and Lemons Service

St Clement Danes, Strand, WC2 (0171 242 8282)

This is the church of the Royal Air Force and it is full of RAF symbols, memorials and monuments. The bells are rung to the tune of Oranges and Lemons at 9am, noon, 3pm and 6pm daily. There is an annual Oranges and Lemons Service for children when each child is given an orange and a lemon.

Hours
Daily 8am-5pm
(closed Dec 25-27). Service Sun at 11am

Travel ⊖
Temple

Oxford v Cambridge Boat Race

(0171 379 3234 for further information)

If you actually want to see the race it is far better watched on tv, but you can't beat the carnival atmosphere as thousands of people turn out to catch a glimpse of the two boats battling their way along the Thames between Putney Bridge and Mortlake. The best vantage points are Putney Bridge, Bishop's Park, Dukes Meadows and Chiswick Bridge. Go early for a good view.

Hours
Usually Sat before
Easter or Easter

Travel
Putney Bridge ⊖
or Mortlake ⇌

EASTER

Easter Kite Festival

(0181 808 1280 for details)

Single line, box, stunt and sport kites, kite ballet and 'rokkuku' (Japanese-style kite flying). If you forget your own kite you can buy one for as little as 80p.

Hours
10am-dusk
Travel
Blackheath ⇌

Easter Parade ☺ ☼ ◑

Battersea Park, SW11

A colourful carnival with a fairground, various stalls and stage acts such as stunt riders, a free-fall parachute team and

Hours
Easter Sunday,
10am-9pm,
Parade starts at
3pm

Prices
Adults £3, children
£1.50, under 10s
free

Travel
⇌ Battersea Park

motorcycle display teams. A special children's village has a bouncy castle, slides, clowns and puppets (and baby-changing facilities). There is also an arts-and-crafts marquee.

APRIL

Hours
Easter Monday
from 9.45am

Travel
⊖ Regent's Park

London Harness Horse Parade ☺ ⬛ ☼ ◖

Regent's Park, NW1

Horses and carts, drays and brewers' vans on parade. Judging is followed by a procession twice round the inner circle.

Hours
9am onwards

Travel
⇌ Blackheath for
the start
⊖ Westminster
for the finish

London Marathon ☺ ⬛ ☼ ◖

(0171 620 4117)

This 26-mile race attracts over 25,000 runners. It starts at Blackheath (just outside Greenwich Park gates), goes via the Isle of Dogs, Victoria Embankment and St James's Park and finishes on Westminster Bridge. Kids love cheering along, and it's fun for the tiny tots to see the fancy-dress brigade while older kids can celebrity-spot. The best place to watch is at the start or finish but anywhere along the route is fun.

Hours
Mid-April over
5 days
Travel
⊖⇌ Victoria

Model Railway Exhibition

Royal Horticultural Society Halls, 80 Vincent Square, SW1
(0171 834 4333)

International collection of model railways including 20 working layouts.

MAY

Hours
May 25–27

Travel
⊖⇌ Waterloo

The Big Workshop ☺ ⬛ ◖

Royal Festival Hall, South Bank Centre, SE1 (0171 960 4242)

Ever wanted to star in a West End musical, shake and shimmy street-style or tap till you zap? Top choreographers will lead dance classes for up to 200 people.

Chelsea Flower Show

Chelsea Royal Hospital, Royal Hospital Road, SW3
(Bookings 0171 344 4343; 24hr info 0171 828 1744)

Open to the public for two days in late May. Very crowded.
Children invariably love the garden gnomes! Under-5s are
not admitted.

Hours
Late May

Travel
Sloane Square ⊖

FA Cup Final

Wembley Stadium, Wembley, Middx (0181 900 1234)

The showpiece event of the England football season. The
match is usually held in early May. Ring for ticket prices.

Hours
Early May

Travel
Wembley Park or
Wembley Central ⊖

Greenwich Festival

(0181 305 1818)

This popular arts festival has various free events for kids and
kicks off with an opening-night fireworks display (10.30pm).

Hours
Late May

Travel
Greenwich ⇌
or Island Gardens
DLR then foot
tunnel

London Dolls' House Festival

Kensington Town Hall, Hornton Street, W8
(0171 937 5464 or 0171 361 2827)

Display of dolls' houses and stalls selling kits, etc. Not suitable for very young children.

Hours
Early May

Travel
High Street
Kensington ⊖

Oak Apple Day ▣

Royal Hospital, Chelsea, SW1

Commemorates King Charles II's escape from Oliver
Cromwell's Parliamentary forces in 1651 when Charles hid in
a hollow oak. Today the Chelsea Pensioners decorate his
statue at the Chelsea Hospital with oak leaves and branches.

Hours
Thurs after May 26

Travel
Sloane Square ⊖

London To Brighton Historic Commercial Vehicles Run (Scania) ▣

(Crystal Palace Park Events Line 0181 778 9496)

Annual drive from Crystal Palace Park to Brighton.

Travel
Crystal Palace ⇌

19

JUNE

Beating Retreat

Hours
June 5 & 6 at
9.30pm
Prices
£5, £8, £10
Travel
➔⇌ Charing
Cross

Horse Guards Parade, SW1 (0171 839 3185)

A military display of marching and drilling bands, with trumpeters, massed bands, pipes and drums. The 'retreat' or setting of the sun is beaten on drums by soldiers on foot and horseback in a colourful ceremony popular with older children. Floodlit performances. Ring the number listed above for tickets, which become available from March 1.

Biggin Hill International Air Fair

Hours
June 15 & 16 from
8am-6pm
Prices
Adults £10, under-
15s £4 (car with
up to six occu-
pants £15);
advance tickets at
£7 and £3
Travel
⇌ Biggin Hill

Biggin Hill Airfield, Biggin Hill, Kent (01959 540959)

An annual aviation spectacle is held on the famous RAF airfield where squadrons of Spitfires and Hurricanes defended London in the Second World War. International flying displays, ground events, a funfair and exhibition stands. Alternatively, park as near the airfield as possible and picnic on the surrounding grassy areas while watching the planes for free.

Blackheath Summer Kite Festival

Hours
Sunday
10am-dusk
Travel
⇌ Blackheath

Blackheath, SE3 (0181 808 1280 for details)

Kite-trading stalls, kite trains, fighting kites, stunt kites and parachuting teddy bears.

Derby Day

Hours
June 8; Derby
starts at 3.45pm
Travel
⇌ Epsom

Epsom Racecourse, Epsom, Surrey (tickets available from January on 013727 26311)

Besides watching the famous Epsom Derby, your children can also enjoy the funfair on Epsom Downs.

Garter Ceremony ■

Hours
Monday pm of
Ascot week
Travel
⇌ Windsor

St George's Chapel, Windsor

Service attended by the Queen, preceded by a colourful procession of Household Cavalry and Yeomen of the Guard. The ceremony dates from the 14th century and takes place on the Monday afternoon of Ascot week (the third week in June).

Henley Royal Regatta ▣ ☼ ◖

(01491 572153)

Take a picnic, arrive early and find a good viewpoint along the towpath to watch the world's oldest rowing regatta. All except the last third of a mile of the course is open to the public and if the wind is right you can hear the commentary.

Hours
Wed–Sat,
late June or
early July

Travel
Henley ⇌

Kenwood Lakeside Concerts ☼

Kenwood House, Hampstead Lane, NW3 (0171 413 1443; box office 0171 344 4444)

Older children or those with an interest in music will love these outdoor concerts of popular classics in the delightful lake-side setting among the trees. Concerts end with a lovely fireworks display. Take a picnic and a rug to keep warm, and pray for fine weather. Call the box office or buy tickets two hours before the concert begins.

Prices
£7 (grass), £10 (deckchair), concs

Travel
Archway,
Hampstead or
Highgate ⊖
Bus 210, 271

Practical Classics Bromley Pageant of Motoring ☺ ☼ ●

Norman Park, Hayes Lane, Bromley, Kent (bookings 0181 658 3531)

The biggest one-day car show in the world has over 3,500 exhibits and attracts 35,000 visitors. Includes hot-air balloons, arena events, children's fun fair and rock 'n' roll band.

Hours
June 30

Prices
Adults £5, children £2 (less if booked in advance)

Travel
Hayes ⇌

Trooping the Colour ▣ ☼ ◖

The route goes from Buckingham Palace, along the Mall to Horseguards Parade, Whitehall, and back again in honour of the Queen's official birthday. The route to Horseguards Parade is very crowded but there is usually space on the Mall (Green Park side). At about 1pm the Queen watches a Royal Air Force jet display from her balcony. For tickets to the event or to the full-scale dress rehearsals (these are on the two preceding Saturdays) apply, enclosing a stamped

Hours
11am, Sat nearest
June 11

Travel
Hyde Park
Corner ⊖

addressed envelope, to the Brigade Major, Household Division, Horseguards, Whitehall, SW1 (state if you also wish your application to be included in the ballot for the dress rehearsal). Only two tickets per application.

Middlesex Show

Hours
June 22 & 23
8.30am–6pm

Prices
Sat, adults £5, children £2.50, under-5s free; Sun, adults £6, children £3

Travel
⊖ Uxbridge

Uxbridge Showground, Uxbridge

This annual two-day country show has attractions such as falconry displays, Morris dancing, showjumping, dog shows, farmyard animals, horticulture and English country crafts.

JULY

Ballroom Blitz

Hours
July 28-Aug 11

Travel
⊖⇌ Waterloo

Royal Festival Hall, South Bank Centre, SE1 (Box office: 0171 928 8800)

Annual festival of dance (performances, seminars and workshops), from reggae to Indian tea dancing, tango, tap, ballroom and ballet (also suitable for under-5s).

Doggett's Coat and Badge Race 🅵

Hours
Late July

Travel
⇌ London
Bridge

River Thames (0171 626 3531)

This sculling race for six Thames watermen originated in 1715. The race goes from London Bridge to Cadogan Pier, Chelsea. Best view is from London Bridge.

The Great Outdoors 🅵

Travel
⊖⇌ Waterloo

South Bank Centre, SE1 (0171 928 8800)

Six weekends of free performances for all the family on the walkways and South Bank Centre riverside. Ring for details.

Royal Tournament

Earl's Court Exhibition Centre, Warwick Road, SW5 (0171 385 1200; box office 0171 373 8141, from January)

This popular military spectacle includes mast manning, cutlass swinging, abseiling, paragliding, marching displays and very noisy massed brass bands. There are also re-enactments of history and forces competitions. The whole show lasts for two and a half hours.

Hours
Two weeks in mid-July
Prices
£9–£17 (concessions available)
Travel
Earl's Court ⊖

Streets of London Festival

(Brochure available from Zap Productions 01273 821588)

Drama, mime, juggling, clowning and dancing on the streets and in shopping centres throughout London.

Hours
July 12–Sept 15

AUGUST

British Teddy Bear Festival

Kensington Town Hall, Hornton Street, W8 (01273 697974)

Largest display of teddies in the UK with over 10,000 antique and new bears for sale.

Hours
Sun from noon–5pm
Prices
Adults £4, children £2
Travel
High Street Kensington ⊖

AUGUST BANK HOLIDAY
Notting Hill Carnival

Ladbroke Grove and Notting Hill, W11 (details on 0181 964 0544)

Europe's largest, and noisiest, street festival where steel bands, flamboyantly costumed dancers and pulsating lorries throb their way through Notting Hill. Dazzling colour and blaring music blend with the tantalising smells of Caribbean food to make an exciting day out for older children (Monday is *the* day but Sunday is best for kids). Anyone with small or even medium-sized children should avoid the main festival area and beat a hasty retreat to the relative safety of the Notting Hill Carnival Family Events. Events include face-painting, juggling, mural-painting, puppet- and mask-making at the Meanwhile Gardens, Great Western Road, W11.

Hours
Bank Holiday Sunday and Monday, all day
Travel
Westbourne Park ⊖
No car access

August Bank Holiday Funfairs

Travel

⊖ Wood Green
⊖ Covent Garden
⊖ Ealing Common
⊖ Hampstead or
⇌ Hampstead
Heath

Alexandra Park, Wood Green, N22.
Covent Garden Piazza, WC2.
Ealing Common, Gunnersbury Avenue, W5.
Hampstead Heath, NW3.

SEPTEMBER

Covent Garden Festival of Street Theatre

Hours
Early September
Travel
⊖ Covent Garden

Covent Garden Piazza, WC2

A week of aerial trapeze artists, stilt walkers, jugglers, escapologists, physical comedy and improvisation by performers from the UK and Europe.

Great River Race ▣

Hours
Early Sept,
10.30am
Travel
Start:
⊖⇌ Richmond
Finish:
DLR Island
Gardens

(0181 398 9057)

Nearly 200 craft with over 40 types of traditional boats including Chinese dragonboats, Hawaiian war canoes, Viking longboats, wherries, whalers, gigs and skiffs race from Richmond to Island Gardens, opposite Greenwich Pier. The start is just below Ham House, Richmond and the race finishes at Island Gardens opposite Greenwich Pier.

Horseman's Sunday ▣

Hours
Late Sept,
service at noon
Travel
⊖ Lancaster Gate or
⊖⇌ Paddington

St John's Church, Hyde Park Crescent, W2 (0171 262 3791)

Annual blessing of horses by the vicar of St John's Church followed by showjumping and other events in Kensington Gardens Paddock (western end of Kensington Gardens).

Spitalfields Show ▣

Hours
Mid-Sept
Travel
⊖⇌ Liverpool
Street

Old Spitalfields Market, Brushfield Street, E1 (entry forms and information on 0171 375 0441)

Entries in anything from herbs and flowers to preserves, with special sections for children's entries.

OCTOBER

Costermongers' Pearly Harvest Festival ▣

St-Martin-in-the-Fields, Trafalgar Square, WC2 (0171 930 0089)

Over a hundred Pearly Kings and Queens, all wearing clothes decorated in thousands of pearl buttons, gather for the harvest festival service.

Hours
Early Oct at 3pm

Travel
Leicester
Square ⊖
or Charing
Cross ⊖ ⇌

Horse of the Year Show

Wembley Arena, Wembley, Middx (0181 900 1234; tickets 0171 900 1919)

Annual equestrian event with top show-jumpers, dressage, shires, hunters and hacks. Ring for times and prices.

Hours
Four days in early Oct

Travel
Wembley Park or
Wembley Central ⊖
Bus N18

Punch and Judy Fellowship Festival ☺ ▣

Covent Garden Piazza, WC2

All-day festival of Punch and Judy shows.

Hours
First Sun in Oct,
10.30am–5.30pm

Travel
Covent Garden ⊖

NOVEMBER

Christmas Lights and Decorations ▣

In mid-November the Bond Street Christmas lights twinkle into action, switched on by a celebrity on the corner of Clifford Street and New Bond Street. The lights are often best in Regent's Street. Look out for the elaborate Christmas decorations in Oxford Street, Regent Street, Carnaby Street, Covent Garden market, Piccadilly and Burlington Arcade.

Travel
Bond Street
Piccadilly Circus
or Covent
Garden ⊖

Christmas Parade

(details on London Tourist Board Christmas Service 0839 123 418)

American-style parade with floats and marching bands through the shopping streets of the West End.

Hours
Sun in late Nov

Travel
Oxford Circus
Piccadilly Circus or
Bond Street ⊖

25

Guy Fawkes Night

Hours
November 5th

London Tourist Board Fireworks Service (0839 123 410, 49p per minute peak time, 39p cheap rate; call from mid-Oct).

Anniversary of the Gunpowder Plot when Guy Fawkes was arrested by Yeomen of the Guard on November 5, 1605 as one of the conspirators in the Gunpowder Plot to blow up King James I and his parliament. Look in your local paper for details of bonfires and fireworks.

London to Brighton Veteran Car Run ◼

Hours
First Sun in Nov
from 7.30am
Travel
⊖ Hyde Park
Corner or
Marble Arch

Hyde Park, Park Lane, W1

The popular annual run commemorates Emancipation Day when it became legal for 'horseless carriages' to go more than 4mph, and without being preceded by a man waving a red flag. Motorists celebrate by destroying their red flags before driving off in a collection of cars, all of which were built before 1905. Spectators can watch anywhere along the route (via Westminster Bridge and Croydon, on the A23). First cars are due at Brighton at 10.30am. Centenary year is in 1996.

Lord Mayor's Show ☺ ◼ ☾

Hours
Second Sat in Nov
Travel
⊖ ⇌ Victoria,
Blackfriars or
Waterloo

Mansion House to Royal Courts of Justice (0171 606 3030 or 0171 332 1455 for details)

The biggest ceremonial event in the City in which 5,000 participants and over 70 floats celebrate the beginning of the Lord Mayor's year in office. There is a state procession, military parade, a fair in Paternoster Square, a firework display from a barge on the Thames (best vantage points are Victoria Embankment, Blackfriars Bridge or Waterloo Bridge) and the Lord Mayor's 18th-century coach pulled by six shire horses.

Remembrance Sunday ◼ ☾

Hours
Second Sun in Nov
at 11am
Travel
⊖ Westminster

Cenotaph, Whitehall, SW1

Service to remember the dead of past wars, with a salute of guns. Poppy wreaths are laid on the Cenotaph by the Queen, the Prime Minister and other major dignitaries.

DECEMBER

For information on Christmas events around London ring the
London Tourist Board Christmas Service (0839 123 418).
For information on a selection of pantomimes and Christmas
shows ring the **School Holiday Service** (0839 123 404). Calls
cost 36p per minute cheap rate, 48p peak time.

Carol Service ▉

Westminster Abbey, Broad Sanctuary, SW1 (0171 222 5152/7110)

Carol services on December 26, 27 and 28.

Hours
Dec 26, 27 & 28

Travel
Westminster ⊖

Carol Singing ▉

Trafalgar Square, WC2

Every evening before Christmas from about December 14.

Hours
Dec 14-24,
4-10pm

Travel
Charing
Cross ⊖⇌

Christmas Funfair ☺

At Covent Garden Piazza, WC2.

Hours
11am-10.30pm

Travel
Covent Garden ⊖

Christmas Tree ▉

Trafalgar Square, WC2

A giant Norwegian spruce (an annual present from the
people of Oslo to thank Britain for liberating them from the
Nazis) is lit from 3–10pm each evening until January 6.
Carols are sung around the tree each evening until December
24 in aid of various charities.

Travel
Charing
Cross ⊖⇌

Ernest Read Concert for Children

Royal Festival Hall, SE1 (0171 928 8800)

The Ernest Read Symphony Orchestra presents a programme
of Christmas music, plus carols for choir and audience. Ring
for full details.

Travel
Waterloo ⊖⇌

Harry Goodman's Grotto 😊 ▣

Hours
Dec–early Jan
4.30–9pm
Travel
◉ Caledonian
Road

On the corner of Mackenzie Road and Roman Way, Islington, N7

Harry Goodman has transformed his large garden shed into a grotto stuffed full of moving models, toys, fake snow, elves, an enormous illuminated manger scene, Santas, gnomes and thousands of fairy lights (Harry's electricity bill comes to over £400 for the winter quarter). Charming, eccentric and very Christmas-sy.

Kew Gardens 😊

Travel
◉ Kew
Gardens

Kew Green, Richmond, Surrey (0181 940 1171)

Call the listed number for details of Christmas events centring around the Christmas Grotto.

London Toy and Model Museum 😊

Hours
Mon–Sat,
10am–5.30pm
Prices
Adults £3.50,
children £2, family
ticket £9
Travel
◉⇌Paddington or
◉ Queensway

21–23 Craven Hill, W2 (0171 262 9450)

Christmas events, toy-making with the elves, a Christmas treasure hunt, carol singing and Santa's grotto (all included in the ticket price).

London Zoo

Hours
Daily, (closed Dec
25) 10am–5pm
Prices
Adults £7.50, chil-
dren (4-14) £5.50,
under-4s free,
concs
Travel
◉Baker Street, or
Camden Town
then **Bus 274**

Regent's Park, NW1 (0171 722 3333)

Living Nativity Play for which children can volunteer to play leading roles, starring with a donkey, sheep and camels in the Christmas story. Santa's grotto and a visit from a real reindeer are all included in the usual admission price.

Syon Park Children's Day 😊 ◖

Hours
Daily (closed Dec
25 & Dec 26)
10am–6pm
Prices
Adults £2.50,
children £2
Travel
⇌ Syon Lane

Syon Park, Brentford, Middx (0181 560 0881)

Father Christmas arrives on a horse-drawn dray. Face painting, miniature railway rides, a magician, free balloons and needlecraft demonstrations.

The following days out have been designed to group attractions together into small areas easily covered by foot. Some are precise step-by-step guides that could be completed in a day and are especially suited to families with small children or babies. Others are more flexible, offering several alternatives along the way, and can be followed fully or partly depending on time, specific interests and stamina. Others could not possibly be undertaken in a single day but offer a starting point with different suggestions so that you can plan a route to suit your family. There are also alternative places of interest for younger or older children as well as suggestions for where to rest, eat, what to do if it rains and things to look out for on the way.

Alexandra Palace to Finsbury Park

Alexandra Palace to Finsbury Park

Running alongside the old railway line between the palace and the park is a four-mile country nature trail with leafy detours through woods (for free Parkland Walk map ring 0181 889 6737 or 0181 348 6005).

At both ends of the walk there are Bank Holiday **funfairs**, **boating lakes** and rainy-day alternatives (ice-skating at Alexandra Palace and **ten-pin bowling** at Finsbury Park). **Alexandra Palace** is best suited to young children as there is a pitch-and-putt golf course, a children's playground, an animal area and summer holiday children's events.

Finsbury Park, despite its noisy and congested roads and litter-strewn pavements, is a fun area for older kids. Behind the tattered façade lies a wealth of excellent eateries ranging from Afro-Caribbean, Greek and Cypriot to Mauritian.

Gunners fans can buy the latest home strip from **Arsenal's World Of Sport** shop before visiting the club's museum at **Arsenal Stadium,** while those keen on participatory sport can head for **Rowan's Ten-Pin Bowling.** There is a boating lake in the park and a good adventure playground.

Listings:

Arsenal Museum (0171 226 0304): see page 58.

Arsenal World of Sport Station Place, N4 (0171 272 1000). Open Monday–Saturday, 9.30am–6pm.

Rowan's Ten-Pin Bowling, 10 Stroud Green Road, N4 (0181 800 1950). Open-all-hours. Venue offers ten-pin bowling, snooker and American pool. Fast food is available all day.

Coco Town Take-Away, Restaurant and Wine Bar, 1–3 Stroud Green Rd, N4 (0171 263 7440). Excellent ground-floor take-away counter sells saltfish fritters and barbecued chicken, and the basement restaurant offers authentic Nigerian cooking.

Travel
For Alexandra Palace:
Wood Green
For Finsbury Park:
Finsbury Park

Highgate and Hampstead

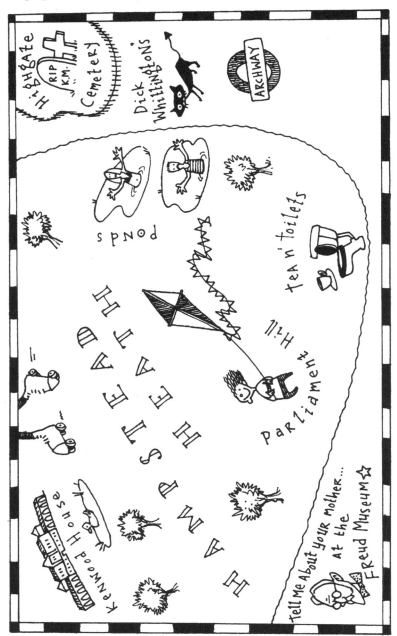

Highgate and Hampstead

Highgate Cemetery is a good starting point if you are coming by tube to Archway. The cemetery is a wonderfully atmospheric Victorian Valhalla of funereal follies, memorials and monuments. Follow the circle-of-Lebanon passageway lined with catacombs, at the heart of which is a large cedar tree. Search among the undergrowth for the sleeping stone lion on the tomb of menagerie owner George Wombwell or the stone dog on the tomb of Tom Sayers, the last of the barefist prize fighters. And don't forget to see the final resting place of Karl Marx.

Continue on to the **Whittington Stone** on Highgate Hill which, according to tradition, marks the spot where Dick Whittington heard the chiming of Bow Bells (and on top perches a cat, his legendary companion), then stop for a spot of lunch at **Lauderdale House.** You should aim to arrive by noon unless you have booked in advance. Alternatively, you can eat their take-away food on the lawn (Italian-run, with home-cooked fare).

There are often puppet shows or craft fairs in the building adjacent to the café. Next, either walk around the historic grounds (originally for locals without their own gardens) or head for any part of Hampstead Heath for a wander round. Most of the Heath is accessible by buggy. If you go on a weekday on your own with under-5s, try the One O'Clock Club at **Parliament Hill** which has attractive gardens, a playground, and is a favoured spot for kite-flying.

Save some energy for a quick look around **Kenwood House** at the top of Hampstead Heath with its Gainsboroughs and Rembrandts (free, leave buggies at entrance). Look out for the portrait of the eccentric 18th-century inventor, John Joseph Merlin, who invented the first roller skates and demonstrated them by making a grand entrance at a masquerade ball in 1760, skating into the ballroom whilst playing a violin. Unable to stop, he smashed into a large mirror, breaking it and injuring himself.

Those with older children might prefer to concentrate on the historic houses in the area. **The Freud Museum** is situated in the house where the father of psychoanalysis moved after fleeing Nazi-occupied Austria in 1938 and has various artifacts and furnishings including Freud's famous couch. You can also visit **Keats House,** where the poet lived in 1818: it has been preserved in its original state.

There is a local history museum in **Burgh House,** off Well Walk, the site of a spring where water was bottled at the turn of the 18th century (note the initials WG on the gates for the physician Dr William Gibbons).

Fenton House has several pieces of 18th-century furniture, English and Chinese porcelain, paintings and a large collection of early musical instruments which are kept in playing order for use by students and occasional musical recitals. In summer, Shakespeare is sometimes performed here.

Listings:

Burgh House, New End Square, NW3 (0171 431 0144); Wednesdy–Sunday noon–5pm, free.

Fenton House, Hampstead Grove (ring 0171 435 3471 for details).

Freud Museum, 20 Maresfield Gardens, Hampstead (0171 435 2002); Wednesday–Sunday noon–5pm; adults £2.50, children £1.50, under-12s free.

Highgate Cemetery, Swain's Lane (0181 340 1834); Archway tube. Daily 10am–4pm (varies in winter). Adults £1, accompanied children free.

Keats House, Keats Grove, Hampstead (0171 435 2062); times vary, admission free.

Kenwood House, Hampstead Lane, NW3 (0181 348 1286); daily 10am–6pm (October–April until 4pm). Free.

Lauderdale House, Waterlow Park, Highgate Hill, N6 (0181 341 4807); café open Tuesday–Sunday 8am–7pm for snacks, hot and cold meals and take-aways. See also Workshops, page 225.

NEARBY: There is a children's zoo at **Golders Hill** and a very popular self-service park café (Golders Hill Park Refreshment House, 0181 455 8010).

Regent's Canal Walk

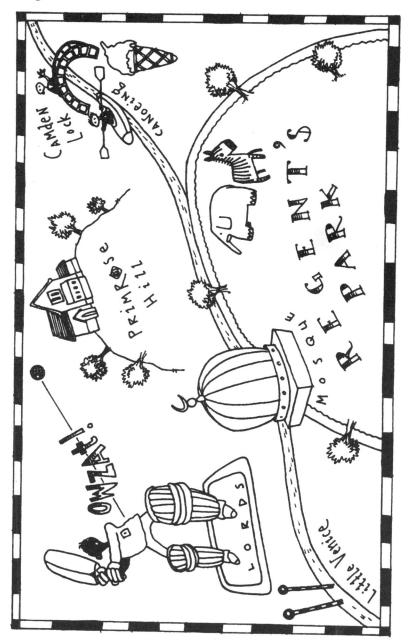

Travel
 Camden Town

Regent's Canal Walk F ☼ ●

To avoid the crowds (which by 1pm in the summer can be unbearable, especially for toddlers) begin your walk at **Camden Lock Market** where you can watch the stallholders setting up shop from 8.30am (trading usually starts at 9.30am on Saturday and Sunday). Walk over the hump bridge from where you can see the drawbridge of the **Pirates' Castle Boatclub** (over-8s can have a go at canoeing in summer at this water sports centre), or pause for home-made ice-creams and sorbets (as well as Italian food) at **Marine Ices** before weaving your way up to **Primrose Hill** for a fine view of the city and a helpful viewing panel at the summit.

Back down the hill you can rejoin the canal at **London Zoo**. Going by the back of the zoo and **Snowdon's Aviary** you pass under **Blow-up Bridge** which was reduced to rubble in 1874 when a working narrowboat carrying gunpowder and benzol exploded as it was towed underneath.

For a visit behind the scenes at **Lords** take the tow-path exit off Park Road. Tours are also available at the **gold-domed mosque** (pre-booking is essential). Continue along the towpath past the brightly painted canal boats to the Lisson Grove exit for lunch at the **Sea Shell** (delicious chips but expensive fish, so share portions).

If it's a Sunday, drop in at the **Church Street Market**. The **Puppet Theatre Barge** is moored in Little Venice until June for children's shows which, if you haven't lingered for too long at any of the sights, you should have plenty of time to catch (shows usually start at 3pm).

Travel
 Hackney Wick

Alternative Route:

A good alternative to this walk is to join the Regent's Canal at Victoria Park, follow the canal through **Old Ford Lock** and down to the Thames with a stop-off at the **Ragged School Museum** where you can catch a glimpse of the lives and schooling of Victorian children in the East End. Then head down to **Limehouse Basin** where the canal joins the Thames; it used to be a busy port and is now being developed into a marina.

Wet Alternative/Younger Children: 😊 🌧

If it is raining, hop on to one of the covered narrowboats which run between Camden Lock and Little Venice. Cruises last 45 minutes and you can get off at London Zoo and pick up a later boat (see Waterways, page 137).

Listings:

Camden Lock Market, see Shopping, page 153.

Church Street Market, Church Street, NW8. Open Monday–Thursday, 8.30am–4pm, Friday and Saturday 8.30am–5pm. Fruit and vegetable market, with household goods, cheap clothes and bric-a-brac on Friday and Saturday.

London Central Mosque, 146 Park Road, NW8 (0171 724 3363). Open dawn to dusk daily, free. Visitors must remove shoes, women should cover their heads.

London Zoo (0171 722 3333): see Animal Attractions, page 131.

Lords (0171 266 3825): see Behind the Scenes, page 98.

Marine Ices (0171 485 3132): see Eating Out, page 171.

Pirates Castle Boat Club (0171 267 6606) see Sport, page 220.

Puppet Theatre Barge (0171 249 6876): see Stage and Screen, page 94.

Ragged School Museum (0181 980 6405): see page 79.

Regent's Canal, NW1 and NW8 (0171 482 0523). Towpaths open dawn to dusk daily. For a free Canal Walks in London Brochure with maps send a stamped addressed envelope to: Canal Info, British Waterways Board, The Toll House, Delamare Terrace, London W2 6ND.

Regent's Canal Information Centre, Camden Lock, NW1 (0171 482 0523). Narrow boat trip departs from here.

Regent's Park (0171 486 7905): see page 114.

Sea Shell of Lisson Grove, 49 Lisson Grove, NW1 (0171 723 8703). Open Monday–Friday noon–2pm, 5.15–10.30pm; Saturday noon–10.30pm, Sunday noon–2.30pm.

The City of London

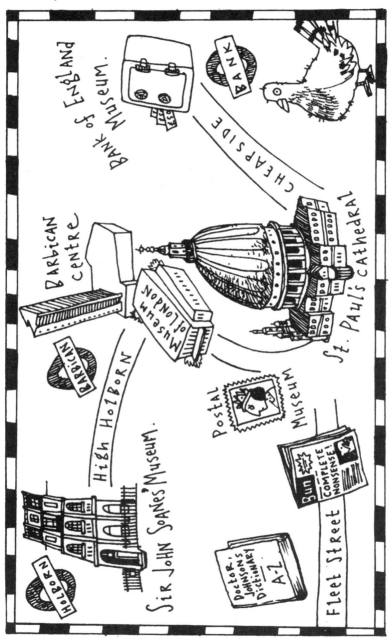

The City of London ⛆ ☼ ●

Start at **St Paul's Cathedral** and climb up to the **Whispering Gallery,** then outside to the **Stone Gallery** for views of the capital (take plenty of change to feed the telescopes). The fit and the brave can continue up to the **Golden Gallery** for a fantastic view of the surrounding skyscrapers.

Leaving St Paul's, any philatelists among you should head north to King Edward Street and the **National Postal Museum** (closed weekends) which houses one of the world's most important stamp collections as well as extensive archives and a reference library. Younger children might enjoy a quick run around **Postman's Park** opposite the National Postal Museum, which is home to a unique and very sentimental memorial wall of ceramic tiles, dedicated to ordinary people who died in acts of heroic self-sacrifice.

From here you can either double back on yourself and head down **Cheapside** to the **Bank of England Museum** (opposite Bank tube) or head north for the **Museum of London** where you can while away a good few hours with children of all ages. If you are with under-5s you will probably be in need of a rest and a train home by now. Stop for a cup of tea at the café opposite the museum then head home from Barbican tube (via the **Barbican Centre** if you have the energy) .

If you wish to save the **Museum of London** for another day, head west from the **National Postal Museum** via **Fleet Street** and **Prince Henry's Room** (the oldest domestic house in the City and one of the few to survive the Great Fire, it has its original Elizabethan timbered façade and now exhibits Samuel Pepys memorabilia) to **Dr Johnson's Memorial House in** Gough Square, where Johnson lived and compiled the first omprehensive English dictionary (the first edition is on display in the dining room).

Next stop is the **Public Record Office Museum** on Chancery Lane which houses the national archive of central government and legal documents. The oldest and most valuable of these is the **Domesday Book,** the first comprehensive survey of England ordered by William the Conqueror in 1085. There are also temporary displays of other documents such as **William Shakespeare's** will, **Nelson's** log book from HMS Victory and **Guy Fawkes'** confession.

Alternatively, have a look at **Sir John Soane's Museum,** once the home of the celebrated designer and architect, which now houses his eclectic collection of funerary objects and some wonderful paintings in the unusual **Picture Room** (designed to hold enough pictures to fill a gallery nearly four times its size — the walls are made up of a series of hinged panels which open out to reveal pictures hung behind them, thus making the most of the confined space). From here you can catch the tube home from Holborn station.

Listings

Bank of England Museum (0171 601 5545): see Museums and Galleries, page 58.

Dr Johnson's Memorial House, 17 Gough Square, Fleet Street, EC4 (0171 353 3745). Monday-Saturday 11am–5pm. Adults £1.70, children £1.

Museum of London (0171 600 3699): see Museums and Galleries, page 72.

Postman's Park, off King Edward St, EC1. Open daily. Free.

National Postal Museum, King Edward Street, EC1 (0171 239 5420). Open Monday–Friday 9.30am–4.30pm.

Prince Henry's Room, 17 Fleet Street, EC4 (0171 353 7323). Monday–Friday 1.45-5pm, Saturday 1.45-5.30pm. Free.

Public Record Office Museum, Chancery Lane, WC2 (0171 876 3444). Monday–Friday 9.30am–5pm. Free.

St Paul's Cathedral, Ludgate Hill, EC4 (0171 248 2705). See Museums and Galleries, page 80.

Sir John Soane's Museum, 12-14 Lincoln's Inn Fields, WC2 (0171 405 2107). Tuesday–Saturday 10am–5pm. Free.

Trafalgar Square

Trafalgar Square ☼ ●

Starting from **Charing Cross Station,** walk into **Trafalgar Square** where the fountains spurt into action at 10am daily, climb on to the lions (something every London child must do if only to test their parents' washing powder against the stains of pigeon droppings) and crane your neck for a view of **Nelson** on his column (depicted correctly without an eye patch, and only one arm).

Before Nelson's statue was erected, 14 stonemasons held a dinner on top of the 145ft-high column – now it is the resting place of pigeons and the odd drunken New Year's Eve reveller. The significance of Nelson's Column was recognised by Hitler who planned to remove it to Berlin after the conquest of Britain as a mark of world domination. The brass reliefs around the bottom show scenes from Nelson's four great battles and every October 21 there is a service here to commemorate Lord Nelson. Look out for **London's smallest police office** – a small hollow pillar built as an observation post for one policeman to monitor political rallies (the lamp on the top allegedly came from Nelson's flagship Victory).

Also look for the brass plaque on the north wall which shows the **British Imperial Standards of Length.** The statue of **Charles I** on horseback looking down Whitehall where he was beheaded in 1660, marks the original site of **Charing Cross** from which all distances from London are measured. Here you can feed the pigeons (in summer you can buy pigeon feed for rather more than tuppence a bag).

At the north-east end of the square stands the church of **St-Martin-in-the-Fields** which has free lunchtime concerts on Tuesdays and is home to the **London Brass Rubbing Centre.** The church also houses the popular **Café in the Crypt** which has home-made snacks and delicious cakes.

At the north side of the square is the **National Gallery** where you can do one of the Gallery's amusing family quiz trails or devise your own tour using the touch-screen computers in the Micro Gallery (the Quick Visit guide directs you to the 16 greatest masterpieces for those in a hurry).

For Saturday or Sunday lunch head north up the Strand to **Smollensky's,** an exceptional restaurant which bends over backwards to accommodate and entertain children.

Alternatively, head south-west of Trafalgar Square through **Admiralty Arch** into **The Mall** and **St James's Park,** a picturesque spot for picnicking and bird-watching by the water (don't expect to see any of the famous pelicans – they were banished to London Zoo because of their upsetting habit of eating the beloved park pigeons).

On the other side of the Mall is the **ICA,** a good place to introduce children to contemporary art. Beyond the ICA is the (Grand Old) **Duke of York's Column** which was paid for by docking a day's pay from every soldier in the British Army (adding to the unpopularity of the man who had already given rise to the derisory nursery rhyme).

From **St James's Palace** you get a less crowded view of the **Queen's Guard** marching to **Buckingham Palace** for the **Changing of the Guard** (but you might have missed this by now unless you were up at the crack of dawn as it takes place at 11.30am daily, and on alternate days in winter).

Your final stop, if you are with older children interested in the Second World War, should be the **Cabinet War Rooms,** Churchill's secret underground headquarters.

Listings:

Cabinet War Rooms: see Museums and Galleries, page 61.

Café in the Crypt: see Eating Out, page 169.

ICA: see Museums and Galleries, page 68.

London Brass Rubbing Centre (0171 437 6023): see Workshops, page 115.

National Gallery: see Museums and Galleries, page 74.

St James's Park: see The Great Outdoors, page 115.

Smollensky's: see Eating Out, page 162.

Covent Garden

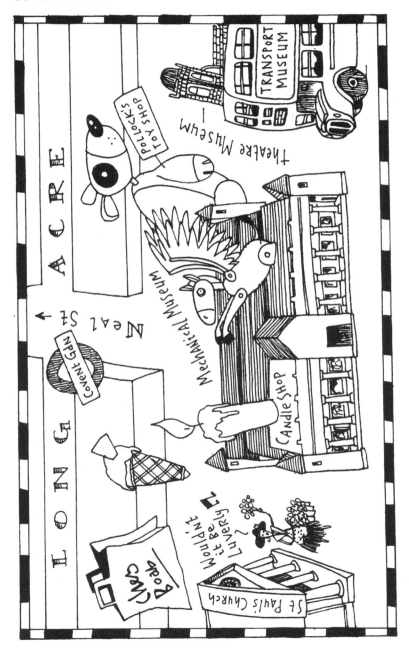

Covent Garden

Travel
Covent Garden ⊖

The site of London's famous fruit and vegetable market is now something of a tourist trap with stalls selling interesting but expensive items set up on restored Victorian cast-iron trading stands, surrounded by arts, craft and designer-clothes shops, expensive cafés and a good 'junk' market at the back. However, if you want to shop with kids who hate shopping, it is ideal and you can have fun even if they are very young.

There are plenty of street performers ranging from fire-eaters and jugglers to Chinese string quartets. You can take a **rickshaw ride** from outside Covent Garden tube (summer only), or climb the stairs to **Benjamin Pollock's** wonderful first-floor toyshop (in the covered market section between Hobbs and the Body Shop) before visiting the **Theatre Museum** or the **London Transport Museum**. Make sure you leave enough time for the **Cabaret Mechanical Theatre**.

There are lots of benches to sit down to eat a packed lunch while watching the entertainers or you can watch candles being made in the **Covent Garden Candle Shop**.

A stroll up Neal Street will take you past several shops with cheap novelties to amuse kids, to **Neal's Yard** and the **Neal's Yard Clock** created by cartoonist Tim Hunkin which fills with water and, on the hour, tips it via a system of bells and watering cans on to flowers which appear to grow.

Listings

Benjamin Pollock's Toyshop (0171 636 3452). Open Monday–Saturday 10am–5pm; closed Sunday.

Cabaret Mechanical Theatre (0171 379 7961): see Museums and Galleries, page 61.

Covent Garden Candle Shop: (0171 836 9815): see Shopping, page 146.

Covent Garden Market Office (0171 836 9136): for information on forthcoming events.

London Transport Museum (0171 379 6344): see Museums and Galleries, page 71.

Theatre Museum (0171 836 7891): see Museums and Galleries, page 82

South Kensington

South Kensington ☺ 🌧 ●

Travel
South
Kensington ⊖

Most of the museums here are linked to South Kensington tube station by a long tunnel, making this an ideal day out when it is cold and raining.

First stop is the **Science Museum** which houses the world's most comprehensive collection of scientific, technological, industrial and medical inventions, with hundreds of working exhibits and lots of interactivity for even very young children.

Next door, the **Geological Museum** tells the story of the Earth and man's use of its resources (more suited to older children – although ten-year-olds Alice, Lucy and Tom found it the least interesting of the three museums). A corridor connects it with the **Natural History Museum** and a quick dash across the road brings you to the **Victoria and Albert Museum** which has an excellent café for rainy days.

If the sun comes out, head for **Kensington Gardens** at the top of Exhibition Road for a picnic and some fresh air. If you are feeling greedy, take the 74 or 14 bus along the Brompton Road to **Harrods** for a blow-out tea in the Georgian Restaurant. This famous shop used to sell anything from hair pins to an elephant, but now more modestly claims to provide 'anything within reason'. The spectacular food halls are popular with children as, more obviously, is the toy department.

Listings:

Geological Museum (0171 938 9123): see Museums and Galleries (Natural History Museum), page 76.

Harrods (0171 730 1234); Fourth Floor Georgian Restaurant tea buffet, £8.95 per head from 4.15pm. See Shopping, page 152 and Eating Out, page 174.

Kensington Gardens: see The Great Outdoors, page 113.

Natural History Museum (0171 938 9123): see Museums and Galleries, page 81.

Science Museum (0171 938 8000/8080): see Museums and Galleries, page 81.

Victoria and Albert Museum (0171 938 8500): see Museums and Galleries, page 85.

South Bank

South Bank 😊 ☼ ●

From Westminster tube, cross **Westminster Bridge** for a quiet, traffic-free walk along the river with lots of things to do and see for small children.

Passing **County Hall** (look out for the lion guarding the deserted building), head for **Jubilee Gardens** (look for the Memorial to the **International Brigade of the Spanish Civil War**) where you can picnic before taking in a free lunchtime concert or evening foyer event in the **South Bank** complex.

Beyond the concert halls, the **National Film Theatre, Royal National Theatre** and **LWT** you come to the **Coin Street** development and the **Jubilee Walkway** which leads you past the market at **Gabriels Wharf** and **Blackfriars Bridge** (from which point, if time and energy allow, you can cross the bridge and continue down-river to the **Globe Theatre**).

Children over four will enjoy **MOMI (Museum of the Moving Image)** where actors playing movie characters make for diverting guides to a museum which traces the history of film and television. There are baby-changing facilities in the **Royal Festival Hall** and a playground in **Jubilee Gardens.**

For six weekends in the summer there are free performances called 'Great Outdoors' for all the family on the walkways and South Bank Centre. **The National Film Theatre** riverside café is fun and those with older children can take out a day membership (40p) and catch a matinée.

Listings:

Great Outdoors Festival: see London by Season, page 22.

MOMI (Museum of Moving Image) (0171 928 3232): see Museums and Galleries, page 73.

National Film Theatre (0171 928 3232). Monday–Friday 10am–6pm; adults £5.95, children £4.00.

Royal National Theatre (0171 928 2252). Free foyer music Monday–Saturday from 6pm until performances start: see Behind the Scenes, page 98.

Royal Festival Hall, South Bank, SE1 (0171 921 0682). Free music daily 12.30–2pm, jazz on Friday from 5.15pm. Education department gives list of special events for kids (ring 0171 921 0886). See Stage and Screen, page 91.

Greenwich

Greenwich

Arrive by boat at **Greenwich Pier** and you sail straight into the view **Canaletto** made famous and which has changed little since 1755. As the boat rounds the pier you will get an uninterrupted view through Wren's spectacular **Royal Naval College**, built in two halves so that from the **Queen's House** royalty would still have a gateway to the river, and beyond up the tree-clad hill of **Greenwich Park** to Charles II's **Old Royal Observatory**, which still marks **Longitude Zero** as the baseline of world time.

Once off the boat you cannot miss the majestic **Cutty Sark,** the famous tea clipper whose main mast towers 152ft above deck. On board (leaving buggies on deck) you can see the sailors' living quarters as they were when the ship transported tea from China — note the stark difference in conditions for officers and crew — and a colourful collection of ships' figureheads in the lower hold.

Compare the grace and splendour of the great clipper with the tiny **Gypsy Moth IV** standing a little farther along the waterfront. This 54-foot yacht, in which Sir Francis Chichester circumnavigated the world single-handed, is particularly popular with young children fascinated by the cramped conditions in which Chichester lived for 274 days, still managing to find room for books, a celebratory bottle of champagne, and some wonderfully antiquated-looking cooking equipment.

Next, walk back past the enormous domed lift of **Brunel's foot tunnel** which links Greenwich Pier to the Isle of Dogs. You should use this to reach Island Gardens DLR for your return journey. (Small children love running along the long pedestrian tunnel, built in 1900 by Brunel to give South London labourers access to Millwall Docks. Even if you do not arrive by DLR it is worth walking through the tunnel to the Isle of Dogs for the views back across the river to Wren's and Jones's skyline — and on really wet days, your kids can always count the 200,000 tiles lining the tunnel.)

As you head up **Greenwich Church Street** (the information centre is on the corner of Greenwich Church Street and College Approach) looking out for **Goddard's Pie 'n' Mash House** on the right, a small family-owned, traditional water-

Travel
DLR to Island Gardens, then **boat** to Greenwich Pier. Ring Riverboat Information Service (0839 123432) for more details (calls cost 39p/49p per minute).

ing hole which has survived since the turn of the century. Almost opposite is the popular weekend **Greenwich Arts and Craft Market (covered)**, which is good for anything from wooden toys and hand-knitted baby clothes to découpage loo seats and flavoured ground coffee (try the vanilla or double chocolate fudge). Prices are reasonable compared with Covent Garden and standards are high. Permanent shops within the covered market which are also open during the week include a Peruvian store, an excellent children's bookshop and a candle shop. The market gets very crowded, especially on Sundays, so if you have a buggy aim to arrive before 11am.

From the Arts and Craft Market cross over **King William Walk** into **Romney Road** and the **National Maritime Museum**, which brings British maritime history vividly to life with plenty of hands-on interactivity and weekend children's events.

From here, if you have young children with you, head for the well-equipped park playground, and small boating pond, but don't let them run off too much steam — it is an arduous climb up to the Old Royal Observatory even without having to push an occupied buggy. If you have older children interested in history and architecture they might enjoy the sumptuous 17th-century splendours of **Inigo Jones's Queen's House (to your right as you leave the Museum)** where you can see how royalty really lived.

Whatever you choose to do, make sure you leave plenty of time for the attractions at the top of the park. In addition to a splendid view of London beneath the **Woolfe Monument, the Meridian Line, Clock** and the **Old Royal Observatory**, there is a bandstand with Sunday afternoon band performances and children's entertainment. Beyond are the beautiful enclosed flower gardens with a duck pond, and deer enclosure.

From here you can leave by **Blackheath Gate** for a stroll across the heath to the village railway station or make your way back down the hill for the return journey.

Listings:

Cutty Sark (0181 858 3445): see Museums and Galleries, page 63.

Fan Museum (0181 305 1441): see Museums and Galleries, page 64.

Greenwich Park (0181 858 2608): see The Great Outdoors, page 111.

Greenwich Foot Tunnel. Open 24 hours daily (lift operates from 5am–9pm). Free.

National Maritime Museum (0181 858 4422): see Museums and Galleries, page 75.

Old Royal Observatory (0181 858 4422): see Museums and Galleries, page 78

Queen's House (0181 858 4422). Ring for details.

Crystal Palace and Horniman Museum & Gardens

Crystal Palace and Horniman Museum & Gardens 😊 🇫 🌳 ●

Crystal Palace itself might no longer be there, ninety-nine fire engines having failed to save the original glass exhibition centre from a terrible fire in 1936, but **Crystal Palace Park** is one of the best-serviced family parks in London.

The park is so jam-packed with things for children of all ages to do and see, your first stop should be the Information Centre near the Penge entrance. Plan your day over coffee at the nearby café or let your children run riot in the large, enclosed children's playground while you spread your map and leaflets over the picnic tables provided.

Dinomaniacs of all ages can stroll round the lake encompassing **Dinosaur Island** which spills over with vast prehistoric models, or hire a boat for a different view of the monstrous creatures.

You can get lost in the **tea maze**, ride the **miniature railway**, drive your own steam engine or pedal car at the small **funfair**, take a leisurely ride on a **horse-drawn cart**, try your hand at *pétanque* or a spot of skiing on the **dry ski-slope** (April-October), before feeding the animals in the Crystal **Palace Farm Yard** and picnicking in the extensive grounds.

On weekends and summer holidays there is a small children's funfair between the car park and playground along with cart rides drawn by two of the farmyard shire horses.

If you are here on a weekday on your own, head for the excellent, free **One O'Clock Club** near the start of the miniature railway ride (50p each). From the playground head south past the **Pétanque Pitch** following signs to the 'Monsters', 29 huge model dinosaurs made in the 1850s and now lurking among the undergrowth.

The paths (all accessible by buggy) take you across wooden bridges, past waterfalls, near hilly slopes where children can scramble up for a better view and round to the boating lake. From here you can backtrack up to the small **Palace Farmyard**, full of rare and common farm animals including **Gertie the pig** and some very friendly goats. There is a picnic table here but I wouldn't rate your chances of eating your food before the goats do.

From here you can either retrace your steps, keeping the **Sports Stadium** on your left, and head up the hill to the tea maze (with hedges just short enough for anxious parents to keep track of young offspring – there is also a special escape gate). Or if you are here on a Sunday with older children head west, past Station Gate, for the **Crystal Palace Museum** (south-west corner of the park) charting the fated history of the great glass exhibition centre.

All the main attractions are on the east side of the park, with the tea maze out on a limb, but if you plan your day so you finish by the maze, you can cut across the park past the site of the old Palace to **Crystal Palace Parade** and catch the 122 bus up to **Forest Hill**. From here, the **Horniman Museum and Gardens** is a 10-minute walk (alternatively the 176 bus from the Penge Entrance or Sydenham Gate will drop you right outside the museum).

Wet alternative

You could easily spend a day in Crystal Palace Park but if it rains or you want something different, head for the **Horniman Museum and Gardens**. This delightful, informal and highly diverting anthropological museum houses a vast, eclectic array of items from Javanese shadow puppets to a mummified crocodile, and a pair of Arabian shoes with flaps to scare away scorpions. If the sun comes out there are lovely gardens with outdoor activities.

Listings:

Crystal Palace Park (0181 778 7141): see The Great Outdoors, page 110.

Crystal Palace Farm (0181 778 4487): see Animal Attractions, page 134.

Horniman Museum (0181 699 2339): see Museums and Galleries, page 66.

Joanna's (0181 670 4052): see Eating Out, page 165.

Horminan Restaurant (0181 291 2901): see Eating Out, page 164.

Uncover medieval London, find a mummified crocodile, sample cooking from Roman and Tudor times, play Victorian games, examine a dinosaur fossil, or follow the children's foot trail. There is a wealth of treasure – and a little trivia – to entice children into London's many museums and art galleries.

Museums & Galleries

Hours
Mon-Thurs
10am-1pm (or by
appointment for
parties of 6 or
more)

Admission
Adults £2,
children &
concs £1

Travel
⊖⇌ Paddington

Alexander Fleming Laboratory Museum

St Mary's Hospital, Praed Street, W2 (0171 725 6528)

Small, friendly museum devoted to the father of penicillin on the site of the original, cramped laboratory where in the 1920s Alexander Fleming discovered a Petri dish contaminated with a mysterious mould – an event marking the beginning of a whole new antibiotic age. The role penicillin then played in the exploration of bacteria and disease is retraced through meticulously arranged displays and a video. Children over 8 with an interest in science, or those doing projects on Fleming, will love this museum which is just the way one would imagine an old-fashioned laboratory to look. Toilets, but no baby changing facilities or toilets for disabled people. No wheelchair or buggy access.

Hours
Fri 9.30am-
4.30pm

Admission
Adults £2,
children £1

⊖ **Travel**
Arsenal

Arsenal Museum

Arsenal Stadium, Avenell Road, N5 (0171 226 0304)

Fans come from miles around to see Charlie George's double medals and Alf Kirchen's kit. You can test your knowledge on the interactive video games and wallow in Arsenal's history while watching the club's life on film. The dedicated can also take the one and a half hour stadium tour (£4; book in advance). Toilets have area on which to change babies but no specific facilities. No wheelchair access or disabled toilet facilities.

Hours
Mon-Fri
10am-5pm,
weekends closed
(except Lord
Mayor's show)

Travel
⊖ Monument or
⊖⇌ Bank
Cannon
Street

Bank of England Museum

Threadneedle Street (entrance Bartholomew Lane), EC2 (0171 601 5545)

A fascinating insight into the 'Old Lady of Threadneedle Street' as the bank is affectionately known, this well-planned, engaging museum is ideal for children of 8 or over (they need to have at least some understanding of money; although Jake and Benja both enjoyed the dealing desks). There are interactive videos in the Banking Today Gallery as well as a dealing desk at which you can work the colour-coded keyboard or use the telephone for up-to-the-minute data about markets and exchange rates. Toilets. Some wheelchair access and buggy access.

Bethnal Green Museum   of Childhood

Cambridge Heath Road, E2 (0181 980 2415/3204)

The national museum of childhood, a branch of the Victoria and Albert Museum, was deliberately located in the poorer East End in 1872 to attract and amuse London's less fortunate children. Not surprisingly this delightful collection of toys, dolls, games and puppets is always over-run with excited kids but there is plenty of space in its cavernous interior to accommodate everyone. Tom liked the 1880 toy butcher's shop complete with split carcasses glistening with blood and Alice was intrigued by the complete wardrobe of Henrietta Byron (including a tiny set of stays) in the collection of children's clothes. But it is the dolls' houses which are the perennial favourites – 46 of them in two long 'streets' which ranging from a 15-room Victorian mansion to little home–made cottages. The temporary exhibitions, including the popular annual 'Spirit of Christmas', often show more imagination in their presentation than the permanent displays. Also holiday activities. The shop sells postcards, books and toys including replicas of old-fashioned games. Café, toilets and baby-changing facilities. Some wheelchair and buggy access.

Hours
Mon–Thurs & Sat 10am–5.50pm (incl Bank Holidays), Sun 2.30–5.50pm (closed Fri, May Day Bank Holiday, Dec 24-26 & Jan 1). Weekly 2–hour Saturday Arts workshops (11am & 2pm)

Travel
Bethnal Green ⊖
Bus 8, 106, 253 or D6

Bramah Tea and Coffee Museum

The Clove Building, Maguire Street, Butler's Wharf, SE1 (0171 378 0222)

If you have ever questioned why Britain is such a great tea-drinking nation or wondered about the origins of the coffee house this is the place to come. The collection of over 1,000 teapots and coffee-makers alone serves to illustrate the many different ways tea and coffee have been made since they were first introduced in the 17th century. Learn about the philosophy behind the Japanese tea ceremony and compare that to the tea-making etiquette of an English family at tea in Richard Collin's famous 1730 painting. Follow the events that culminated in the Boston Tea Party of 1773 and led to the great Clipper races of the 1860s (see also Cutty Sark clipper ship). The museum turns its nose up at the tea bag as well as instant coffee – it does not sell or serve them on the premises, but is

Hours
Daily 10am-6pm

Admission
Adults £3, children under-14 and concs £1.50, family ticket (2+4) £6

Travel
Tower Hill ⊖

less dogmatic about the choice between China and Indian tea. The shop sells tea and coffee and related items (tea towels, caddy tins, etc). Café serves Bramah blends (cup of coffee 60p; pot of tea £1; tea, hot scones, butter, jam and cake £3). Toilets. No baby-changing facilities. Wheelchair access and disabled toilet facilities, ring in advance.

British Museum

Great Russell Street, WC1 (0171 636 1555, info 0171 580 1788)

Hours
Mon-Sat 10am-
5pm; Sun 2.30-
6pm (closed
Christmas,
New Year's Day,
Good Friday,
1st Mon in May)

Admission
Free (charge for
some temporary
exhibitions). First
Tue of every
month (excl Jan)
evening openings
6-9pm: admission
£5 (good value to
avoid crowds)

Travel
⊖ Holborn,
Russell Square or
Tottenham Court
Road

This vast museum houses the national treasury of art and artifacts from all over the world, all periods and all civilisations, and the 4 million artifacts increase daily with new bequests and recent finds. You cannot possibly do even a quarter of the museum in one visit so don't try – Jake and I only managed one 'civilization' the first time round. Since then we have done about 20 rooms at a go which takes about 2 hours. Start with the Ancient Greeks and Romans, and the Egyptians – every aspect of life and death is examined with easy-to-read informa-tion cards. The Egyptians are particularly popular especially for those obsessed with death – see mummies of fish, falcons and cats as well as humans (note the jars of human organs standing next to the mummies). Also popular with kids is the Lindow man (room 35) who was found in a Cheshire peat bog 2,000 years after having been murdered, probably by Druids. The Treasure Trails are popular with even very young children. Café and restaurant. Shop and children's shop. Toilets for disabled and baby-changing facilities. Wheelchair access by prior arrangement only. Buggy access (but stairs to each floor).

Bruce Castle Museum

Lordship Lane, N17 (0181 808 8772)

Hours
Wed-Sun

Travel
⊖ Seven Sisters
or Wood Green
⇌ Tottenham
Hale

Excellent local history museum for those wanting to know more about the area in which they live. Good for children interested in or doing projects on the postal system as there is an important exhibition on the subject (the castle was once home of Rowland Hill who introduced the Penny Black stamp). Small shop sells postcards and books. Toilets. Wheelchair and buggy access on the ground floor.

Brunel's Engine House

Railway Avenue, Rotherhithe, SE16 (0181 318 2489)

The engine house contains the sole surviving example of a compound horizontal V steam pumping engine, built in 1885, as well as the exhibition 'Brunel's Tunnel and Where It Led'. Unless you have an interest in engineering you need similar skills of perseverance to keep the kids amused during the video display and guided tour, but a short visit can be fun if combined with a walk round the St Mary's Rotherhithe conservation area with its restored warehouses, craft workshops and riverside walks. No toilets or baby-changing facilities. Wheelchair and buggies restricted access.

Hours
Open first Sun of every month noon-4pm; every Sun in Aug & Sept

Admission
Adults £1.50, children & concs 50p, family ticket (2+2) £4.50

Travel
Rotherhithe ⊖ (East London Line)
Bus P11, 47 or 188

Cabaret Mechanical Theatre

33-34 The Market, Covent Garden Piazza, WC2 (0171 379 7961)

Although this delightful museum will not fail to entertain all age groups, it is particularly suitable for under-5s who love the bizarre world of moving wood and metal sculptures because they can make each of the 100 hand-carved moving models operate by pushing buttons without any help from adults. Little red stools are provided to reach the higher exhibits and they can go back again and again to their favourite automata. Older children are fascinated by the mechanics of the pieces, all of which can be seen working, as well as the witty play on words. There is a man eating spaghetti all day, a bucking bronco in a bath, a typing tiger, a brightly painted Noah's Ark and a man flogging a dead horse. No toilets or baby-changing facilities. No wheelchair access.

Hours
Mon-Sat 10am-6.30pm, Sun 11am-6.30pm or 7pm in summer, closed 25 Dec

Admission
Adults £1.95, children & concs £1.20, under-5s free, family ticket (2+3) £4.95 (group discounts)

Travel
Covent Garden ⊖

Cabinet War Rooms

Clive Steps, King Charles Street, SW1 (0171 930 6961)

Churchill's secret underground headquarters are a great place for older children or those with some interest in or understanding of the Second World War but there is no interactivity for younger children. There are 21 rooms including the Cabinet Room, Transatlantic Telephone Room, Map Room and Prime Minister's Bedroom all just as they were left at the end of the war. Among the maps, telecommunication equipment and

Hours
Daily 10am-6pm (last admission 5.15pm; closed Dec 24-26)

Admission
Adults £4.20, children £2.10, under-5s free, various other concs, family ticket (2+2) £10.50

Travel
⊖ St James's Park
or Westminster

scrambling devices there are also more personal things belonging to Churchill – the desk from which he made his famous broadcasts and his chamber pot (there were no toilets in this cramped bunker). The audio guides are good value for money. Shop. No refreshments. Baby-changing facilities in men's and women's toilets. Wheelchair access. Toilets for the disabled.

Hours
Daily 10am-
5.30pm,
Oct-March
10am-4.30pm,
(closed Dec 25 &
26)

Admission
Adults £4.95,
students & OAPs
£2.75, under-15s
£3.75, under-3s
free,
disabled in
wheelchairs free,
family ticket (2+2)
£13

Travel
⊖ ⇌ London
Bridge
(NCP car park)

Churchill's Britain at War 😊 🌰 ◐ Experience

Tooley Street, SE1 (0171 403 3171)

A relatively new hands–on theme museum presenting the sounds, smells and visual effects of the London Blitz. Starting with an elevator descent to an underground tunnel of bunkers where dummies shelter from an air raid, you can re-live the drama of everyday life on the home front during the Second World War. The best bit comes at the end of the tour in The Black Out where you wander through a London street that has just been hit by a doodlebug. It all gets a bit gory with a man whose face has been blown off and a woman half buried beneath a pile of rubble but needless-to-say Tom liked those details best. This is a superb museum for children (although the noises might frighten sensitive under-4s) which makes history really come alive. Families or small groups of children can play the Blitz Zone game where volunteers are transformed into ARP wardens complete with gas masks and tin helmets. They then embark on a two-and-a-half minute race against time to find an unexploded bomb buried in the street rubble. No café on site. Toilets (no disabled or baby-changing facilities). Disabled access.

Hours
Tues-Sat
10am-5pm

Travel
⊖ Elephant
& Castle

Cumming Museum 🇫 🌰 ◐

155-157 Walworth Road, Walworth, SE17 (0171 701 1342)

Award–winning local history museum charts Southwark's history from the Romans to the present day including displays of medieval life, Shakespeare's Bankside theatre and the Southwark of Charles Dickens. Call for details of themed hands-on exhibits. No toilets or baby-changing facilities. No wheelchair or buggy access.

Cutty Sark Clipper Ship 😊 ☼ ◑

King William Walk, Greenwich, SE10 (0181 858 3445)

Now standing in dry dock, the Cutty Sark, launched in 1869, was the fastest, most famous tea clipper ever built and the only one to survive. The name comes from Robert Burns' poem *Tam O'Shanter* in which Tam is chased by a witch wearing a 'cutty sark' (short dress). If you look at the Clipper's figurehead you will see her clutching hair from the tail of Tam's horse. Other more bizarre figureheads are housed in the lower hold, and the history of the Cutty Sark is told through pictures and models on the 'tween deck. Toilets nearby on Greenwich Pier. See Ten Days Out page 51. Wheelchair access deck only.

Hours Summer Mon-Sat 10am-6pm, Sun noon-6pm; winter Mon-Sat 10am-5pm, Sun noon-5pm

Admission Adults £3.25, children 7-16 & concs £2.25, family ticket (2+2) £8.

Travel Greenwich or Maze Hill, ⇌ **DLR** Island Gardens

Design Museum 🌧 ◑

Butlers Wharf, Shad Thames, SE1 (0171 403 6933)

Displays everyday things and explains why and how mass-produced consumer objects work and look as they do, from cars to toothbrushes. Children's workshops and events in the summer and school holidays which have included Design Your Own Street and Designing from Fiction. Best for older children. Day-long museum workshops run June-October (included in price of admission). Bookshop and library. Bar, café, toilets, baby-changing facilities in men's and women's, toilets for disabled people. Full wheelchair and buggy access.

Hours Mon-Fri 11.30am-6pm, Sat & Sun noon-6pm

Admission Adults £4.50, children, OAPs & students £3.50, under-5s free

Travel Tower Hill ⊖ London Bridge ⊖⇌ **Bus** 15, 42, 47, 78, 188, P11

Dulwich Picture Gallery ☼ ◑

College Road, SE21 (0181 693 5254)

The oldest art gallery in the country exhibits works by Rembrandt, Gainsborough, Rubens and Murillo. It is rarely crowded, the staff are friendly and helpful and there is a nearby park, making it a good way to introduce quite young children to art. Tea tent in summer. Toilets (no disabled or baby-changing facilities). Buggy and wheelchair access.

Hours Tues-Fri 10am-5pm, Sat 11am-5pm, Sun 2-5pm

Admission Adults £2, under-16s free, concs £1 (free admission Fridays)

Travel North Dulwich or West Dulwich ⇌ Brixton ⊖

Fan Museum 🌧 ⏱

12 Crooms Hill, Greenwich, SE10 (0181 305 1441)

Hours
Tue-Sat 11am-
4.30pm; Sun
noon-4.30pm

Admission
Adults £3,
children £2,
under-7s free

Travel
⇌ Greenwich

The only venue in the world devoted to the art and craft of the fan with over 2,000 fans on display. Demonstrations on the craft of fan making and restoration. Also changing exhibitions. Best for older children with an interest in art and design. Shop, wheelchair access and toilets for disabled people. Large surface on which to change babies but no specific facilities.

Florence Nightingale Museum ☀ ⏱

2 Lambeth Palace Road, SE1 (0171 620 0374)

Hours
Tue-Sun & Bank
Holidays 10am-
4pm

Admission
Adults £2.50,
children, OAPs &
students £1.50,
family ticket £5

Travel
⊕ Westminster
⊕ ⇌ Waterloo

On the site of St Thomas's hospital the museum tells the history of the famous 'lady with the lamp' using original objects, audio–visuals, period settings and a life-size reconstruction of a ward scene from the Crimean War. Ideal for 7-11-year-olds doing projects on the Victorians and any budding young nurses. Takes one to one and a half hours. Take a picnic to eat here or overlooking the Thames in Jubilee Gardens or Lambeth Palace. Shop. Toilets, no baby-changing facilities. Facilities for disabled. Wheelchair and buggy access.

Geffrye Museum ▮ ⏱

Kingsland Road, E2 (0171 739 9893)

Hours
Tues-Sat 10am-
5pm (also open
Bank Holidays),
Sun 2-5pm (closed
Good Fri,
Dec 25 and
Jan 1)

Travel
⊕ ⇌ Liverpool
Street or Old
Street

Highly recommended, very popular museum with rooms decorated in different period styles from the 1600s to 1939 which give a real insight into the way homes looked in the past and the type of people who lived in them. Walk through history, from the oak furniture and panelling of the 17th century to the splendours of the Georgian period, the cluttered, high style of the Victorians and on to 20th century art deco and post-war utility. Imaginative children's holiday and weekend activities for toddlers to teenagers. Family workshops, summer evening events, music and picnics on the lawns. Café. Shop. Toilets for disabled and baby-changing facilities. Wheelchair access to the ground floor.

Shakespeare's Globe Exhibition ☼ ◐

New Globe Walk, Bankside, SE1 (0171 928 6406)

Multi-media exhibition detailing the rebuilding of the Elizabethan Globe Theatre at its Bankside location. Toilets. Admission: adults £4, concs £3, children (5–14) £2.50, under-5s free, family ticket (2+2) £11 (subject to increase May '96).

Hours
Daily 10am-5pm

Travel
Mansion House or Monument ⊖ Cannon Street ⊖⇒

The Grange Museum Of ☺ 🄴 🌧 ◐ Natural History

Neasden Roundabout, Neasden Lane, NW10 (0181 452 8311)

A great place to bring kids for an hour or two to explore the history of Brent. The museum is crammed full of old photos, costumes and the stories of local peoples' lives from the 1920s to today. Try on the old-fashioned hats, imagine having to wear the corsets and suspenders on display, gawp at the ludicrous longjohns, draw your favourite exhibits on the drawing paper provided, or fill in a quiz. Look out for the wigs, cut-throat razors and the Eugene Perm Machine. Take a picnic to eat in the enclosed garden and look out for unusual plants, identify herbs in the Victorian Herb Garden, or toss pennies in the old well from the original farm. If it rains, shelter in the conservatory. Changing and feeding facilities on request. Free activity sheets. Wheelchair and buggy access to downstairs and garden.

Hours
Mon-Fri 11am-5pm, Sat 10am-5pm, (open Sundays 2-5pm May-Sept only)

Travel
Neasden ⊖ Bus 16, 112, 182, 245, 297, 302. By car North Circular & park on the roundabout

Guards Museum

Wellington Barracks, Birdcage Walk, SW1 (0171 414 3271)

The story of the Foot Guards told through a collection of uniforms, weapons and memorabilia spanning 350 years. It's worth a pop-in visit for military-minded boys if you are already in the park or visiting other things nearby, otherwise only for the real enthusiast. No toilets. No baby-changing facilities or wheelchair access.

Hours
Mon-Fri 10am-4pm (last admission 3.30pm)

Admission
Adults £2, children & OAPs £1

Travel
St James's Park ⊖

Gunnersbury Park Museum

Hours
April 1-Oct 31
Mon-Fri 1-5pm,
Sat & Sun 1-6pm,
Nov 1-March 31
daily 1-4pm.
Regular
programme of
weekend and
holiday workshops
(ring for details).

Travel
Acton Town
Free on-site
parking

Gunnersbury Park Museum

Gunnersbury Park, W3 (0181 992 1612)

Popular local museum where captions to the exhibits have been specially written to appeal to children and there are lots of kids' activities. You can dress up in Victorian sailor suits or pinafores, try on hats, play hopscotch and parlour games, and colour in penny–plane pictures. Imagine yourself a Victorian child as you copy work on to a slate at an old school desk, then become a chimney sweep and climb the replica chimney. The changing exhibits in the gallery always have hands-on elements for children. There is a café but if it's fine weather take a picnic to the park which has a boating pond, lake, playgrounds, a pitch-and-putt course, orangery and mock ruins. Wheelchair and buggy access.

Hours
March 1-Oct 31
daily 10am-6pm;
Nov-Feb daily
10am-5pm (closed
Dec 25).

Admission
Adults £4, children
£2, under-5s free,
OAP/concs £3,
family ticket (2+2)
£10.

Travel
London Bridge
or Tower Hill
Tower Gate **DLR**
Ferry from Tower
Pier

HMS Belfast

Morgans Lane, Tooley Street, SE1 (0171 407 6434)

Moored on the Thames near Tower Bridge this Second World War cruiser is Europe's largest preserved warship. From the captain's bridge to the boiler rooms you see the mess decks, galley, sick bay, gun turrets and punishment cells. Experience a four-minute recreation of surface action – what might have happened if the ship were hit by a shell and how it would control the danger. See what the sailors ate for breakfast or hunt for the ship's cat. Look out from the bridge and imagine what it would have been like to have relied only on visual observation to navigate, then see the huge guns which have a range of 14 miles. Confined spaces and ladders. Toilets for disabled people in which you can change babies, but no specific facilities. Wheelchair access to some parts. Leave pushchairs on quarterdeck.

Hours
Mon-Sat 10.30am-
5.30pm, Sun 2-
5.30pm (closed
Dec 24-26)

Travel
Forest Hill
Bus 176, 185, 94,
122, 63, 115
Parking in roads
off London Rise

Horniman Museum and Gardens

100 London Road, Forest Hill, SE23 (0181 699 2339/1872)

This delightful, informal and indispensable anthropological museum was founded by Frederick Horniman, a 19th century tea merchant who made his fortune selling tea in packets and then spent a good deal of it shipping back bizarre artifacts gathered on his travels. The dozens of masks,

head-dresses and Egyptian mummies are most popular with young children, but be prepared to step over art students sprawled in front of the cases. Prising Jake away from the goggle-eyed African wooden mask and the mother figure with infants draped from her breasts, we went in search of the puppets – Polish stick puppets, Javanese shadow puppets and a family favourite, the Punch and Judy selection whose annotations can be read like a story to the younger children. Living Waters – An Aquarium for the Future – is an excellent underwater conservation centre for endangered species. The Perspex water tanks reach right down to the ground enabling crawlers and toddlers to see the fish for themselves. The natural history section has a spectacular 100–year-old stuffed Canadian walrus, an ancient mummified crocodile, huge elephant skulls, stuffed vultures, ostriches and eagles and massive models of insects (there's also half a fruit bat and the foot of an orang-utan). The animals are displayed to illustrate the story of evolution or the history of flight as well as according to species, so this section is an invaluable source for study. In the recently revamped music room there are 6,000 instruments that make up the Dolmetsch collection, 1,500 of which have been included in revolutionary new hands-on displays. This is one of the best museums for really young children because they can't knock anything over, they can see everything from their level and the wide variety on offer never fails to fascinate. Ambitious series of weekend and holiday workshops. Outside in the beautiful Horniman Gardens are nature trails, formal and water gardens, an animal enclosure and spectacular views of London. Toilets for disabled people. Baby-changing facilities. See Ten Days Out page 56.

Houses of Parliament 🄴
(Palace of Westminster)

Parliament Square, SW1 (0171 219 4272)

When the old Palace of Westminster burnt down in 1834, architects Charles Barry and Augustus Pugin won a national competition to rebuild the present day gothic masterpiece. It took nearly 20 years and went £2m over budget. All that remains of the medieval royal palace is Westminster Hall with

Hours
Opening times of each House vary (ring for details). Victoria Tower Gardens daily 7am–dusk

Worksheets. To find out more about Parliament and its workings send a postcard with your name and address to The Parliamentary Education Unit, Room L210, 1 Derby Gate, London SW1A 2DG, indicating one of the following publications: The Palace of Westminster, The Work of an MP, Education Sheets on Parliament or The Glorious Revolution 1688-89.

Travel
⊖ Westminster

its impressive hammerbeam roof decorated with massive carved angels. It was here that Guy Fawkes was tried for his part in the Gunpowder Plot in 1605, and where Charles II had Cromwell's exhumed head impaled on the roof where it remained for 20 years. You can look at, but not go into, the Hall at the first of a series of security checks before being ushered through St Stephen's Hall, Central Hall and into a small room where all visitors have to sign a form vowing not to cause a disturbance. From here you go up steep staircases to the Strangers' Gallery above the chamber (you get a guide to the House, explanatory diagrams, notes on procedure and a Points of Order sheet so you can follow what is being debated). Shop, post office, toilets for the disabled people. Wheelchair access.

ICA (Institute of Contemporary Art)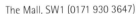

Hours
Daily noon-7.30pm, Fri to 9pm (centre open to 11pm)

Admission
Day pass £1.50

Travel
⊖ Piccadilly

The Mall, SW1 (0171 930 3647)

A good place to expose children to contemporary art in the three galleries with changing exhibitions. There is also plenty going on – kids' weekend cinema club (see theatre and film), bookshop, theatre, restaurant and bar. Toilets for disabled. No baby-changing facilities (but there is a flat surface in the toilets on which to change a baby).

Imperial War Museum

Hours
Daily 10am-6pm

Admission
Adults £3.90, children (5-16) £1.95, under-5s free, concs £2.90, family ticket (2+4) £10.50; free admission 4.30-6pm daily

Travel
⊖ Lambeth North or Elephant & Castle
⊖⇌ Waterloo
Some parking nearby

Lambeth Road, SE1 (0171 416 5000)

Voted Museum of the Year in 1990, this museum does a superb job, telling the story of war from Flanders to the Gulf as tastefully as is possible, with thousands of exhibits from ration books to rockets, all beautifully lit, labelled and mounted. You can see the large exhibits like tanks, planes and submarines from above and below, and there are 4 balcony art galleries featuring work by war artists. The Home Front display is popular with children of any age and you can watch archive film and listen to sound-recordings of people's war-time experience. The Blitz and Trench Experiences are multi-sensory displays where you can see, hear and feel what it was like to be at the front or in London during the Blitz (to avoid long queues for this popular experience go on Monday or weekday term-time afternoons). Special events and workshops during school holidays. Shop is well stocked with recruitment posters, books, videos, and very good value 'photo packs' (£3.50) and 'document packs' (£9.99) based on the museum's collection (available mail order). Film shows on Saturday and Sunday. Wheelchair and buggy access, toilet for disabled people, breast-feeding and baby-changing facilities. Restaurant and picnic area in nine acres of parkland.

Livesey Museum

682 Old Kent Road, SE15 (0171 639 5604)

Excellent small, local history museum with changing, hands-on exhibitions particularly suited to children under 12. From May 1 The Great Rubbish Show – an interactive exhibition for under-12s who can try their hand at can recycling, play musical instruments made out of rubbish and see just how much rubbish they generate in one day. Soft corner with cushions, toys and books for under-5s. Shop with toys, cards, games and small gifts. Disabled access to ground floor. Disabled toilets and baby-changing facilities. Picnic area in courtyard.

Hours
Mon-Sat 10am-5pm

Travel
Elephant & Castle ⊖ ⇌
Bus 53 or 177
Free parking in side streets

London Canal Museum ☼ ◗

12/13 New Wharf Road, N1 (0171 713 0836)

Beside Regent's Canal on Battlebridge Basin the museum occupies an old ice warehouse originally owned by Carlo Gatti who shipped ice from the frozen Norwegian lakes, in the days before fridges. The museum is a good starting point before a canal walk or boat trip and children get a real insight into what it would have been like living in the cramped quarters of a barge's cabin – the pull-down bed was for adults, and the children had to sleep upright on hard wooden benches after an 18-hour day leading the horses, steering the boats and helping with the daily chores. Good for those doing projects. Toilets (not for disabled people). Can change babies in the education room upon request.

Hours
Summer months Tues-Sun and Bank Holidays 10am-4.30pm

Admission
Adults £2.50, children and concs £1.25

Travel
King's Cross ⊖ ⇌

69

London Dungeon

Hours
Daily 10am–
5.30pm

Admission
Adults £7.50,
students £6,
children (under-
14) £4.50 (no
unaccompanied
children)

Travel
London
Bridge

28–34 Tooley Street, SE1 (0171 403 0606)

Dreamt up by London housewife Annabel Geddes whose children were disappointed by the lack of 'blood and thunder' to be found at the Tower of London, the vaults under London Bridge Station are full of gruesome scenes of torture, murders and executions. An 11-year-old Canadian friend who stomped unimpressed around the rest of London reading Spiderman comics was really 'wowed', especially when Anne Boleyn is beheaded, 'and she was in the middle of talking – that shut her up.' As well as the historic figures of Boudicca, Richard the Lion Heart, Anne Boleyn *et al* there are exhibits detailing the history of the Great Plague, Newgate Prison and the Norman Conquests. The blood-curdling sounds, dank, gloomy nooks and musty smell all add to the atmosphere but the dummies could be a bit more lifelike – they are beginning to look tatty. Not suitable for young children or those prone to nightmares (best for over-8s). Go Monday–Thursday before noon to avoid crowds. Café. Toilets for the disabled. Baby-changing facilities.

London Planetarium

Hours
Summer daily
9.40am-5.40pm;
winter Mon-Fri
12.20-5pm, Sat &
Sun 10.20am-5pm

Admission
Adults £4.75,
children £2.95,
OAPs £3.65, family
ticket (2+2)
£12.45. Reduced
prices if combined
with tickets for
Madame Tussauds.
Preferably no
children under 5

Travel
Baker Street

Marylebone Road, NW1 (0171 935 6861)

Wander through the gallery of astronomy and space travel before taking your reclining seat for the audio-visual star show. As you gaze up into the dome of stars the usually impossible-to-comprehend habits of the planets, of time and the universe are explained before your very eyes. The images are created by the Zeiss Planetarium Projector which can recreate the night sky as seen from any place on earth and at any time through history. No prior knowledge of astronomy necessary. Shows last 30 minutes. Phone for times. Wheelchair access (book in advance). Toilet for disabled people; baby-changing facilities in Madame Tussaud's. See also page 72.

London Toy & Model Museum 😊 🐾 ◐

21–23 Craven Hill, W2 (0171 402 5222/706 8000)

This wonderful museum started life as two large Victorian houses joined together to create a labyrinth of small rooms with the best collection in Europe of dolls, teddies, Dinky toys, Meccano, clockwork planes, cars and rows of shops, regiments of soldiers, nursery toys and dolls' houses. Despite a £4 million facelift, the museum has managed to retain its eccentricity while the themed galleries on 5 floors mean more space to display the 7,000 or so toys and models ranging from an ancient Roman gladiator doll to a modern toy robot. Collection of scale models include a highly decorated, fully functioning 1920s funfair and the miniature Axford village. There's a wooden Noah's Ark with 90 pairs of animals, and a showcase of Paddington, the most famous London bear. A model railway circles the garden and there is a miniature railway that trundles children through tunnels and across the pond (it is steam-driven at weekends). Those under 10 can ride the highly decorated, hand-cranked vintage fairground carousel for just 10p, before playing the end-of-pier penny slot machines with their older siblings. Summer events include a model boat regatta, a teddy bear's picnic and a train fair. Excellent place for children's birthday parties (ring for details). Not suitable for double buggies. Toilets for disabled. Baby-changing facilities.

Hours
Mon-Sat 10am-5.30pm; Sun & Bank Holidays 11am-5.30pm

Admission
Adults £4.95, children £2.95, concs £3.95, family ticket (2+2) £13.50

Travel
Lancaster Gate, Bayswater or Queensway ⊖ Paddington ⊖ ⇌
Bus 12, 88, 94

London Transport Museum 😊 🐾 ◔

Covent Garden, WC2 (0171 379 6344)

Horse-drawn, motor and trolley buses, trams and underground trains illustrating London public transport from 1829 are housed within the impressive and ornate, cast-iron arched frame and glazed roof of the 1870s Flower Market. When we went, the actors playing characters associated with the past 200 years of transport in London had shrunk to a lone road sweeper (from whom Jake ran in terror) but the interactive video displays next to each exhibit will turn on any budding tube, bus or tram spotter. Pace yourselves, the first exhibits are the most exciting — and use your imagination. Sit on an old bus and imagine what it was like to go to work in days gone

Hours
Daily 10am-6pm (last admission 5.15pm) closed Dec 24-26

Admission
Adults £3.95, children & concs £2.50, under-5s free & family ticket £10

Travel
Covent Garden or Leicester Square ⊖

by during one of London's famous 'pea-soupers'. Don't miss the 'Padded Cell', an 1890 carriage which has no windows because designers reasoned that passengers might be frightened to see the tunnel walls flashing by so fast, or the Ladies Only carriage on the Metropolitan underground train. There is plenty of room for toddlers to run around (mostly accessible by buggy). Holiday events such as puzzles, hunts for a missing ticket or storytelling on the top of a tram. Shop. Allow one hour for under-5s, two or more for over-7s, then head for the Cabaret Mechanical Theatre which toddlers and teenagers will enjoy, see page 61. Toilets for disabled. Baby-changing facilities.

Madame Tussaud's

Hours
Mon-Fri 10am-
5.30pm, Sat & Sun
9.30am-5.30pm

Admission
Adults £8.35,
children £5.25,
OAPs £6.25, family
ticket (2+2)
£21.95. Beat the
queue and book
tickets by credit
card on 0171 465
0077

Travel
⊖ Baker Street

Marylebone Road, NW1 (0171 935 6861)

Nearly 3 million visitors come here every year so don't be surprised if you have to queue for several hours at Easter and in the summer holidays. Best times to arrive are before 11am and after 3pm. The Chamber of Horrors is a wonderfully gruesome place for bloodthirsty kids (but not the very young). You can see the wax heads of guillotine victims King Louis XVI and Marie Antoinette taken from the death masks made by Madame Tussaud by order of the French Government during the French Revolution. You can enjoy the sights and sounds of the seaside at The Promenade Pier Café or meet the Royal Family in all their finery, see a rather grey-looking Henry VIII surrounded by his six wives or spot the man in grey out of the selection of modern Prime Ministers. The Spirit of London, the new dark-ride finale, takes you off on a whistle-stop tour of London's history in a 'time taxi' (replica of a black cab) which visits Elizabeth I, Shakespeare, Sir Christopher Wren, Queen Victoria, Charles Dickens, Churchill, Twiggy and Benny Hill. Toilets for disabled and baby-changing facilities. See also The London Planetarium page 70.

Museum of London

Hours
Tues-Sat 10am-
5.50pm
(last admission
5.30pm), Sun
noon-5.50pm
(last admission
5.30pm). Open
Bank Holidays

150 London Wall, EC2 (0171 600 3699)

See what a Roman room would have looked like, stand in an 18th-century debtors' prison cell and walk through the door of Newgate prison, wander down a Victorian street and look into the grocer's and pawnbroker's shops. Listen to the sounds of London at war and imagine what it was like to spend the night in an air-raid shelter. Marvel at the ornate splendour of the Lord Mayor of London's 1757 stagecoach. Look out for a pair of leather bikini-style trunks dating from Boudicca's sacking of London in AD61 and the skulls of some of her decapitated victims. Displays are imaginative and there are numerous changing exhibits from an extensive collection. There is a film about the Great Fire which devastated London in 1666. Accessible by buggy with a lift between floors. Picnic area on nearby lawns. Full wheelchair access. Seasonal events and workshops. Restaurant next door (closes 5pm). Shop. Good facilities for disabled people. Baby-changing facilities.

Admission
Adults £3.50 children & concs £1.75, under-5s free, family tickets (2+2) £8.50 Admission free after 4.30pm.

Travel
St Paul's, Moorgate or Bank ⊖
Barbican ⊖ ⇌

Museum of Mankind

6 Burlington Gardens, W1 (0171 437 2224)

This ethnographic museum houses a series of changing exhibitions which give an excellent insight into the way non-western societies live with a collection of costumes, weapons, statues and domestic items. Look out for the enigmatic Ancestor Figure from Easter Island (in the foyer), and the rare and valuable Aztec treasures in Room 1, including a sacrificial wooden knife, used to take the heart out of a living victim. The masks, many of which are worn to give the wearer the power of the animal, bird or demon the mask represents, are popular with young children. Look out for the shrunken human heads with lips sewn up into a deathly grin from Equador and the Botswanan hat made from spiders' webs. Free film shows on Tuesday-Friday afternoons linked to current exhibitions. Shop, library. Toilets for disabled. Baby-changing facilities. Wheelchair access by prior arrangement.

Hours
Mon-Sat 10am-5pm, Sun 2.30-6pm (closed some Bank Holidays).

Travel
Green Park, Oxford Circus or Piccadilly Circus ⊖

Museum of the Moving Image (MOMI)

South Bank, SE1 (0171 401 2636/928 3535)

Popular hands-on museum which tells the story of moving images from Chinese shadow puppets through to film, television, video, satellite and holograms. Children can be inter-

Hours
Daily 10am-6pm (closed Dec 24-26)

Admission
Adults £5.95, children & concs £4, students £4.85, under-5s free, family ticket (2+2) £16

Travel
◉ Embankment
◉⇌ Waterloo

viewed by a televisual Barry Norman then watch themselves on the TV monitor, make their own cartoons in the animation room, read the News at Ten from autocue, try-out for a Hollywood audition, take part in a cowboy film or fly across London like Superman. Actors are on hand to liven up the proceedings. The workshop has a programme of events, lectures, films and magic-lantern shows. Best for children of six and over, although younger ones will still get something out of it. Restaurant. Buggy access restricted (book in advance for wheelchair access). Toilets for disabled. Baby-changing facilities.

Hours
Daily 10am-
5.30pm

Travel
◉ Sloane Square
then **bus** 1, 19 or
22 to Smith Street

National Army Museum

Royal Hospital Road, Chelsea SW3 (0171 730 0717)

The emphasis is on the lives of individual soldiers from the first men to join Henry VII's Yeomen of the Guard to the present-day men and women of action. Particularly popular is the 400sq ft model of the Battle of Waterloo complete with over 70,000 model soldiers, and the skeleton of Napoleon's horse Marengo. Summer holiday activities include model making, drawing, trails and films. Café. Shop. Wheelchair and buggy access. Toilets for disabled. Baby-changing facilities.

Hours
Mon-Sat 10am-
6pm, Sun 2-6pm

Admission
Free (charge for
special exhibitions)

Travel
◉ Leicester
Square or
Embankment
◉⇌ Charing
Cross

National Gallery

Trafalgar Square, WC2 (0171 839 3321)

As you cannot possibly see everything in one go your first stop should be the high-tech micro-gallery in the Sainsbury Wing where colour touch-screen computer terminals allow you to explore the collection then plan and print out your own personalised tour. It is worth investing in the 'National Gallery Children's Book' and/or the 'Twenty Great Paintings' booklet rather than joining a guided tour, or let younger children just roam around – you will be surprised by what they find, the way they see paintings and what they like. Those in a hurry should pick up the information sheet entitled *A Quick Visit to the National Gallery* which directs you to the 16 greatest masterpieces. The rooms are laid out logically in broadly chronological order so older children can get a real feel for the development of art through the ages. Best times to go are weekday mornings or late afternoons. Wheelchair access (entrance Sainsbury Wing or Orange Street). Shop. Buggy Access. Toilets for disabled people. Baby-changing facilities.

National Maritime Museum

Romney Road, Greenwich, SE10 (0181 858 4422)

National Maritime Museum galleries include Navy Board models, Captain Cook Explorers, Barge House, Nelson and 20th-Century Sea Power. Look out for Nelson's uniform worn at the Battle of Trafalgar. In the Neptune Hall you can walk around the engine room of the Reliant steam tug, go aboard a steam-liner, peek into the luxury steam yacht of biscuit baron Alfred Palmer where the table is set for tea with china cups and Bourbon biscuits. Watch the lighthouse light flash across the hall or ring the bell of the Mauretania. A wonderful museum for all things nautical with a collection of the most friendly, helpful and entertaining staff we've come across. It's also real value for money. Passport Ticket gives you entry to the Museum, the Queen's House and the Old Royal Observatory (and allows you to return to one site on one other day). Toilets for disabled people. Baby-changing facilities. Shop. Wheelchair access to ground floor only. Buggies can be carried upstairs and used in most galleries.

Hours
Summer Mon-Sat 10am-6pm, Sun 2-6pm. Winter Mon-Sat 10am-5pm, Sun 2-5pm

Admission
Adults £5.50, children (7-16) £3, under-7s free, concs £4.50, family ticket (2+3) £16.

Travel
Maze Hill
DLR Island Gardens then walk through foot tunnel
Boats from Westminster, Charing Cross or Tower Pier

National Museum of Cartoon Art

15–17 Saint Cross Street, EC1 (0171 405 4717)

Ever-changing exhibition of British cartoons, caricatures and comic strips. Daytime and evening classes for children and adults in the art of cartoon-making. No baby-changing facilities or toilets for disabled people.

Hours
Mon-Fri noon-6pm
Admission
Free but donations requested
Travel
Farringdon

National Portrait Gallery

St Martin's Place, WC2 (0171 306 0055)

This is a great place for children doing the Tudors and Stuarts at school or those who like to put faces to historic figures (and the present Royal Family who feature extensively)

Hours
Mon-Sat 10am-6pm, Sun 2-6pm

Admission
Free (sometimes
charge for special
exhibitions).

Travel
⊖ Leicester
Square
⊖⇄ Charing
Cross

as well as more contemporary icons such as Jagger or Geldof. The top floor is full of Tudor royalty, notorious traitors, po-faced prelates and the only painting of Shakespeare for which he actually sat. Look out for a rather tired-looking Charles II next to a room housing portraits of his many mistresses including the orange-seller-turned actress Nell Gwyn. We found it best suited to children over nine. Children's holiday events, painting, and study groups. Quiz and worksheets available. No café but there is one next door in the National Gallery (see above). Shop. Toilets for disabled. Baby-changing facilities. Wheelchair access.

Hours
Mon–Sat
10am–5.50pm,
Sun 11am–5.50pm

Admission
Adults £5.50,
children and concs
£2.80, under-5s
free, family ticket
(2+4) £5.00. Free
Mon–Fri
4.30–5.50pm, Sat
& Sun 5–5.50pm

Travel
⊖ South
Kensington.
Quite a number of
parking meters in
neighbouring
roads; weekend
parking at Imperial
College £1

Natural History Museum 😊 🐛 ▶

Cromwell Road, South Kensington SW7 (0171 938 9123)

The giant skeleton of a Diplodocus marks your arrival in the great Central Hall in this monolithic, neo-Gothic bastion of Victoriana which is full of moving beasts, press-button gadgets and 3D-video magic. You can't go wrong with the major permanent dinosaur exhibition with some bloodthirsty scenes to enjoy or Discovering Mammals – a display of the biggest, tallest and rarest animals in the world including the blue whale. The Creepy Crawlies gallery teems with spiders, insects, centipedes and other arthropods while Wonders introduces visitors to the museum's more unusual exhibits – a 40-million-year-old spider trapped in amber, an extinct giant ground sloth, and an elephant-bird egg. Discovery Room for children (Easter and summer holidays) which is aimed at 7–11-year-olds but younger children will also have fun here with the 'feely box', trying to guess what's inside by touch, or collecting data about their bodies. The building also houses the Geological Museum, reached by a linking passage, which portrays the story of the Earth through models, mineral displays and various special effects including an earthquake simulator (a moving platform that gives you the same sensation as being in a real earthquake tremor). Field excursions and films. Shop. Café and restaurant. Toilets for disabled people. Baby-changing facilities. Wheelchair access.

North Woolwich Old Station Museum

Pier Road, E16 (0171 474 7244)

Set in the restored North Woolwich Old Station this delightful little museum charts the history of the Great Eastern Railway and the Docklands rail system. There is a reconstructed Victorian ticket office, display cases with easy–to–understand illustrations of how steam is made and what it is used for, and lots of model trains. Outside on the station platform (which you can arrive on if you take the train) stands the 'Coffee Pot' engine (the oldest GER engine), old carriages, signalling devices and so on. Engines are put in steam on Easter Sunday and the first Sunday of the month in summer. pub opposite has good views of the Thames. Arriving via the free foot tunnel is fun for under-4s, or take the train into the actual museum station. There is a shop and very clean toilets so you can even change babies on the floor (no specific facilities). No disabled toilets. If you are going by car a visit here could be combined with one to the Museum of Artillery. Both are free, as is the ferry.

Hours
Mon-Wed & Sat 10am-5pm, Sun & Bank Holidays 2-5pm

Travel
North Woolwich ⇌ then **ferry** or **foot tunnel**
Bus 69, 101, 276

Old Operating Theatre, Museum and Herb Garret

9a St Thomas Street, SE1 (0171 955 4791)

This is the only surviving example of an early 19th-century operating theatre. The herb garret has a fascinating collection of objects revealing the horrors of medicine before the age of science, displayed alongside pickled bits of 19th-century bodies. In the operating theatre patients would be propped up on the wooden table so they could watch the surgeon – if they could stand the pain. Ask the kids to shut their eyes and imagine the screams of the unanaesthetised amputees (alcohol was used to dull the patient's senses but surgeons relied on swift techniques – one minute or less for an amputation). Look out for the box of sawdust which the surgeon would move round with his foot to catch the blood. Toilets (with space for baby-changing though no specific facilities). No wheelchair access or toilets for disabled people.

Hours
Tues-Sun 10am-4pm (times vary)

Admission
Adults £2, children £1, concs £1.50

Travel
London Bridge ⊖⇌

Old Royal Observatory ☼ ◗

Greenwich Park, SE10 (0181 858 4422)

Hours
Mon-Sat 10am-
6pm, Sun noon-
6pm

Admission
Adults £4, children
(5-16) £2, concs
£3, family ticket
£12. For Passport
Ticket to the
Observatory,
National Maritime
Museum and
Queen's House see
National Maritime
Museum above

Travel
⇌ Greenwich,
Maze Hill

Recent renovations to the home of Greenwich Mean Time and Longitude Zero, Prime Meridian of the World, have transformed the once gloomy, specialist museum into a compelling and accessible display area with hands-on science stations for children, a light-and-sound show in the Telescope Dome (reached via a spiral staircase), exhibits illustrating the story of time-keeping and astronomy, and the apartments of the Astronomers Royal. On the roof is the red 'time ball' which rises to the top of its mast and drops at 1pm every day, controlled by the 24-hour clock on the wall below (once used as a time signal for ships on the Thames). Toilets for disabled people. Baby-changing facilities.

Pollock's Toy Museum 🌧 ◗

1 Scala Street, W1 (0171 379 7866)

Hours
Mon-Sat 10am-
5.30pm (last
admission 4.30pm)

Admission
Adults £2, children
(3-18) 75p (Sat
accompanied
children free)

Travel
⊖ Goodge Street
Bus 14, 24, 29, 73

This charming museum, named after Benjamin Pollock, the toy-theatre designer, is like a child-size doll's house. Occupying two small, adjoining 18th-century houses connected by narrow winding staircases, the tiny, red-painted rooms with their low ceilings are jam-packed with toys from all over the world. Ideal for children aged 7–12, who will love the large collection of dolls and dolls' houses, but younger children (4–6 years) need to exercise rather a lot of self-control. Some of the exhibits are high up in glass cases so small children need to be lifted, which can be a problem in the confined space. Stairs are a problem with toddlers, and buggies must be left at the entrance. Among my favourite toys were the tiny Egyptian clay mouse with moving jaw and tail which is over 4,000 years old, the exhibit which shows how composition dolls were made, and the fascinating collection of dolls' houses. Jake liked the collection of puppets, especially Punch and Judy, and the reconstruction of a 1920s toy shop. Benjamin liked the farm animals and the fort, both of which were at ground level, and the teddy bears which popped up in unexpected places. Everything is meticulously labelled. There is a games room where you can try out old-fashioned board games. The delightful, well–stocked shop sells all you need to stage your own Aladdin, Cinderella or Ali Baba and the 40 Thieves. No café. Small toilet with narrow shelf for emergency baby-changing. No disabled toilets. No wheelchair or buggy access.

Puppet Centre Trust ⬛ 🌧 🕐

Battersea Arts Centre, Lavender Hill, SW11 (0171 228 5335)

A registered charity set up to promote and develop the art of puppetry in Britain, the Puppet Centre provides information and resources on all aspects of puppetry, training workshops and an exhibition of puppets from all over the world. The exhibition is suitable for all children with an interest in puppets while older children with a genuine desire to learn more will find the centre invaluable. Parents who remember Muffin the Mule will have fun boring their kids about how children's tv used to be so much better than it is today. Toilets and baby-changing facilities, café, bookshop.

Hours
Mon-Fri 2-6pm

Travel
South Kensington ⊖ then 45A **bus** or Clapham Junction ⇌

Ragged School Museum ⬛ 🌧 🕐

46-48 Copperfield Road, E3 (0181 980 6405)

This museum of the East End examines the experiences of children who attended the Ragged School during the late-Victorian period. This canal-side warehouse once housed Dr Barnado's Ragged Day School set up in the 1880s in response to the terrible living conditions of London's poor children. School groups can attend a typical Victorian lesson in the recreated classroom and see how it compares with today's schooling. Shop and café. Toilets. No disabled toilets or baby-changing facilities.

Hours
Wed, Thurs 10am-5pm, first Sun of each month 2-5pm

Admission
Free (donations appreciated)

Travel
Mile End ⊖

Rock Circus ☺ 🌧 🕐

London Pavilion, Piccadilly Circus, W1 (0171 734 7203)

The rock 'n' roll counterpart to Madame Tussaud's is hugely popular with children and teenagers. A non-too-young Tim Rice look-a-like compères the half-hour concert during which electronically controlled moving, speaking and singing versions of your favourite pop stars, from the

Hours
Mon, Wed, Thurs, Sun 11am-9pm, Tues noon-9pm, Fri & Sat 11am-10pm (extended hours in summer)

Admission
Adults £7.50,
children (under-
16s) £5.75, under-
5s & disabled free,
family ticket (2+2)
£19.95
Travel
⊖ Piccadilly
Circus

Beatles, Elvis and Madonna to the nine-minute wonders of the day, strut their stuff (complete with lips synchronised to the recorded singing). You can then wander around the wax figures with a set of headphones which pick up infra-red signals from whichever display you happen to be looking at (Prince, Status Quo, Jim Morrison, Bruce Springsteen, Janis Joplin). Shop has souvenirs, books and T-shirts. Snack bar and refreshments available. Disabled toilets and baby-changing facilities. Wheelchair and buggy access.

Hours
Daily 10am-6pm
(closed Dec 24-26,
Jan 1)
Admission
Adults £5.20,
children (5-15),
students & OAPs
£2.60, disabled and
under-5s free,
family ticket (2+2)
£12.60
Travel
⊖ Colindale
⊼ Mill Hill
Bus 303 from
Edgware, Mill Hill
or Colindale,
free on-site
parking

Royal Airforce Museum (including Battle of Britain Hall and Bomber Command Hall) 😊 🌧 ◑

Grahame Park Way, Hendon, NW9 (0181 205 2266)

Standing on the site of the old Hendon Aerodrome this impressive collection, which will turn any child into a plane spotter, includes a display of 70 full-size aircraft. You can walk around and underneath the planes and sit in the cockpits. Have a go in the Tornado flight simulator (preferably before your lunch – it's stomach-churningly realistic) or the Jet Provost Trainer. The Aircraft Hall, made from two huge First World War hangars, and the Battle of Britain Hall house original Spitfires, a Vulcan bomber and the Hawker Hurricane, and you can watch a 20-minute video showing the complete story (which will interest older children only). Restaurant (10am–5pm daily). Wheelchair and buggy access. Disabled toilets and baby changing facilities.

Hours
Daily 7am-6pm,
Galleries, crypt and
ambulatory open
Mon-Fri
10am-4.15pm, Sat
11am-4.15pm
Admission
Donations
requested.
Galleries: adults
£2.75, under-16s
£1.15; Crypt adults
£1.75, under-16s
75p
Travel
⊖ St Paul's

St Paul's Cathedral 🄴 🌧 ◑

EC4 (0171 248 2705)

However much one might like to think otherwise, the only real interest for children in Christopher Wren's masterpiece is in the dome itself – how high up it they can climb and how quietly they can whisper and still be heard. Catch a quick glimpse of Wren's epitaph in the centre of the floor ('If you seek his monument, look around you') before heading for the south transit stairs leading to a series of galleries in the dome. The first, after 250 steps, is the Whispering Gallery, a balcony running round the inside of the dome and so called because a whisper directed along the wall on one side can be very clearly heard over 100ft away on the other side. Up another 118 steps to the Stone Gallery and a wonderful view of London. Finally you can ascend the last 153 rather narrow steps to the Golden Gallery — but this is not for the faint-hearted or very young. Shop. Toilets for disabled people. Baby-changing facilities.

Science Museum

Exhibition Road, SW7 (0171 938 8000/8080)

This is by far the most popular national museum as far as children are concerned – five floors of interactive galleries and marvellous displays of scientific invention allowing children to explore basic scientific principles. Children love Flight Lab where 24 hands-on exhibits demonstrate the principles of flight – you can climb up onto the Cessna light aircraft while listening to a pre–flight check on tape and there is a full size replica of Apollo 11 Lunar Lander. Launch Pad is a brilliant hands-on interactive children's gallery full of do-it-yourself experiments exploring basic scientific principles, including building a bridge or becoming a human battery. Science Nights offer children of 8–11 and accompanying adults a chance to camp overnight in the museum, take part in workshops, go on spooky torchlit museum tours and listen to late–night story-telling as they snuggle up in sleeping bags (book on 0171 938 9785). Dramatised gallery talks and family lectures in school holidays. Café, well-stocked shop and book store. Toilets, baby-changing facilities. Wheelchair and buggy access.

Hours
Daily 10am-6pm

Admission
Adults £5, children (5-15) and concs £2.60; disabled and under-5s free. Free admission after 4.30pm. Season ticket available

Travel
South Kensington ⊖
Meter parking in surrounding streets, weekends at Imperial College for £1

Story of Telecommunications

(Also known as BT Museum)

145 Queen Victoria Street, EC4 (0171 248 7444)

British Telecom's museum charts the rise of telecommunications from the telegraph to the age of digital transmission and fax. Ringing phones, flashing lights, video sound tracks and clicking switchgear make this fun for all kids. Allow an hour for small children and longer for older, mechanically-minded children. Toilets. No baby-changing facilities.

Hours
Mon-Fri 10am-5pm (& Sat of Lord Mayor's Show)

Travel
St Paul's or Mansion House ⊖

The Tate Gallery 😊 📧 🌧️ ◖

Hours
Mon-Sat 10am-
5.30pm, Sun 2-
5.30pm (closed
Dec 24-26, Jan 1,
Good Fri, May
Bank Holiday)

Admission
Free (charge for
special exhibitions)

Travel
⊖ Pimlico
Parking meters in
Atterbury Street

Millbank, SW1 (0171 887 8000)

You will see mothers with new-borns and children of all ages here – the toddlers love the animals depicted in the first 4 galleries while older children can spend ages sorting out the images in the cubist paintings or finding their own in the abstract works. Exhibits range from 16th-century world art to the works of present-day artists with the national collection of British art permanently displayed. Trails and special children's tours. Shop and coffee shop. Baby-changing facilities. Wheelchair access and toilets for disabled people.

Thames Barrier and Visitors'   Centre

Admission
The Visitors' Centre
– adults £2.50,
concs £1.55, family
ticket (2+3) £6.80

Travel
🚂 Charlton
Bus 177, 80
Boat from
Greenwich or
Westminster Piers
Car park 50p

Unity Way, Woolwich, SE18 (0181 854 1373)

A short boat trip takes you from Greenwich Pier past the least scenic part of the Thames to the enormous shining fins of the Thames Barrier, one of the most remarkable feats of engineering this century, to say nothing of its architectural beauty. The Visitors' Centre, open daily, has a foyer exhibition and audio-visual presentation of the construction of the Thames Barrier (of interest to children doing river or engineering projects – mine weren't and fell asleep!). The Barrier is raised for tests once a month which you can watch from the bank but you cannot go through the barrier by boat. Souvenir shop, riverside walk, picnic and outdoor play area, café. Baby-changing facilities. Disabled toilets. Wheelchair and buggy access.

The Theatre Museum 😊

Hours
Tues-Sun 11am-
7pm

Admission
Adults £3, children
(6-14) £1.50,
under-5s free

Travel
⊖ Covent Garden

1a Taviestock St, WC2 (0171 836 7891)

A permanent exhibition of memorabilia from all the major performing arts with stage models, costumes, prints and drawings, puppets, props and posters. Popular exhibits include John Lennon's black Beatles suit and the rather more flamboyant costumes worn by Mick Jagger and Elton John. Look out for the wheelbarrow of the legendary tightrope walker Charles Blondin with which he crossed Niagara Falls in 1859, and display cases featuring Grimaldi, the Father of all Clowns, and Phineas T Barnum, showman extraordinaire who coined the phrase 'there's a sucker born every minute'. There is usually a make-up artist on hand to give you a hideous scar or bloody flesh wound. Café, induction loop for the hard of hearing, wheelchair access. Toilets for disabled people and baby-changing facilities.

Tower Bridge Museum: 😊 🐾 🌓
The Celebration Story

Tower Bridge, E1 (0171 378 1928)

This famous piece of Victoriana is brought to life in an imaginative multi-media exhibition inside the bridge itself. The 75-minute walking tour (and stair-climbing unless you have small children in a buggy, in which case the extremely friendly staff will take you from floor to floor in the lift) takes you on a journey through time to the 1890s where "Harry", an animatronic worker, takes over acting as guide and commentator, telling the story of the most famous draw-bridge in the world. He doesn't mention that, in 1952, a double-decker London bus, route number 78, jumped a 3-foot gap over the open bridge when the traffic lights didn't switch to red: "I had to keep going," said the driver, "otherwise we should have been in the water." Toilets for disabled. Baby-changing facilities. Buggy and wheelchair access in lifts.

Hours
Daily in April-Oct 10am-6.15pm, Nov-March 10am-5.15pm (closed Good Friday, Dec 24-26, Jan 1; last admission 1 hour before closing)

Admission
Adults £5, children & OAPs £3.50, family ticket (2+2) £14

Travel
Tower Hill ⊖
London Bridge ⊖ ⇌
Bus 15 to Tower Hill

Tower Hill Pageant 😊 🐾 🌓

Tower Hill, EC3 (0171 709 0081)

Via a glass lift through which you see the different layers of London hidden beneath street level, all reconstructed as an archaeological dig, you enter a computer-controlled time car which transports you through 2,000 years of history in an hour – from Roman London, past Viking ships, Norman conquerors, scenes from the Great Plague and the Fire of London, through the Blitz to the present day. You get a glimpse and a whiff of each era (and believe me London smelt) but don't blink or you will miss great chunks of history. Also a Waterfront Finds Museum with hundreds of archaeological discoveries excavated under the streets of London over the

Hours
April 1-Oct 31 daily 9.30am-5.30pm; Nov 1-March 31 9.30am-4.30pm

Admission
Adults £6.25, children £4.25, OAPs £4.95, under-4s free, family ticket (2+2) £15.75

Travel
Tower Hill ⊖
DLR Tower Gateway
Fenchurch Street ⇌
Bus 15, 25

past 20 years (jewellery, pottery and even a bubonic plague victim). Purpose-built car takes wheelchairs. Café. No toilets (public toilets on hill outside).

Tower Of London

Tower Hill, EC3 (0171 709 0765)

Hours
March-Oct, Mon-Sat 9am-6pm, Sun 10am-6pm (sometimes 6.30pm); Nov-Feb Mon-Sat 9.30am-5pm, Sun 10am-5pm (closed Dec 24-26, Jan 1, Good Friday)

Admission
Adults £8.50, children £5.50, under-5s free, family ticket £21.95

Travel
⊖ Tower Hill
DLR Tower Gateway
⇌ Fenchurch Street
NCP car park nearby

If possible, go on a clear autumn or winter day to avoid summer and spring holiday queues and allow plenty of time – this is a deceptively large area with lots to see. It is worth filling in children on the background of the tower, especially the gory bits, embellishing the facts if you have to as it does make it more fun for them, whatever their age (ask the Tower to send you a leaflet in advance – it has some historic information). You get a lot for your money – executions, murder most foul, assignations, incarcerations, treachery, dungeons, an armoury and, of course, the ravens (who have been known to bite). There's the Bloody Tower, so called after the two young princes who were murdered at the behest of their uncle, Richard III; the White Tower, in which Guy Fawkes was tortured three times on the rack before finally confessing to the Gunpowder Plot; Tower Green where Lady Jane Grey was beheaded at the instigation of her half-sister Princess Mary – particularly popular with our friend's daughter who expressed a wish to become a Princess, looking murderously at her sister who was whingeing because she could not buy a raven as a pet. Tower Green is also where the Changing of the Guard takes place daily in summer and on alternate days in winter, usually at 11.30am. The Crown Jewels are now housed in a separate Jewel House round which visitors are conveyed on an airport-style moving walkway. Queues are still long (Easter Bank Holiday up to 50 minutes) but you could always take heart at the words of the Tower's resident governor, quoted as saying 'we like to think that what we are offering is not a queue but a line of anticipation'. You cannot overtake and it gets very crowded. Café and picnic area on wharf nearby. Very restricted wheelchair and buggy access. Toilets for disabled and baby-changing facilities.

Vestry House Museum

Vestry Road, Walthamstow, E17 (0181 509 1917)

This 1730s brick workhouse is now a local history museum with an extensive collection of photographs (many of which can be bought as postcards) and a fine example of a Victorian parlour full of kitchenalia. Highlights with the kids include an original police cell, which survived from 1840 when it used to be the local police station, and the Bremer Car – the first all-British car to be made in London by local Frederick Bremer in 1892. No toilets for disabled or baby-changing facilities. Partial wheelchair and buggy access.

Hours
Mon-Fri 10am-1pm & 2-5.30pm, Sat to 5pm

Travel
Walthamstow

Victoria and Albert Museum

Cromwell Road, SW7 (0171 938 8500)

This museum of decorative arts and design is situated, perhaps surprisingly, across the road from the Science Museum and is popular with children. There are seven miles of gallery across this 13-acre site so you do have to know what you are doing – pick up a free *Guide To The V&A* at the information desk, sit down for five minutes and plan what you are going to see that day. Don't miss Tipoo's Tiger (it's just outside the restaurant), a painted wooden figure of a tiger mauling a British soldier. Inside it there is a pipe organ and bellows that produce roars and groans as the tiger attacks. Other things to locate are the Bed of Ware, the largest four-poster bed in England (made in 1580, it was big enough to hold eight people and by tradition those who slept in it carved their names on the oak), the beautiful glistening jewellery, and the Cabinet of Mirrors, an oval room with mirrored walls and a star-patterned floor. The Young Visitor's Guide is sold in the shop and has suggestions for a Treasure Trail and nine things to look out for. Free guided tours for children are aimed at 6–11-year-olds (ring for dates and times). Holiday workshops. Restaurant (0171 938 8358). Good café. Shop. Toilets with baby-changing and disabled facilities. Wheelchair and buggy access.

Hours
Mon noon-5.50pm, Tues-Sat 10am-5.50pm, Sun 2.30-5.40pm

Admission
Free but "voluntary" donations expected (adults £4.00, concs £1.50)

Travel
South Kensington

Westminster Abbey ▣ 🌳 🕐

Hours
Mon–Fri
9.30am–4pm, Sat
9.30am–2pm &
3.45–5pm (Sun
closed – service
only). Museum
open daily

Travel
⊖ Westminster
or St James's Park

Broad Sanctuary, SW1 (0171 222 5152)

The best time to go is weekday mornings (and on Wednesday evenings when photography is allowed). Westminster Abbey has been the scene of every royal coronation since William the Conqueror was crowned on Christmas Day in 1066. Nine English kings and queens are buried in Saint Edward's Chapel and there are more in Henry VII's beautiful chapel including Elizabeth I and the bones found hidden in the Tower of London (probably those of the princes murdered there at the behest of their uncle who became Richard III). The things that caught 10-year-old Shay's lurid imagination were the scraps of skin preserved on the door of St Faith's Chapel – the remains of someone who attempted to rob the Abbey in the 1500s and was subsequently flayed to death.

William Morris Gallery 😊 ▣ ☼ ◐

Hours
Open Tues-Sat
10am-1pm, 2-5pm
& first Sun of
month 10am-noon
& 2-5pm

Travel
Walthamstow
⊖ ⇌ Central
Bus 34, 97, 215,
257, 275

Lloyd Park, Forest Road, E17 (0181 527 3782/5544 ex 4390)

Although welcoming children of all ages, this is an excellent museum for over-5s, or toddlers happy to remain in their buggy, as the museum has recently been redesigned with open display areas (furniture and carpets are on open display, not roped off). Unless your under-5s are very restrained we suggest you go with another adult so you can take turns to enjoy the exhibits with older children while younger children run around in the beautifully landscaped Lloyd Park, which has lots to appeal to toddlers including an aviary, a moat with black swans, geese and ducks, and play areas. For children 'doing' the Victorians the gallery is a great place to start. As a poet, writer, textile and furniture designer, conservationist, socialist, printer and manuscript illuminator, William Morris's life and work touch on all aspects of the period. Shop (with a mail-order service). Take a picnic in fine weather. Toilets, no disabled or baby-changing facilities. Wheelchair and buggy access. Disabled toilet outside entrance to Lloyd Park.

Looking for something to amuse, divert and delight? Look no further — whether it's drama, comedy, circus, film or music, London is full of entertainment aimed at and suitable for children of all ages. Call **KIDSLINE** (0171 222 8070) open term-times from Monday–Friday 4–6pm, or during school holidays from Monday–Friday 9am–4pm, for details of children's entertainment in London.

Stage & Screen

CINEMAS

Barbican Children's Cinema Club

Barbican Centre (Cinema 1), EC2 (0171 638 8891)

Hours
Sat 2.30pm
Prices
Annual membership £3, then children £2.50, accompanying adult guests £3
Travel
◐ Moorgate or Barbican

Shows a wide range of films and cartoons suitable for 6-12-year-olds. There is a restaurant, several cafés, car park, shops, disabled toilets and wheelchair access. Arrive early because everyone gets lost in this concrete jungle and remember where you have parked your car, and in which car park.

Clapham Picture House

76 Venn Street, SW4 (0171 498 2242)

Hours
Sat 11.45am
Prices
Annual membership £3, then £2.50, adult guests £4.50
Travel
◐ Clapham Common

Kids' Film Club with competitions, prizes and movie. If one child takes out a membership, brothers and sisters are entitled to join the club at reduced rates. Phone for details.

National Film Theatre

South Bank, SE1 (0171 928 3232)

Hours
Sat & Sun 4pm
Prices
Children £2, adults £3
Travel
◐⇌ Waterloo

Monthly programme available by sending stamped addressed envelope to the Junior NFT.

Phoenix

52 High Road, N2 (0181 444 6789/883 2233)

Hours
Sat 11am
Prices
Children £2, adults £3
Travel
◐ East Finchley

Children's Cinema Club on Saturday mornings.

Rio Cinema ☺

107 Kingsland High Street, Hackney, E8 (0171 249 2722/254 6677)

Hours
Sat 11am
Prices
Children £1.50, accompanying adults £2.50
Travel
⇌ Dalston Kingsland

Children's Picture Club. Under-5s must be accompanied by an adult but you can drop off over-5s, do your shopping and pick them up at the end of the film.

Willesden Green Library Centre

95 High Road, NW10 (0181 830 0822)

Kids' Cinema Club. Admission charge includes free popcorn and a drink.

Hours
Sat at 11am
Prices
All tickets £2
Travel
Willesden
Green ⊖

Whiteley's Cinema

Queensway, W2 (0171 792 3332)

There is no particular kids' club but children love watching movies at this mutliplex cinema with eight screens, good seating, lots of ticket offices so no long queues, and a host of food bars to choose from before or after the shows.

Prices
Adults £3.50-
£5.95, children
£3.50.
Travel
Queensway
or Bayswater ⊖

CIRCUS

There are no permanent circuses in London (the nearest being at Chessington – see Theme Parks, page 123) but they are held frequently in parks and open spaces throughout London from around October to the end of January.

Billy Smart's Circus

(details on 01903 721200)

An international cast of performers displaying spectacular traditional skills including comedy and mime, dressage horses and a troupe of dogs. Usually in London during October and November. Ring for details.

Chinese State Circus 😊

(details on 01260 297589)

Rope-dancers, foot-jugglers hoop-divers and others perform an array of breathtaking acts. Fresh, simple presentation free from slapstick, ring masters, over-loud music or animals. Traditional Chinese musicians. Highly reccommended for very young children who might be frightened by other types of circus. Usually in December or January. Ring for details.

The Cottle Sisters' Circus 😊

(details on 01932 857779)

While Gerry Cottle is off experimenting with a host of new entertainment ideas his three daughters are carrying on the family tradition touring England all year with their show. Representing a return to the real roots of circus the only animal acts are feats of horsemanship. New to their exciting show is the first ever woman-cannonball act. Ring for details.

Moscow State Circus

(details on 01932 830000 or 0421 432215).

The very popular animal-free Moscow State Circus is touring Britain, from March to December 1996. Acts include a flying trapeze duo, a hula-hoop dancer, magicians, jugglers, a bendy Russian rag-doll and illusionists. Ring for details.

Prices
Adults from £4.50,
children from
£3.50

Zippo's Circus 😊

(details on mobile 0374 811811)

A delightful circus with virtuoso balancing acts, death-defying aerial stunts, exhilarating acrobatics, bizarre contortionists and many of the traditional circus tricks and treats. And, of course the ever popular clown Martin 'Zippo' Burton. This year Zippo is introducing horses for the first time but they will not be doing anything 'unhorsey'. Particularly suitable for under-8s. Ring for details.

DANCE

Hours
May-Sept
12.30pm

Travel
Liverpool
Street

Broadgate Arena ☼ 🇫

Liverpool Street & Eldon Street, EC2 (0171 588 6565)

Although this outdoor amphitheatre is used mainly for concerts it often has visiting dance companies, martial arts displays, race days and Giant Games which are suitable for children.

90

Chisenhale Dance Space 😊

64–84 Chisenhale Road, E3 (0181 981 6617/980 8115)

This venue does four shows a year specially designed for young children.

Prices
All tickets £2
Travel
Mile End ⊖

Royal Festival Hall

South Bank Centre, Belvedere Road, SE1 (0171 960 4242)

Every year the English National Ballet performs *The Nutcracker*, which opens in mid-December and runs for a month.

Hours
7.30pm
Prices
£8–£32
Travel
Waterloo ⊖ ⇌

Sadler's Wells Theatre and Lilian Baylis Theatre

Rosebery Avenue, EC1 (0171 278 8916)

As well as playing host to major dance companies from home and abroad featuring anything from flamenco to classical ballet, the Whirligig Theatre, Britain's leading company for children presents a season every autumn. The adjoining Lilian Baylis Theatre offers amazingly cheap tickets for what are often excellent and usually experimental dance, theatre and music shows.

Prices
£4–£25 (Lilian Baylis Theatre £1.50-£8)
Travel
Waterloo ⊖ ⇌

THEATRES

Of the many touring theatre companies aimed particularly at children look out for Pekko's Puppets, Pop-Up Theatre, Soap Box, Whirligig and Oyly Cart at a theatre near you.

The Albany Empire

Douglas Way, SE8 (details 0181 692 0231)

As well as many excellent children's shows the Albany usually does a very up-beat, streetwise panto (suited to cynical children rather than wide-eyed innocents who still believe in fairies and Tinkerbell).

Travel
Deptford ⇌

Battersea Arts Centre ☺

Prices
£3, children &
concs £2.50
Travel
⇌ Clapham
Junction
Bus 45, 77, 156

Old Town Hall, Lavender Hill, SW11 (0171 223 8413)

Excellent range of visiting theatre companies performing shows on Saturday afternoons.

Half Moon

Travel
⇌ Limehouse

43 White Horse Road, E1 (0171 265 8138)

As well as producing plays for children, this bilingual British/Bangladeshi theatre company offers theatrical and technical training courses. Ring for details.

Lauderdale House ☼ ☺

Hours
Sat 11.30am
Prices
£1-£4
Travel
⊖ Archway

Waterlow Park, Highgate Hill, N6 (0181 348 8716)

A family venue with fairs and puppet shows for under-10s.

Little Angel Marionette Theatre ☺

Prices
Adults £4.50-£6,
children
(under-17) £4-£5
Travel
⊖ Angel
⊖⇌ Highbury
and Islington

14 Dagmar Passage, off Cross Street, N1 (0171 226 1787)

This delightful venue is London's only permanent puppet theatre, with regular weekend and holiday performances and a visiting company in August. It usually caters for 3-7-year-olds and it specialises in traditional and folk tales using all kinds of puppetry.

London Bubble

5 Elephant Lane, SE16 (0171 237 4434)

A mobile arts company whose summer 'tent' tour travels through London's parks from May to September each year. In spring they do a community tour. The musicals, plays and cabaret are usually entertaining, and there is a large range of participatory theatre projects. Minimum age is 11 unless otherwise specified. Times and prices vary.

Lyric Hammersmith ☺

King Street, W6 (0181 741 2311)

Special plays for children. The Lyric hosts a very good Christmas panto, and you should also look out for the return of David Wood's superb *Noddy* show for over-2s. Book well in advance. The café has children's portions.

Hours
Sat 11am and 1pm
Prices
£3
Travel
Hammersmith ⊖

Malden Centre ☺

Blagdon Road, New Malden (0181 949 3330)

Saturday Splash offers occasional afternoon shows on Saturdays for under-5s with free swim before or after the show.

Prices
Adult and one child £4.40, one adult and two children £6.60.
Travel
New Malden ⇌

Nomad Puppet Studio ☺

37 Upper Tooting Road, SW17 (0181 767 4005)

Popular folk and fairytales have been adapted for this delightful little studio theatre, which also does private parties by arrangement. Phone bookings only.

Hours
Sundays 11.30am & 2.30pm
Prices
£2.50, includes squash and biscuits)
Travel
Tooting Bec ⊖

Old Vic ☺

Waterloo Road, SE1 (0171 928 7616)

The Wind in the Willows, Alan Bennett's hugely successful, wonderfully magical adaptation of Kenneth Grahame's children's tale, has transferred following four sell-out seasons at the Royal National Theatre for what is hoped will be an annual run at the Old Vic as well as a national tour. Suitable for children over four. Ring for details.

Hours
Mon-Sat 7.30pm, Wed and Sat 2.30pm
Prices
£10-£19.50
Travel
Waterloo ⊖⇌

Polka Theatre For Children ☺

240 The Broadway, SW19 (0181 543 4888/0363)

As well as hosting top visiting companies this splendid, purpose-built complex stages colourful, imaginative, specially-commissioned children's plays and puppet shows geared to different ages (ring to check details and suitability before booking). There are four shows a day in school holidays and two a day in term-time. The fine facilities include an adven-

Hours
Box office Tue-Fri 9.30am-4.30pm, Sat 11am-5.30pm
Prices
£3.50-£6.50
Travel
Wimbledon ⊖
South Wimbledon ⊖⇌

ture room, playground, and free puppet and toy exhibitions which relate to the performances. There is also a café, plus an induction loop for the hard-of-hearing and wheelchair access. The Christmas shows here are always very popular.

Puppet Theatre Barge 😊

Hours
Times vary so ring for details
Prices
Adults £5.50, children £5
Travel
Warwick Road

Little Venice, Blomfield Road W9 (0171 249 6876 or mobile phone 0836 202 745)

Movingstage Marionettes company gives performances throughout the year on an old Thames barge converted into a delightful miniature auditorium complete with a proscenium arch and raked seating. The venue is almost as much of a treat for children as the imaginative marionette and shadow puppet shows themselves. In Little Venice on the Regent's Canal from October to May, and sailing up the Thames between June and September (performances at Kingston and Richmond etc). 50 seats. Not all shows for kids.

Questors Theatre 😊

Travel
Ealing Broadway

Mattock Lane, W5 (0181 567 5184)

Family shows at Christmas and drama groups for children throughout the year.

Saturday Sausages 😊

Hours
First Sat of month 2pm
Prices
£2.40
Travel
West Norwood

Nettlefold Hall, West Norwood Library, 1 Norwood High Street, SE27 (0171 738 3801)

First Saturday of the month shows for 2-9 year olds. Book early. For booking on the day phone 0181 670 6212.

Tricycle Theatre 😊

Hours
Performances Sat 11.30 am & 2pm (extra matinées in Christmas and summer holidays)
Prices
£1.75 in advance; £2.25 on the day
Travel
Kilburn

269 Kilburn High Rd, NW6 (0171 328 1000)

Excellent children's shows are on offer as well as after-school and holiday workshops. The theatre puts on two productions a year during half-term. Children under seven must be accompanied by an adult. There is wheelchair access and an induction loop. Children's menu in the café on Saturdays.

Unicorn Theatre 😊

Great Newport St, WC1 (0171 836 3334)

London's oldest professional children's theatre has an adventurous programme of specially commissioned plays, puppet and magic shows, weekend and holiday workshops throughout the year, and special birthday workshops for children's parties. There is a café downstairs.

Hours
Sat 11am, 2.30pm
& Sun 2.30pm
during school
holidays
Prices
£3.50 and £7.50
(plus 20p day
membership)
Travel
Leicester
Square ⊖

Young Vic

66 The Cut, SE1 (0171 928 6363)

Known for its commitment to school-aged children, the Young Vic commissions plays for children that parents and teachers will also enjoy. They usually do at least one play from the GCSE list and excellent Shakespeare productions. Most plays are aimed at over-10s. There is a good café.

Prices
Under-16s £7.50-
£8
Travel
Waterloo ⊖⇌

MUSIC

Arthur Davison Orchestral Concerts

Fairfield Halls, Croydon, Surrey (0181 688 9291)

Season tickets are available for the monthly concerts for children. The pieces are short, use a wide range of instruments and are a very good introduction to music. Book well in advance.

Hours
Once a month
(ring for dates)
11am-1pm
Prices
£4-£4.50
Travel
Croydon ⇌

Ernst Read Children's Concerts

Royal Festival Hall, South Bank Centre, SE1 (info 0181 942 0318; tickets 0181 336 0777)

A varied range of music aimed to captivate young first-timers with theme concerts, choirs and stories put to music, all suitable for children over seven. Season tickets are available for the six concerts held between October and May. Book well in advance (tickets issued from May) as they are very popular.

Prices
£4-£9
Travel
Waterloo ⊖⇌

Hours
Sat 10.30am-
12.30pm
Prices
Adults £2,
children £1
Travel
⊖ Westminster

Morley College Family Concerts

61 Westminster Bridge Road, SE1 (0171 928 8501 ext 238 or 236)

Six informal family music-and-dance concerts from classical to pop, folk and electronic from October to June.

Travel
⊖ High Street
Kensington,
Knightsbridge or
South Kensington

Music for Youth

4 Blade Mews, Deodar Road, SW15 (0181 870 9624)

Every November three public concerts are held at the Royal Albert Hall featuring over 1,200 young performers chosen from the National Festival of Music for Youth. Ring Music for Youth for details.

Travel
⊖ High Street
Kensington,
Knightsbridge, or
South Kensington

School Proms, Royal Albert Hall

Kensington Gore, SW7 (bookings 0171 589 8212)

Held in November. Over 1,000 young musicians perform their own prom at the Albert Hall. Ring for details.

If you are nosy by nature, this is the chapter for you! Sneak behind the scenes of the Houses of Parliament, through the changing rooms of two of London's best football clubs, backstage at the Royal National Theatre and on a tour round the home of world cricket. Wherever your interests lie, there are plenty of secrets just waiting to be uncovered...

Behind the Scenes

Chelsea FC 🇪 ☼ ◐

Hours
Fri 11am

Travel
⊖ Fulham
Broadway

Stamford Bridge, Fulham Road, SW6 (0171 385 0710)

Tours around this Premier League football club's home take place each week except during school holidays. You must book in advance.

The Glasshouse 🇪 ☔ ◐

Hours
Tues-Fri
10am-6pm
Sat 10am-6pm

Travel
⊖ Angel

St Alban's Place, N1 (0171 359 8162)

You can watch four artists at work from the gallery at this glass-blowing workshop. Glass is for sale in the shop and in the gallery.

Houses of Parliament 🇪 ☔ ◐

Travel
⊖ Westminster

St Margaret Street, W1 (0171 219 3000)

Write to your local MP to attend a debate in the House of Commons or for a tour of Westminster Hall and Palace of Westminster, or queue at the St Stephen's entrance. See Museums and Galleries for details, page 67.

Lords Cricket Ground ☼ ◐

Hours
Daily at noon and
2pm (10am only
during Tests, cup
finals and
preparation days).

Prices
Adults £4.95,
children and OAPs
£3.95

Travel
⊖ St John's Wood
Bus 13, 74, 82, 113

St John's Wood, NW8 (0171 266 3825/432 1033)

Tour the home of world cricket. The Gestetner Tour of Lords is a guided tour of the Long Room, the museum, the history of cricket brought to life, and the real tennis court (where you can see how tennis was played in Henry VIII's day). Minimum age seven years. Tour starts from the Grace gates.

Royal National Theatre ☔ ◐

Hours
Mon-Sat 10.15am,
12.45pm and
5.30pm

Prices
Adults £3.50,
children £3

Travel
⊖ ≈ Waterloo

South Bank, SE1 (0171 633 0880)

You can see the prop room, costume room, wardrobe, workshops and witness just how much effort goes into a production. Children must be accompanied. Reduced prices are available for some performances, workshops, lectures and study courses. Phone or write to arrange tours, which last about one hour.

Royal Shakespeare Company 🌧 ▶

Barbican, EC2 (0171 628 3351, ask for Backstage Tours)

The backstage tour includes the scenery, prop and costume departments. Advanced booking only (minimum six people).

Hours
Mon-Sat noon &
5.15pm
Prices
Adults £3.50,
children & concs
£2.50
Travel
Barbican ⊖

Theatre Royal 🌧 ▶

Drury Lane (0171 494 5091)

If, like Mrs Worthington, you don't want your daughters on the stage, then don't bring them here – the most popular of the 'arty' tours, according to our kids. We went backstage, under the stage, into the Royal Box, the Royal Retiring Room, the grand saloon and the boardroom.

Hours
Daily (times vary)
Prices
Adults £4,
under-14s £3
Travel
Covent Garden ⊖

Twickenham Rugby Football Ground ☼ ▶

Whitton Road, Twickenham, Middx (0181 892 8161)

The home of British rugby has been impressively developed and enlarged. Write to arrange a tour. Minimum age seven years. Tours start with a 15-minute video, followed by a walk around the grounds, pitch, and players' tunnel, ending in the museum.

Hours
Tues-Sun 10.30am,
noon, 1.30pm
and 3pm
Prices
Adults £4,
children £2.50
Travel
Twickenham ⇌

Wembley Stadium Tour ☼ ▶

Wembley, Middx, HA9 0DW (0181 902 8833)

The venue for FA Cup Finals, and the stadium where England's football team play their home games, as well as the host to many other great sporting encounters. This might be your only chance ever to climb the famous steps and collect the 'Cup'. You can walk down the players' tunnel and see the pitch close up, check security at Event Control, see the players' changing rooms and watch the special cinema presentations of Wembley's greatest moments. Party packages are available.

Hours
April-Sept 10am-
4pm, Oct-March
10am-3pm. No
tours when there
is a stadium event.
Prices
Adults £6.45,
children (5-16)
£4.50, under-5s
free, family ticket
(2+2) £17.50,
various other
concs.
Travel
Wembley Park ⊖

West Ham United FC ☼ ▶

Green Street, Upton Park, E13 (0181 548 2707)

The home of the 'Hammers'. Tours held on first Thursday of each month. Additional tours during school holidays.

Hours
10.30am, 2pm & 6pm
Prices
Adults £2, children
free
Travel
Upton Park ⊖

WALKING TOURS

Canal Walks 🅴 ☼ ●

Hours
Towpaths open daily from dawn to dusk
Travel
⊕ Camden Town or Warwick Avenue

For details ring the Inland Waterways Association (0171 586 2556). The best walks for children are Camden Town to Little Venice (about two and a half miles) and Little Venice to Willesden Junction (just over three miles).

Docklands Tours ☼ ◓

Hours
By appointment
Prices
Adults £4.50, children £3.50

60 Bradley House, Aspinden Road, Bermondsey, SE16 (0171 252 0742)

Guided coach, mini-bus and walking tours of Docklands by local people. The friendly service is tailored to the individual needs of families or groups. See where pirates were executed and where smugglers hid their goods. Recommended for over-7s, and especially 10-12 year olds doing Dockland or East-End projects.

Gallows, Gardens and Goblins ☼ ◓

Hours
Ring for dates and times
Prices
£4, £3 concs, accompanied children free
Travel
⊕ Marble Arch exit 3, by Marble Arch itself

(0171 435 4782)

Grim tales of gruesome executions at the site of Tyburn Gallows get this exciting walk off to a great start before taking you in search of the 'real' Peter Pan, then the Elfin Oak and ending at the London Toy and Model Museum (entrance to which is an optional extra – see Museums and Galleries, page 71, for details). Children really enjoy this walk, especially the horses stabled on the Bayswater Road.

Greenwich Treasure Trail ☼ ◓

Hours
Sat 2pm; Sun 11.30am
Prices
Adults £5, concs, £3.50, accompanied children free
Travel
⇌ Greenwich

Greenwich Park, King William Walk (0181 444 1559)

A series of literal and cryptic clues guide visitors on a route around Greenwich's classic buildings and park, leading to the treasure. You can either follow the trail competitively, in teams, or as a stroll for pleasure. Clues are based on general knowledge. Takes two hours. Suitable for over-9s. Meet opposite the Gloucester Pub.

Historical Walks of London Tours ☼ ◑

(0181 668 4019)

There are a large variety of themed walks on offer. Tours last approx two hours. The following are of particular interest to children: Jack the *Ripper Murder Trail; Graveyards, Ghouls and Ghosts of the Old City; Charles Dickens' London;* and *A Walk in the Footsteps of Sherlock Holmes.* Ring for a leaflet.

Prices
Each walk: adults £4.50, concs £3.50, under-14s free if accompanied by an adult

London Wall Walk ▣ ☼ ◑

Museum of London, London Wall, EC2 (0171 600 3699)

This two-mile self-guided walk takes you round Roman and medieval city walls from the Museum of London to the Tower. You can buy a leaflet, *Roman Wall Walk,* from the museum, or use the explanatory panels at each of the 21 sites.

Travel
Barbican, Moorgate or St Paul's ↔

The London Silver Jubilee Walk ▣ ☼

London Tourist Board, Tourist Information Centre, Victoria Station, SW1

This ten-mile walk, created to celebrate the Queen's Silver Jubilee in 1977, is divided into seven sections. Each is guided with markers set in the pavement. The walk starts at Leicester Square, goes through Westminster and over Lambeth Bridge, along the south bank to Tower Bridge then back through the City, Fleet Street, Holborn and Covent Garden.

Travel
Leicester Square ↔

SIGHTSEEING TOURS

Original London Sightseeing Tours ◑ 🌧

(0181 877 1722)

One-and-a-half-hour tours round the capital in double decker buses, some of which are open-topped.

Prices
Adults £10, children (under-16s) £5

Hours
April-Sept
Prices
Adults £15,
children £10

Star Safari ◑ ☂

(01932 854721)

See the haunts and homes, with full commentary, of London's rich and famous from Prince Charles to Michael Caine. Ring for days and times.

DIY Sightseeing Tours ▣ ☺ ☂

Children of all ages love exploring the capital at the top of a double-decker bus and it is a cheaper way of taking in the sights than a sightseeing tour. A day's travel pass allows you to get on and off the buses as you wish. Try one of the following:

Bus 4 from Waterloo station via Aldwych, Fleet Street, St Paul's, Barbican, Islington and Finsbury Park to Archway.

Bus 11 from Liverpool Street station via Bank, St Paul's, Fleet Street, Aldwych, Strand, Trafalgar Square, Whitehall, Westminster, Victoria, Sloane Square, Chelsea and Fulham to Hammersmith.

Bus 38 from Victoria station via Hyde Park Corner, Piccadilly, Shaftesbury Avenue, Bloomsbury and Islington to Clapton.

Up a tower, on top of a hill, in a roof garden,
under a hot-air balloon or above a bridge —
if you've got a head for heights and want to put
London in perspective, then head for a high spot.

Travel
⇌ Woking

Alan Mann Helicopters ☼

Fairoaks Airport, Chobham, Surrey (01276 857471)

For a vast amount of money (£526.50 to be precise) Alan Mann Helicopters will take up to four passengers for a spectacular ride following the route of the River Thames in a single-engined helicopter. Under-8s must be accompanied.

Hours
24 hours daily
Travel
✆ Wood Green
⇌ Alexandra
Palace

Alexandra Palace ☺ ▣ ☼

Muswell Hill, N22 (0181 365 2121)

Excellent views over north London, Kent, Surrey, Essex and Hertfordshire from the 250ft-high terrace round 'Ally Pally', the Palace at the top of this steep park. Children's activities take place daily June–September with Bank Holiday funfairs and a free fireworks display on November 5. Animal sanctuary, boating lake, café, pitch and putt, dry ski slope. See also Ten Days Out page 31.

Balloon Safaris ☼

27, Rosefield Road, Staines, Middx (01784 451007)

For a real bird's-eye view you can't beat a hot-air balloon flight over London and south-east England (but at £99 per person, you might want to try). Venues in Surrey and Kent. Not suitable for under-10s.

Hours
Daily 5am-dusk
(open to traffic
from 7am)
Travel
⇌ Greenwich,
Blackheath or
Maze Hill
Boat to Greenwich
Pier (ring 0171 930
3373)

Greenwich Hill ☺ ▣ ☼

Greenwich Park, Charlton Way, SE10 (0181 858 2608)

Blackheath railway station is the best place to arrive if you want to start at the top of the park where the splendid view is, before walking down to Greenwich itself (from where you can get the train at Greenwich or Maze Hill stations). It is a longer, but less steep walk to the viewing platform and Blackheath is a pretty village. From the Wolfe Monument the view of Wren's naval college and the Thames as it loops round the Isle of Dogs is breathtaking (despite the recent erection of Canary Wharf which does its best to ruin the skyline by being off-centre).

Hampstead Heath 😊 F ☼

NW3

The views from here of London as painted by Constable are so wonderful they have special legal protection. Best views are on the high ground by Jack Straw's castle, Whitestone Pond and Parliament Hill. See below, and pages 33 and 111.

Hours
Daily 24 hours
Travel
Hampstead
Heath ⇄

The Monument ☼

Monument Street, EC2 (0171 626 2717)

The Monument was commissioned by King Charles II in 1666 in memory of the Great Fire of London. When it was completed in 1677 it was the world's highest free-standing column at 202ft, this being equal to the distance due east to the site of the bakery in Pudding Lane where the five-day fire began. Ironically almost as many lives have been lost from the top of the monument as during the Great Fire (to prevent further jumps an iron cage was erected). Although the view is slightly obscured by modern high-rises it is worth the clamber up the narrow 311-stepped spiral staircase if you have older children (don't try carrying toddlers or heavy babies unless you are hyper–fit).

Hours
Apr–Sept Mon–Fri
9am–5.40pm; Sat
and Sun 2pm–
5.40pm; Oct–
March Mon–Sat
(closed Sun)
9am–3.30pm
Admission
Adults £1,
children (5-16)
25p, under-5s free
Travel
Monument ⊖

National Westminster Tower

25 Old Broad Street, EC2

This is the tallest cantilevered building in the world at a height of 600ft 4ins. It is only open to National Westminster Bank account holders (but you can open a bank account with NatWest with as little as £1). Contact your local branch manager for details.

Travel
Liverpool
Street ⊖⇄

Parliament Hill 😊 F ☼

Hampstead Heath, NW3 (0171 485 4491)

At the south end of Hampstead Heath this kite-flyers' heaven affords a spectacular view right across central London (you can even see Crystal Palace on a clear day). Helpful notices point out landmarks. There is also a café and toilets.

Hours
Daily 24 hours
Travel
Kentish Town ⊖
then
Bus C2
or Hampstead
Heath or Gospel
Oak ⇄

The Roof Gardens 🇫 ☼

Hours
Ring for details

Travel
⊖ High Street
Kensington

99 Kensington High Street, entrance Derry Street, W8
(0171 937 7994)

High above the bustle of Kensington High Street this secret garden in the sky — one and a half acres of lush greenery with a waterfall, wisteria and roses — is open to the public when not being used for private functions. Two pink flamingoes live in the English woodland pond and from a small hole in the brick wall you get a great view of west London.

St Paul's Cathedral ☼

Hours
Daily 7am–6pm
(Golden Gallery
open 9am–4.30pm
Mon–Sat)

Admission
Adults £2.50,
children (5–16) £2,
under-5s free

Travel
⊖ St Paul's

EC4 (0171 248 2705)

The Golden Gallery was used to spot fires all over the city during the blitz in the Second World War. This is not a good place to discover your kids have vertigo as the 627 steps are usually crowded. From the top you get a glorious view of the Tower, London Pool and the other 50 churches Wren built. See also pages 39 and 80.

Tower Bridge   ◐

Hours
April–Oct
10am–6.30pm;
Nov–March
9.30am–4.30pm

Admission
Adults £5,
children £3.50,
under-5s free

Travel
⊖ Tower Hill
⊖ ⇌ London
Bridge

SE1 (0171 407 0922)

There are stunning views over London and up and down the Thames from the high, glazed walkways which kids can run along safely. The museum and displays are imaginative and it is good value for money. Last admission 1hr 15min before closing. See also page 83.

Westminster Cathedral ☼

Victoria Street, SW1 (0171 798 9055)

Hours
7am–8pm. Lift
open Apr–Sep
9am–5pm
Mon–Sun (small
charge)

Travel
⊖ St James's Park
⊖ ⇌ Victoria

The 280ft-high viewing platform of Sir Edward's Tower can be reached by lift. From the top there is a splendid view of Westminster and the Thames and you can even see into the gardens of Buckingham Palace. Much of the West End is obscured by modern office blocks but the views south over the Thames and west towards Kensington are impressive (take a map as there are no signs).

From the wild expanses of Richmond Park to the ordered formality of St James's, from royal hunting grounds to common grazing land, there are literally hundreds of parks in London. The capital also has a surprising amount of heathland, nature reserves and woodland where kids can discover Roman remains, find ancient burial sites and follow nature trails. Here are those most suited to entertaining and exhausting children.

The Great Outdoors

TEAROOM

toilets

KEEP OFF THE GRASS

PARKS AND GARDENS

Most parks have sports facilities, playgrounds and special children's events in the summer. For information on events in the Royal Parks ring 0171 298 2000 or send an A5 stamped, addressed envelope to Old Police House, Hyde Park, London W2 2UH, asking for a copy of '*Summer Entertainment Programmes*'.

Alexandra Palace Park 😊 F

Hours
Daily 24 hours
Travel
Wood Green

Muswell Hill, N22 (0181 365 2121)

The glorious setting for Alexandra Palace, this large, steep park has stunning views over London. There are children's activities daily from June to September and a popular free fireworks display around November 5. There's also a boating lake, a café, a pitch-and-putt golf course, an animal sanctuary and a dry ski slope, plus ice-skating and ice hockey. See also Ten Days Out, page 31 and Birds-Eye Views, page 104.

Avery Hill Park 😊 F

Hours
Mon–Sun
7am–9pm or dusk
Travel
Eltham

Bexley Road, SE9 (0181 850 2666)

The Winter Garden is full of tropical and sub-tropical Asian and Australasian plants. The wonderful Victorian greenhouses are open Monday–Thursday 1–4pm, Friday 1–3pm; Saturday and Sunday 10am–6.30pm (to 4pm in winter). There are also tennis courts and a small playground.

Battersea Park 😊 F

Hours
Dawn to dusk.
Zoo: Easter–Oct
daily 10am–5pm,
winter Sat and
Sun only
11am–3pm
Prices
Zoo: adults £1,
children over-2
50p

Albert Bridge Road, SW11 (0181 871 7530/1)

This very pretty, extremely well-equipped riverside park is famous for its Festival Gardens, Grand Vista fountains, the London Peace Pagoda and the annual Easter Parade. There is an exceptionally good free Adventure Playground (0181 871 7539) for 5–15-year-olds with helpers on hand at weekends, after school and during school holidays. The boating lake in the south-east corner (open noon–7pm weekends only; daily during school summer holidays) is by far the best and most reasonably priced in London. Several fishing lakes and theatre shows and pony rides for kids in summer. The zoo has larger animals including cattle, an aviary, a new reptile and amphibian house, a zoo shop and a picnic area. There is a One O'Clock Club and a very good dog–free play area. There is a café on the lakeside and toilets.

Travel
Sloane Square ⊖
Battersea Park
or Queenstown
Road ⇌
Bus 19, 36, 44, 45, 49, 130, 137 or 170

Blackheath 😊 F

SE3 (0181 854 8888)

Blackheath is a large open common which is popular with kite flyers (annual conventions are held here on Easter Bank Holiday Monday and in June), and there are funfairs on some Bank Holidays and at Easter. People sail their model boats on the Prince of Wales Pond. There are good pubs backing on to the heath where the kids can play football while you relax. Thousands of runners start the London Marathon here every spring. Backs on to Greenwich Park (see below).

Hours
Daily 24 hours
Travel
Blackheath ⇌

Bushey Park F

Hampton Court Road, Middx (0181 979 1586)

Across the road from Hampton Court Palace, Bushey Park has two large ponds where fishing is allowed, dozens of swans (on Heron Pond) and the most accessible herd of red deer in London. The deer usually congregate between Cobblers Walk and Leg o' Mutton Pond. There is children's entertainment throughout the summer.

Travel
Hampton
Court ⇌
Car park near
Diana Fountain

Clapham Common F

Clapham Common West Side (top of Broomwood Rd)

The common has two dog-free playgrounds both with rubber matting. Windmill Drive is an enclosed area with slides, swings, a see-saw and a sand-pit with public toilets and a pub nearby. It gets busy in summer but a good place to make friends is at The One O'Clock Club (Monday–Thursday). There's a café near the bandstand with a dog–free picnic area nearby. There are tennis courts, a bowling green and another café near the Nightingale Road end of Westside, a smaller

Hours
Daily 24 hours
Travel
Clapham
Common ⊖

playground near Grandison Road, and a good paddling pool opposite The Pavement. The Long Pond has model boat yachting regattas during the summer.

Coram's Fields Children's Playground 🄴

Hours
9am–8pm or dusk
Travel
➜ Russell Square

93 Guildford Street, WC1 (0171 837 6138)

A shady seven-acre playground with paddling pool, play equipment, sports area, pets' corner and duck pond. Adults or over-16s are not admitted unless accompanied by a child.

Crystal Palace Park 🄴

Hours
Daily
7.30am–30mins
before dusk
Travel
➜ Crystal Palace

Thicket Road, SE20–Crystal Palace Park Road, SE26 (0181 778 7148; Crystal Palace Eventsline 0181 778 9496; Bromley Leisureline 0181 313 1113)

This is one of the best family parks in London with dinosaurs, a farmyard, maze, mini funfair, horse-and-cart rides, and a dry ski slope. Call 0181 778 7155 for details of **Crystal Palace Camping Site**. Crystal Palace National Sports Centre is Britain's major athletics venue and home to Fulham Rugby League Club. See also page 54.

Dulwich Park 🄴

Hours
Summer daily
8am–9pm; winter
daily 8am–4.30pm
Travel
➜ North Dulwich

SE21 (0181 693 5737)

This park has a children's playground and an ecology area. There are tennis courts and you can buy refreshments in the Rose Garden.

Finsbury Park 🄴

Hours
Daily 6am–dusk
Travel
➜➜ Finsbury
Park

Seven Sisters Road, N4 (0171 263 5001)

Finsbury Park has a running track, bowls, tennis courts, a children's playground and summer boating, and bank holiday funfairs. The Parkland Walk, a beautiful rural corridor linking Alexandra Palace and Finsbury Park, follows the old railway line on a four-mile nature trail with detours through Queen's and Highgate Woods. See also page 31.

Green Park

SW1 (0171 930 1793)

Popular with 18th-century duellers, Green Park is now sim-
ply that – a green expanse with no water, no statues, no
facilities, no flower beds. It is still pretty in spring when the
daffodils are out. Good place to picnic if you are in the area.

Hours
Daily dawn–dusk
Travel
Green Park ⊖

Greenwich Park

Charlton Way, Greenwich, SE10 (0181 858 2608)

This is my favourite park for its avenues lined with chestnut
trees, its view across the Thames, its beautiful flower gardens
and ancient oaks. At the top of the park near the duck pond and
inside the dog-free zone is a deer enclosure kept in memory of
royal hunts. You can visit the **Old Royal Observatory** (0181 858
4422) which crowns the park (see page 78), cross the Meridian
and watch the famous Greenwich Timeball which is raised and
dropped at 1pm. There is a bandstand (concerts in summer) and
at the bottom of the hill a tiny boating pond and a good playground. Lookout for the Queen's Oak, a hollow oak stump
waround which Henry VIII danced with Anne Boleyn. The park
has tennis courts, cricket, hockey and rugby pitches and a good
cafeteria, despite very expensive ice-creams. See Ten Days Out,
page 51, for full details of Greenwich.

Hours
Summer
dawn–dusk, winter
7am–6pm daily
Travel
Greenwich
or Maze Hill ⇌
Bus 177, 180, 286.
Boat to
Greenwich Pier
from Westminster
Pier (riverboat
information 0171
930 2062/4721)

Gunnersbury Park 🅴

Popes Lane, W3 (0181 992 1612)

You'll find two playgrounds, a boating lake, miniature golf, a
fishing lake and a café at this park. The house is a local
history museum (open afternoons only).

Hours
Sundays only
Travel
Chiswick Park ⊖

Hampstead Heath 🅴

NW3 (0171 485 4491)

Once the stamping ground of poets Keats and Shelley, London's most natural park has 800 acres of rolling hills and
fields, so buy a local map to avoid getting lost. Funfairs are
held at Easter, and on May and August Bank Holidays.

Hours
24 hours daily
Travel
Belsize Park
or Hampstead ⊖
Gospel Oak
or Hampstead
Heath ⇌

Despite its size it gets crowded at weekends. Free summer brass band and jazz concerts and children's shows take place at the bandstands at Golders Hill and Parliament Hill throughout the summer, every other day in August. Children and adults can swim in **Parliament Hill Lido** (0171 485 3873; Gospel Oak tube) from May to late September. There's a marvellous panoramic view from Parliament Hill (near the South End Green on the south end of the park) so named after the 1605 gunpowder plotter Guy Fawkes, whose accomplices planned to light fires here to signal that Parliament had been successfully blown up. Constable painted his famous view over the city from this spot; it is now popular for weekend kite-flying. Nearby there are ten tennis courts (changing facilities are primitive), a play park, a paddling pool, a running track, orienteering, cricket, football, rugby, rounders and a One O'clock Club. There are toilets, and fishing pond for the disabled. At the north end of the park, near **Kenwood House**, on Saturday evenings in summer there are popular open-air lakeside concerts, some with fireworks (June–September; ring 0171 413 1443).

Holland Park ▣

Hours
Daily dawn–dusk

Travel
⊖ Holland Park
or High Street
Kensington

Kensington High Street, W8 (0171 602 2226)

This park has an excellent adventure playground with ever-changing tree walks, rope-swings and a One O'Clock Club. Weekend jazz. Peacocks and pheasants strut by the Yucca lawn and squirrels dart across the woodland paths of The Wilderness. There is a Japanese garden and a lovely orangery as well as an aviary, a small zoo and a café.

Hyde Park ▣

Hours
5am–midnight
daily. The Gun
Salute takes place
on the Park Lane
side near the
Dorchester (arrive
11.30am) on the
Queen's Accession
(February 6),
Queen's birthday
(April 21), Corona-
tion Day (June 2),
Prince Philip's
birthday (June 10),

W2 (0171 298 2100)

Try to plan your visit on a Gun Salute day for the exciting, if noisy, free spectacle of the splendidly uniformed King's Troops of the Royal Horse Artillery galloping down the park to fire the big guns on the dot of noon. Other special events include Riding Horse Parade on Rotten Row on the first Sunday in August and the **London-to-Brighton Veteran Car**

Run which starts at Hyde Park Corner 8–9am on the first Sunday in November, (see page 26). Rowing and pedal boats for hire on the Serpentine Lake open 9am–7pm daily. You can swim in the **Serpentine Lido** (May–end September); the water is chlorinated. The swimming area is enclosed by booms, a grassy area for sunbathing and picnicking, plus a small children's paddling pool, sand-pit and slide. There is a putting green and four tennis courts. **Speaker's Corner**, in the north-east corner of the park below a bower of London plane trees, is the historic home of the soap box orator. Sunday mornings are best for this colourful event but be warned – your kids are likely to pick up every four-letter word under the sun as well as some pretty cranky views (Marble Arch tube). There are military bands every Sunday during summer. Playground and underground car park on Park Lane. Toilets for disabled people. See page 214 for details on riding through Hyde Park.

(cont...)
and on the Queen Mother's birthday (August 4).
Travel
Hyde Park Corner, Knightsbridge, Lancaster Gate, Marble Arch or Queensway ⊖

Kensington Gardens

W8 (0171 724 2826)

Adjoining Hyde Park are the royal gardens of Kensington Palace. The most famous attraction for children is Sir George Frampton's statue of Peter Pan which stands on the spot where Peter's boat is supposed to have landed in the 'Never, Never Land of the child's mind'. Just outside the playground is the Elfin Oak with its carvings of fairies and animals. There are puppet shows in August at 11am and 3pm from Monday to Saturday, and the playground, as well as workshops, are free and suitable for under–11s.

Hours
5am–30 mins before dusk daily
Travel
Bayswater, Lancaster Gate, Queensway or High Street Kensington ⊖

Kew Gardens

(0181 332 5000)

Gape at the 10-storey pagoda which was built in 1761 or stand dwarfed beside the Chilean Wine Palm raised here in 1846 from seed and now over 60ft tall in the greatest botanical garden and seed bank in the world (also home to the world's largest collection of orchids). The Prince of Wales Conservatory has 10 different habitats from desert to tropical

Hours
Daily 9.30am to dusk (closed Christmas Day and New Year's Day)
Prices
Adults £4, children aged 5–16 and concs £2, Under 5s free, family ticket (2+4) £10, season tickets available

Travel
⇌ Kew Bridge
⊖ Kew Gardens.
Bus 65, 391, 237,
267.
One-and-a-half
hour ride by
riverboat from
Westminster Pier
(river boat
information 0171
930 2062/4721)

pools and houses orchids, palms, ferns, cacti, and giant water–lilies which grow up to 6ft in diameter in one week. The impressive curved-glass Palm House holds banana, cocoa, papaya and rubber plants, beneath which is the marine display with flowering marine plants and a coral reef. The conservatory also houses the ever-popular carnivorous plants – particularly popular with Benja who offered his bacon frazzles to every passing plant. The conservatories and tropical palm and water-lily houses make it a great day out even in winter when it's raining. If it is a clear day bring a picnic. Otherwise you can have tea in the Orangery (also a shop) or better still in the Maids of Honour tea room just outside Cumberland Gate. No dogs. Wheelchair hire (free), wheelchair access and toilets for the disabled.

Travel
Walthamstow
⊖ ⇌ Central
Bus 34, 97, 215,
257

Lloyd Park 🟥

Forest Road, E17 (0181 527 5544 ext 4568)

The park has an aviary, a moat with black swans, geese and ducks, six tennis courts, safe-surface play areas for under-twelves, under-sevens and under-5s (the last of which has little equipment) and a kick-about area with goal and netball posts. Toilets are outside the park near the William Morris Gallery. Dog-free zones.

Hours
5am–dusk daily

Travel
⊖ Baker Street,
Camden Town,
Great Portland
Street or Regent's
Park

Regent's Park 🟥

NW1 (0171 486 7905)

This beautiful park, once the hunting ground of Henry VIII, is surrounded on three sides by terraces built by John Nash and on the fourth by Regent's Canal. It has a large boating lake, a mosque (write or phone for guided tours Monday–Thursday: **Mosque Tours**, 146 Park Road, NW8; 0171 724 3363), tennis courts, four playgrounds (open daily from 10.30am), cricket, baseball and football pitches and a child-friendly café. In the Inner Circle is Queen Mary's rose garden with its bandstand and open-air theatre (May–September; bookings 0171 486 2431/1933) and summer puppet shows (August Monday–Saturday 11am and 3pm). The theatre has annual Shakespeare productions and is one of the best ways to introduce young children to Shakespeare in a beautiful setting. The north end of the park houses **London Zoo** (see Animal Attractions, page 131). A boating lake offers rowing boats at £5.50 per hour plus £5 deposit. There is also a shallow children's lake with single pedal boats for hire at £1.60 for 20 minutes. There is a running track, and softball and football at weekends. Toilets for disabled people and a car park.

Richmond Park ▣

Surrey (0181 940 0654)

This is the largest park in London. It is great for cycle rides, long walks or even a drive. The herds of wild red and fallow deer are popular with the kids but can be quite dangerous in the autumn rutting season or after the birth of their young (they particularly dislike dogs). There are two public golf courses by Roehampton Gate (0181 878 1795). Refreshments can be found at Roehampton Gate, where there is a restaurant, and near Richmond Gate at the **Pembroke Lodge Restaurant** which has a lovely open terrace with extensive views.

Hours
Daily March–Sept
7am–30 mins
before dusk;
Oct–Feb
7.30am–30 mins
before dusk

Travel
Richmond ⊖ ⇌

St James's Park ▣

The Mall, SW1 (0171 930 1793)

A pretty park, popular with children despite the lack of amenities for them. The park used to house several pelicans (whose ancestors were given to Charles II in 1665 by a Russian ambassador) but due to their unsavoury habit of eating the park pigeons they were finally banished to London Zoo. Duck Island still has flocks of water birds and mandarin ducks. There are brass and military band concerts on summer lunchtimes, a playground with a sand pit and, if you stand on the Mall, you can see St James's Palace Foot Guards on their way to Buckingham Palace for the Changing of the Guard. In the 17th-century a herd of cows was kept in the park and the cows were milked on the spot to provide refreshment for the public at 1d a shot. Now you have to make do with the Cake House tea shop. Toilets for the disabled are at Marlborough Gate.

Hours
Daily dawn to
midnight

Travel
St James's Park ⊖

Syon Park Gardens

Hours
Daily 10am–6pm
or dusk (closed
Dec 25–26)

Prices
Adults £2.50,
children £2. House
open April–Sept
Sat, Sun and Bank
Holidays
11am–5pm (and
Suns in Oct). Tick-
ets for house and
gardens
combined adults
£5.50, children £4

Travel
↔ Gunnersbury
then **Bus** or
⇌ Syon Lane
then walk.
Car park

Brentford, Middlesex (0181 560 0881)

The gardens of Syon House have a Great Conservatory building housing an aquarium and aviary. There is also a garden
centre, six acres of rose garden, an art centre, a wholefood
shop, an aquatic centre and the Syon Craft Show on first
weekend in August. England's first botanical gardens were
laid out here in the 16th century (two of the original fruit-
bearing mulberry trees are still here). A ten-and-a-quarter-
inch gauge railway (daily, April–October then weekends and
Bank Holidays) runs from the entrance to the picnic area
(adults £1, children 50p). The **London Butterfly House** is
home to hundreds of free-flying exotic butterflies as well as
tarantulas and scorpions.

Wandsworth Common 🄴

Hours
Daily dawn to dusk

Travel
⇌ Wandsworth
Common

SW18 (0181 871 6391)

The common has a duck pond, an adventure playground,
swings and a highly recommended One O'Clock Club. In the
middle of the common, next to the tennis courts and bowling green, is **Neal's Lodge Restaurant**, off Baskerville Road,
SW18 (0181 870 7484). Open daily 10am–10pm. It has high
chairs and is fairly child-friendly.

Wimbledon Common/Putney Heath 🄴

Hours
Daily dawn to dusk

Travel
↔⇌ Wimbledon
then 93 **Bus**

SW19/SW15 (0181 788 7655)

A vast open space for walking and riding. The nineteenth
century **Wimbledon Windmill**, with a museum inside, is
open to the public from Easter–end October (ring for opening
times). For pub grub head for the **Hand-in-Hand**, 6 Crooked
Billet, SW19 (0181 946 5720) and take your drinks on to
Wimbledon Common.

WOODS, OPEN SPACES, NATURE RESERVES AND TRAILS

Beckenham Place Park ▣

SE6

If you live in the area or on the Ravensbourne line then this delightful wood and meadowland is an ideal spot for children of any age – there are excellent trees to climb (that even toddlers can have a go at), open meadows for picnics, tributary paths for little ones to explore, butterflies, mushrooms, birds to look out for and a good sloping field for kite-flying. If you have the stamina you can walk right across the park from one station to the other (approx 1 mile). There is also a public golf course, putting green and tennis courts.

Hours
Daily dawn to dusk

Travel
Ravensbourne or Beckenham Hill ⇄ stations are at the entrances to the woods

Camley Street Natural Park ▣

12 Camley Street, NW1 (0171 833 2311)

Originally a coal drop on the Grand Union Canal, this tiny two-acre wildlife park has a pond, a wood and a marsh.

Hours
Mon–Fri 10am–5pm, Sat and Sun 11am–5pm

Travel
King's Cross ⊖⇄

East Ham Nature Reserve ▣

Norman Road, E6 (0181 470 4525)

East London's largest churchyard is now a nature reserve. If you follow the nature trails (one of which is suitable for wheelchairs and buggies) you will spot anything from butterflies to pheasants. There are quiz sheets, a bird-watching hide (by appointment), natural history displays, a Victorian schoolroom, a wartime kitchen and a Braille guide. Gift shop with pocket-money toys. Toilets for the disabled.

Hours
Mon–Fri 9am–5pm, Sat and Sun 2–5pm

Travel
East Ham ⊖
DLR Beckton
Bus 101 or 104 stops at reserve

Epping Forest ▣

Essex (0181 508 0028)

Epping Forest, to the north-east of London, forms a vast crescent of land stretching from Wanstead in the south and northwards towards Epping, with an isolated portion, the Lower For-

Hours
Daily, 24hrs

Travel
Epping, Theydon Bois, Loughton or Snaresbrook ⊖

117

est, just north of Epping town. Ancient woodland, grassland and heath, rivers, bogs and ponds make it an ideal place to get lost. **The Epping Forest Centre**, High Beach, Loughton, Essex IG10 4AF (0181 508 7714) runs children's safaris and summer holiday activities. There are also environmental children's parties (£30 for up to 12 children includes use of room and tutor).

Fryent Country Park ◼

Hours
Daily 24hrs

Travel
Fryent Way
(A4140)
⊖ Kingsbury or
Wembley Park

Kingsbury, NW9 (0181 206 0492 for leaflets and maps)

For a bit of real countryside in town, head for this lovely unspoilt woodland, meadows and ancient hedgerows, accessible via a good network of paths (easy for wheelchairs and buggies). Various holiday activities for children.

Green Chain Walk ◼

Green Chain Working Party, John Humphries House, Stockwell Street, London SE10 9JN

A network of footpaths linking green open spaces. A popular walk is Thamesmead to Oxleas Wood which is approximately six miles (takes about five hours with children over six).

Gunnersbury Triangle ◼

Hours
Sun 2pm–4.30pm

Travel
⊖ Chiswick
Park

Entrance in Bollo Lane, W4 (0181 747 3881)

Set between the District and Northern lines this nature reserve covers six acres of woodland and grassland with a large pond. Birdlife includes tawny owls and green spotted woodpeckers. There are regular workdays where families are encouraged to help with the conservation programme. Leave buggies at the entrance. Toilets and catering facilities.

Highgate Wood ◼

Hours
Daily 24hrs

Travel
⊖ Highgate

Muswell Hill Road, N6 (0181 444 6129)

A stone's throw from the Archway Road and you are in the heart of an ancient woodland bursting with wildlife. On the other side of Muswell Hill Road is the slightly smaller, wilder Queen's Wood. Playground and sportsground. Take a picnic.

Lee Valley Park ▣

Lee Valley Park Countryside Centre, Abbey Gardens, Waltham Abbey, Essex (01992 713838)

Lee Valley Park follows the River Lee from Ware in Herefordshire to London's East End. Large areas of water offer sailing, rowing, fishing and boat trips and there are guided walks, children's activities, riding, swimming, quizzes and nature trails. The Leisurebus takes you around the park and on Sundays links up with Liverpool Street station. Ring for leaflets and events diary for indoor and outdoor activities.

Hours
Daily dawn to dusk

Travel
Tottenham
Hale ⊖
Various ⇥
stations on
Liverpool Street-
to-Cambridge line

Lesnes Abbey Woods ▣

Lesnes Abbey Road, Belvedere, Kent (0181 312 9717)

The name comes from the twelfth-century abbey whose remains still stand in this 200-acre wood. It is a riot of colour in the spring with daffodils, bluebells and woodland anenomes. Popular with children is the fossil bed where you can search for prehistoric remains. Best for older children and good walkers as the woods are very hilly.

Hours
Daily 24hrs

Travel
Abbey Wood ⇥

Morden Hall Park ▣

Morden Hall Road, Morden, Surrey (0181 648 1845)

Originally laid out as a deer park, this is now a wildlife and ecology centre. There is a complex system of waterways coming off the river Wandle which were designed to power the snuff mill. Visit the craft workshops to see artists wood-turning, sculpting and making stained glass (closed Tuesdays). The environmental study centre runs day sessions for children in the holidays (ring Gillian on 0181 542 4239) with games and projects. Garden and aquatic centre. National Trust shop, tearoom, toilets for the disabled, picnic area.

Hours
Daily dawn to dusk

Travel
Morden ⊖

Oxleas Wood ▣

SE1

This is one of London's last remaining ancient woodlands. Approximately 8,000 years old, it was recently saved from the road-builder's bulldozers (a festival every June celebrates the event). Part of the Green Chain Walk, see page 118.

Hours
Daily 24hrs

Travel
Falconwood ⇥
By car off Shooters
Hill A207; free
parking in wood

Hours
Mon–Fri
10am–5pm (ring
to confirm)

Travel
⊖ Manor House
⇌ Haringey,
Green Lanes

Railway Fields ▰

N4 (0181 348 6005)

This former British Rail goods yard has been turned into a conservation park designed for teaching primary school children about nature. There is a visitors' centre, woodland, meadow and pond. Don't miss the unique hybrid plant, the Haringey Knotweed.

Hours
Daily 24hrs

Travel
⊖ Ruislip
then **Bus** H13 or
114

Ruislip Woods ▰

Middlesex (01895 250635)

Head for Bayhurst Wood Country Park for a barbecue site – there is a charge to book them but you don't have to pay if you are prepared to take what's left. Picnic sites. Leaflet available in local libraries or write to Recreation Unit, Civic Centre, Uxbridge, Middx UB8 1UW.

Hours
Dawn to 9pm daily

Travel
Bus P11, 225

Russia Dock Woodland and Stave Hill Ecological Park ▰

off Redriff Road, nr Onega Gate, SE16 (0171 237 9165)

Britain's largest man-made ecological park, adjoining the woodlands. Look for signs to the Angel pub with its balcony built out on wooden piles over the river, and the Cherry Garden which was popular with Samuel Pepys and Turner, who painted The Fighting Termeraire from here.

Hours
Daily dawn to dusk

Travel
⇌ Streatham,
Streatham
Common

Streatham Common, Norwood Grove and Rookery Gardens ▰

Streatham Common South (for car park), SE1 (0181 764 5478)

The grassy hill is good for kite-flying while at the eastern end of the common up the hill is the Rookery Garden which sometimes has jazz at the seasonal open-air theatre. There is a large safe picnic area in the orchard, rambling woodland paths to explore and a pond full of frogs. Tennis court and great views across south London. Good café near toilets.

Fun, fun, fun — whether you want to visit the pyramids of Egypt or ride the Rocky Mountain Railway, test your courage on the ultimate white-knuckle rides or relax on a boat ride through fantasy land; whether you are a tiny tot or a tearaway teenager, you will find something to thrill and delight in Britain's theme parks. And if you are looking for a couple of hours' distraction on a rainy day there are plenty of indoor fun parks in the centre of London from which to choose.

WELCOME to DiLLO WoRLD

Alton Towers

Alton, Staffordshire (01538 702200; Alton Towers Hotel 0990 001100)

Hours
Daily 9am–dusk
(with some rides
opening and
closing from
10am-7pm)

Admission
Adults
£16.50,under-14s
£12.50, under-4s
free, OAPs £5.50;
£6 second day.
Alton Towers Hotel
open all year.
Family of four for
one night
including entry to
park £142.50 –
£162.50

Travel
➤ Stoke-on-
Trent
then service bus.
M6 to junction 15

This theme park is immensely popular, although it is too far from London to do in a day. The huge landscaped grounds mean the adults can escape into the peace of some beautiful gardens while the children enjoy white-knuckle rides such as Nemesis (where you'll experience four seconds of weightlessness), Thunder Looper, Energizer, The Beast and Corkscrew (with two 360-degree turns). It is an excellent place to take sulky teenagers as well as younger siblings (but minimum-height restrictions apply on quite a few rides, so ring first if you are unsure). Toddlers will enjoy Old MacDonald's Tractor Ride, the Doodle Doo Derby and a relaxing Canal Boat Ride. Newly opened is the Alton Towers Hotel, a family-orientated, well-equipped four-star hotel full of weird and wonderful suprises. All rooms are themed and sleep up to four people with an interconnecting door – adults 'garden' room and childrens 'travel' room.

Butlin's South Coast World

Bognor Regis, West Sussex (01243 822445)

Hours
Daily April–Oct
10am–11pm;
Winter times and
dates vary

Admission
Adults and over-4s
£5.99, 2–3 year
olds £3, under-2s
free

Travel
➤ Bognor Regis
(60 miles south of
London)

Butlin's provides the traditional holiday camp environment complete with Redcoats (who mercifully don't rush around organising you into wet-T-shirt competitions and the like if you are just a day tripper). Our family favourites include Aquasplash sub-tropical water world (which is regulated into sessions), the large funfair and junior funfair, shows, bowls, darts and sports facilities. Regular entertainers include 'stars' such as Bobby Davro, Mike Reid and Freddie Starr. There is wheelchair access to most of the complex. Cafés, restaurants, picnic areas, baby-changing facilities, toilets and a variety of shops. You could combine this trip with a visit to the Weald and Downland Open Air Museum (nine miles).

Chessington World of Adventures

Leatherhead Road, Chessington, Surrey (01372 727227)

Chessington offers nine theme lands and 15 rides, the most thrilling of which are the Vampire roller coaster, Dragon River Log Flume and Terrortomb Dark Ride. Jared and his three-year-old brother enjoyed the bustle, hated the weekend queues (20 minutes to get in, then, on average, a 30-minute queue for each ride), didn't think much of the height restrictions (3'10"), and were upset by what they thought were scruffy, sad–looking animals in the zoo. Even in Toy Town there were 20-minute queues for the mini–rides, little to do indoors when it rained and neither child was impressed by the Mobster Magic Family Show. However, 16-year-old Gemma and her brother were having the time of their lives. They had spent most of the day on, or waiting to get on, the Ramses Revenge (total queuing time was three hours ten minutes, for 4 rides, the combined duration for which was 12 minutes) but thought that was 'all part of the fun'. The restaurants are expensive but the themes extend to the food areas so you can sample food from around the world. There is good double-buggy access, toilets are plentiful and easy to get to with a recently potty-trained toddler, baby-changing facilities and mother-and-baby room. Jared liked the people-shaped talking dustbins best and spent a lot of time picking up rubbish.

Hours
Daily April 1–Oct 29 10am–6pm, and until 9.30pm in summer holidays (last admission 3pm/7pm)

Admission
Adults £14.50, children (4–14 yrs) £11.50, OAPs £6.25, disabled £5.75, under-4s free. Children under 10 must be supervised on all rides, children under 12 not admitted without an adult.

Travel
Chessington South ⭾ then 10-min walk.
Flightline Bus 777 from Victoria; M25 junction 9 to A243

Dreamland White Knuckle Theme Park

Belgrave House, Belgrave Road, Margate, Kent (01843 227011)

As the name suggests the 26 rides at this theme park are really only for those hardy children who are in search of ultimate thrills and have strong stomachs. There are, however, a few rides for smaller children, as well as Britain's biggest big wheel.

Hours
June–Aug 10.30am–6pm, Easter–May & Sept weekends 10.30am–6pm

Admission
All tickets £7.99

Travel
Margate ⭾
A2, M2 & A28

Hours
March 29-Oct 27
daily 10am-6pm
(Oct open
weekends only).
Park closes when
full

Admission
Adults £15,
children (3-15)
£12, OAPs £11,
under-3s free (£1
off advanced
bookings)

Travel
By car on the
B3022 Windsor-
Bracknell Road
On-site parking

Legoland® Windsor

Windsor, Berks (booking on 0990 626364 or 01753 626364; information 0990 626375 or 01753 626375)

Although still under construction at the time of going to press, if Legoland® Windsor is half as good as Legoland® Denmark (see page 208) it will become an extremely popular attraction. Anticipating this, Legoland® has introduced an advanced booking system and will close the park when it reaches capacity to minimise queues which so often spoil visits to other theme parks. There will be five main activity areas in the park with interactive rides, shows, playscapes, building workshops and driving schools, with plenty to amuse and delight adults and children of any age. Full disabled facilities and baby-changing areas.

Hours
Daily mid
March–Oct
10am–6.30pm
(last admission
4.30pm, earlier in
spring and
autumn)

Admission
Adults £7.50,
children under 14
£6.50, children
under 1 metre
free, various
different family
tickets, disabled
£4.50

Travel
Just off Junction
2, M27

Paultons Park

Ower, nr Romsey, Hampshire (01703 814455)

This park is designed with 4–14-year-olds in mind with no white-knuckle rides. Some rides have height restrictions. Allow at least 5–6 hours (all rides included in price except go-karts – £2 extra). To get your bearing take a ride on the Rio-Grande train around the park, then follow the eerie marshland trail through the Land of the Dinosaurs or make your way through the Hedge Maze. Have a go in a Krazi-Kart whose steering will lead you all over the place. Play crazy snooker or crazy golf, take a ride on a pirate ship, whizz down the Astroglide and try Percy's Bouncer before getting splashed on the Bumper Boats. Kids' Kingdom is a popular adventure play area with a huge structure where 7–13-year-olds can slip down the giant tube slide, scramble over the Super Spiral Spider's Web and haul themselves along the cableways, while 3–7s enjoy frolicking in the play village. Young ones will also enjoy a visit to the Magic Forest, where nursery rhymes come to life at the push of a button, or the farmyard where they can pet the animals. In the Romany Experience you can see, smell and hear the world of gypsies – visit a horse fair, learn about gypsy crafts and customs and listen to 'characters' reminisce about the olden days. There are plenty of secluded picnic spots, extensive and very beautiful gardens, a huge wildfowl lake, a working 19th-century watermill, Romany museum and Village Life museum. Plenty of kiosks, cafés and refreshment stalls. Full buggy access. Paultons Park is, on the whole, good value for money and much prettier than most theme parks.

Thorpe Park

Staines Road, Chertsey, Surrey (01932 562633)

This is by far the best theme park for young children (over-12s with their hearts set on white-knuckle rides might find it a bit tame). The most popular and thrilling rides (and therefore those with the longest queues) are Logger's Leap, Thunder River, Flying Fish roller coaster and Depth Charge water slide. Despite the patronage of Royals — most noticeably the Princess of Wales and her sons, the hoi polloi have to queue for hours for the most popular rides at the height of the season. One friend went with her three children (aged five, eight and 10) on a hot day in July and found the crowds were unbearable, the queues far too long, the toilets filthy, refreshments expensive, no water fountains in sight and the whole place rather tacky (nevertheless, the kids were already planning their return trip in the car on the way home). We went with children of a similar age in term-time in October, didn't have to queue for a single ride, found the toilets clean, baby-changing facilities good and the staff very helpful. There were lots of parents with toddlers and under-5s enjoying themselves enormously (there is total buggy access and room to park them while on rides). Good adventure playground (but can be difficult to keep tabs on children when crowded). Pool and beach area, good partly shaded picnic areas, Burger King, Pizza Hut, etc. An excellent day out off-peak but, at the height of the season, take headache pills.

Hours
Daily March 23-Oct 27
10am–sometime after 5pm

Admission
Adults £13.25, under-14s £11.25, free if you are under a metre tall (although most height restrictions only apply to children under 90cms), family of four £40

Travel
Staines ⇌
Bus 718 from Victoria;
M25 junction 11 or 13

INDOOR FUN PARKS

Discovery Zone

Hours
Daily 10am–8pm

Admission
Children (2–12)
£3.99 (weekends,
£4.99), under-2s
£2.99, babes in
arms and accom-
panying adults
free (no time limit
to sessions). Week-
day toddler group
limited sessions
£1.99 per child
under five

Travel
⇌ Clapham
Junction

First Floor, The Junction Shopping Centre, Clapham Junction, SW11
(0171 223 1717)

The lack of natural light, the bright colours and the music at Discovery Zone are guaranteed to give carers a headache but children love this large indoor FunCentre with its Mini-zones, Multi-zones, bouncy castles, ball ponds, slides, tunnels, swings, pulleys and various other obstacle courses. Adults are encouraged to join in with the kids. There is a Burger King, tv room for parents and a Skill Zone slot machine area (extra charge). This is a perfect place to spend a wet winter day when the kids are driving you up the wall, but it is popular, so arrive early on weekends and holidays.

Fantasy Island Playcentre

Hours
Daily 10am–7pm

Admission
Children 5–13
years £3.95 per
90-minute session
(5ft height
restriction), Under-
5s £2.50

Travel
⊕ North Wembley

Vale Farm, Watford Road, Wembley (0181 904 9044)

Fantasy Island Playcentre is a purpose-built adventureland with amusements such as slides, rope bridge, climbing nets, ball pond, witch doctor's den and a monster serpent slide. Under-5s have their own Fantasy Adventure Island with talking animals and scaled-down equipment. Carers can escape to the relative safety of the Island Café while leaving the kids to let off steam.

The Fun House

Hours
Daily 10am–7pm

Admission
£2.45-£2.85 per 90
minutes for 2-12s

Travel
⇌ Edmonton
Green

Edmonton Leisure Centre, N9 (0181 807 0712)

There is a ball pool, slides, climbing ropes, a separate area for under-5s and various summer holiday activities. A height restriction of 4'9" applies.

House of Fun

78a Frith Road, Croydon, Surrey (0181 781 1661)

The House of Fun offers a variety of amusements including an adventure area with ball ponds, fun rides, rope climbing frames and a soft play area for toddlers. There is a Happy Hippo snack bar for refreshments. Ring number listed above for details of coffee mornings. Sessions last for one hour during holidays and weekends; at other times they last for as long as the House is not full.

Hours
Daily 10am–6pm

Travel
East or West Croydon ⇌

House of Fun 2

The Bridge Leisure Centre, Kangley Bridge Road, Colindale, NW9 (0181 201 3580)

Offers soft play equipment, a ball pond, rope bridges and slides — all along the same lines as House of Fun, listed above.

Hours
Daily 10am–6pm
Admission
Children (2–9) £2
Travel
Lower Sydenham ⇌

Kidstop

Corner of Collindale Avenue and Edgware Road, Colindale, NW9 (0181 201 3580)

Kidstop boasts London's largest indoor play area with a roller skating rink (for £2 extra), over-3s adventure area with slides, ropes, bouncy castles, large play frame and soft area for toddlers. There is also a cartoon cinema and restaurant. Roller-skating sessions take place in the evening for 12–16 year olds. Ring for details.

Hours
Daily
10.30am–6.30pm
Admission
Children £3.50,
adults £1
Travel
Colindale ⊖

Krazy Kids

213–217 Mile End Road, The Courtyard, Stepney Green, E1 (0171 790 4000)

Slides, climbing frames, rope walkways, etc. Krazy Kids is best for 1–12-year-olds.

Hours
Daily 10am–7pm
Admission
£2.50 per 2-hour session
Travel
Stepney Green ⊖

Hours
Daily 10am–7pm

Admission
Under 5s £2.50,
5–13s £2.75

Travel
⬤ Wood Green

Monkey Business

Lodge Drive Public Car Park, Green Lanes, Palmers Green, N13 (0181 886 7520)

Monkey tree house, twizzle maze, biff-bash bags, tube slides, spooky room, roller challenge. Toddler area with toddler mornings in term time. Height restriction of 4'10". Café.

Hours
10am–8pm

Admission
Under-5s £2.65,
5–11s from £3.65

Travel
⬤ ⇌ Gunnersbury
⇌ Kew Bridge
then **Bus** 237, 267

Snakes and Ladders

Syon Park, Brentford, Middx (0181 847 0946)

Slides, ropes, ball pond, climbing frame, roller skating (£1 extra), electric cars (50p extra). Height restriction of 4'8".

Hours
Daily
10.30am–6.30pm.
Carers and
toddlers (under-4s)
on Mon 10.30am–
12.30pm

Admission
Children £3.50,
adults £1.

Travel
⇌ Hackney Downs

Sunshine Safari

King's Hall Leisure Centre, 39 Lower Clapton Road, Hackney E5 (0181 533 6013)

Inflatable and soft adventure play area for children from 18 months up to about 10. Kinder Crocs for Under 5s, Safari Explorers for 5–12s.

Have you ever wanted to adopt an aardvark, pet a pig, ride a camel, milk a cow or see a snake? In London's zoos, farms and animal sanctuaries not only can you see all kinds of animals, often at very close range, but you can also watch sheep-shearing, cheese-making or lambing, clamber over old tractors and adventure playgrounds.

Animal Attractions

Battersea Dogs Home

4 Battersea Park Road, SW8 (0171 622 3626)

Hours
Mon-Fri 10.30am-
4.15pm, Sat & Sun
10.30am-3.30pm
(strays and
unwanted dogs
accepted any time)

Prices
Adults 50p,
children 20p

Travel
⇌ Battersea Park
Queenstown Road
or **Bus** 44

Since Britain's largest sanctuary for lost or unwanted dogs opened in 1860 nearly 3 million dogs have found shelter here. When we visited, the canine population stood at 542 but during the Christmas and summer holidays it can swell to over 700. Human visitors fall into three categories: those searching for a lost companion; those wishing to find a new addition to their household and those looking around. Prospective owners are carefully screened for suitability and compatibility with the dog of their choice and are required to fill out a long form. Expect to pay between £20-£60 for a dog (customers returning animals within seven days get their money back). Don't expect to find puppies – they are kept at Bell Mead in Old Windsor which is a canine nursery and maternity home. Toilets (no disabled or baby-changing facilities). Wheelchair and buggy access.

Battersea Park Children's Zoo

SW11 (0181 871 7540)

Hours
Easter-Oct daily
10am-5pm, winter
Sat & Suns only
11am-3pm (closed
for 2 weeks in Feb)

Prices
Adults £1, children
50p, OAPs 25p,
disabled and
under-2s free

Travel
⇌ Battersea Park

Yum Yum the pot-bellied pig has quite a fan club at this small zoo which boasts a reptile house, meerkat and mongoose enclosures, monkeys, flamingoes, ponies, deer, wallabies. Pygmy goats and sheep wander freely and can be safely handled by children of all ages. Buggy and wheelchair access. Loos. Picnic area. Very popular park (see page 108 for further details). Thomas the Tank Engine ride round the park in summer leaves from here (50p). Toilets for disabled and baby-changing facilities outside park gates. Toilet and baby-changing facilities in zoo Easter–October only.

Golders Hill Park ☺ ◼ ☼ ◗

NW11 (0181 455 5183)

Hours
Daily 7.30am to
half an hour after
sunset

Travel
⊖ Golders Green

Pygmy goats, wallabies, black buck and fallow deer, pheasants, cranes, flamingoes and rheas in pens at the bottom of park near the children's play area (where they have inflatables and kids entertainment during summer hols). Toilets by café at top of park although it's a bit of a trek. Toilets for disabled people and baby-changing bench.

London Butterfly House 😊 🌧 ◐

Syon Park, Brentford, Middx (0181 847 0946)

Huge collection of free-flying butterflies in tropical green-house gardens and ponds which do not excite children nearly as much as the spiders, stick insects, snakes and locusts in the Insect House. Also Snakes and Ladders indoor adventure playground (daily 10am-5pm, adults and babies free, over-5s £3.65-£4.25, under 5s £2.65-£3.25; roller skating, crazy golf and go-karting extra). Toilets for disabled people and baby-changing facilities.

Hours
Daily 10am-6.30pm (last admission 5pm)

Prices
Adults £2.75, under 16s & OAPs £1.75, family ticket (2+4) £6.95

Travel
Gunnersbury ⊖ ⇄ Kew Bridge ⇄ then **Bus** 237 or 267 to Brentlea Gate

London Zoo 😊 🌧 ●

Regent's Park, NW1 (0171 722 3333 24 hr info; Zoo-line 0891-505767)

Collect a free daily events guide on your way, and take some time studying the map and planning your day carefully (otherwise you will find yourself at the wrong end of the zoo at the wrong time). Over 12,000 mammals, birds, reptiles, fish and insects live in this wonderful zoo – Chinese alligators, Sumatran tigers, Nile crocodiles, African eagles, Asiatic lions. The famous aquarium has sharks and piranhas, while the eery Moonlight World has nocturnal animals including the Leadbeater Possum, once thought to be extinct. In the summer there are Meet the Animals sessions, pony and camel rides and elephant bath time (watch out!). We found children get more out of the zoo if they come without friends (otherwise all they want to do is head for the playground). Jake wants to spend all his time with the monkeys and Benja just wants to watch the penguins so we try to split up and meet back at an agreed place (usually an ice-cream kiosk – there are lots of them). There is a recommended Rainy Day Route (ask at ticket kiosk). Pushchair and wheelchair hire at the gate. Total double buggy and wheelchair access. Very child-and-baby-friendly restaurant with babyfood, nappies, rusks, toddler and children portions (children's saussages and vegetables £2.25, toddler portion £1.25; juice 65p). Baby-changing and feeding room. Grass area for picnics near Barclay Court. Toilets for disabled people.

Hours
Daily 10am-5.30pm (closed Christmas Day). Elephant weighing 3pm, camel and pony rides 11am-4pm, crocodile, piranhas and shark feeding time 2.30pm. Discovery Centre workshops daily 2-4pm. Cows milked in Children's Farmyard daily 3pm. Summer Workshops for children 6 and over (booking essential 0171 722 3333).

Prices
Adults £7.50, children (4-14) £5.50, OAPs & Students £6.50, under-4s free

Travel
Camden Town or Baker Street ⊖ then **Bus** 274 London Water Bus along Regent's Canal (Car park & meter parking near zoo entrance)

Young's Brewery 😊 🇫 ☼ ◐

Hours
Sun 11am-1pm

Travel
🚉 Wandsworth
Town

Wandsworth High Street (entrance Ram Street), SW18 (0181 870 0141)

On a Sunday morning you can visit the dray horses, donkeys, goats, geese and sheep. Ring for details prior to journey. No baby-changing facilities or toilets for disabled.

CITY FARMS

These genuine working farms give children of all ages a chance to see a wide variety of farm animals as well as getting involved in the day-to-day activities such as milking, feeding and mucking out. Most also offer other activities like sheep-shearing demonstrations, riding, milking and craft sessions. And don't forget your wellies.

College Farm 😊 ☼ ◐

Hours
Daily 10am-6pm

Prices
Adults £1.25,
children 70p, OAPs
£1 (on open days
£2, £1, £1.50
respectively)

Travel
⊖ Finchley Central

45 Fitzalan Road, N3 (0181 349 0690)

Small children's farm with usual variety of animals and special Open Day on first Sunday of the month (1-6pm) with craft fair, donkey rides, puppet shows. Toilets with baby-changing area. No facilities for disabled people.

Dean City Farm 😊 🇫 ☼ ◐

Hours
Open all year daily
9am-4pm

Prices
Free but donation
appreciated

Travel
⊖ Colliers Wood
or South
Wimbledon

1 Batsworth Road (off Church Road), SW19 (0181 543 5300)

Farm with variety of animals, riding school for able bodied and disabled children, and organic horticulture. Discovery Week for 11-15 year olds in August;. £27.50 for the week. Toilets for disabled people. No baby-changing facilities.

Freightliners Farm 😊 🇫 ☼ ◐

Hours
Tues-Sun 9am-
1pm & 2-5pm

Travel
⊖ Highbury &
Islington
Buses 43, 271, 4,
19, 17

Sheringham Road, N7 (0171 609 0467)

Lots of chances to get involved with the care of animals in this small busy farm including feeding sheep, cows, pigs, goats, ducks, geese and chickens. Sensory Garden. Playgroup for under-5s on Wednesday and Saturday morning. Café and farm shop. Toilets for disabled people. baby-changing facilities.

Hackney City Farm 😊 🇫 ☼ ◑

1a Goldsmiths Row, E2 (0171 729 6381)

Bees, pigs, sheep, goats, ducks & rabbits. Cobbled yard, small orchard, ecological pond, butterfly tunnel and wildflower area. Regular children's events and activities including pottery, spinning and weaving workshops. Toilets for disabled people. Baby-changing surface.

Hours
Open daily 10am-4.30pm
Travel
Cambridge Heath ⇌
Bus 26, 48, 55

Kentish Town City Farm 😊 🇫 ☼ ◑

1 Cressfield Close, NW5 (0171 916 5421)

Horses, sheep, pigs, chicken, ducks, cows, geese and rabbits. Toilets for disabled people. No baby-changing facilities but you can use the office.

Hours
Tues-Sun 9.30am-5.30pm
Travel
Chalk Farm ⊖
Kentish Town ⊖⇌
Gospel Oak ⇌

Mudchute Farm 😊 🇫 ☼ ◑

Pier Street (off Manchester Road), Isle of Dogs, E14 (0171 515 5901)

The largest city farm in Britain which includes a working farm, wildlife area, horses, woodland and parkland. Children can meet Mary the Aberdeen Angus cow, Perky the rare breed pig, and Larry the Llama. A lot of walking involved. Good riding facilities (for lessons ring 0171 515 0749). Café (not as cheap as other farms). Agricultural Show mid-August. Wheelchair access and toilets for disabled (no baby-changing facilities).

Hours
Daily 9am-5pm
Travel
DLR Mudchute

Newham City Farm 😊 🇫 ☼ ◑

Stansfeld Road, E6 (0171 476 1170)

Barbecues, pony rides, craft sessions, picnic area. Toilets for disabled people (no baby-changing facilities).

Hours
Open Tues-Sun 10am-5pm
Travel
DLR Royal Albert

Spitalfields Farm Association 😊 🇫 ☼ ◑

Weaver Street, E1 (0171 247 8762)

Learn to feed, muck out, milk and bed down the animals which include pigs, goats, sheep, cows, rabbits, donkeys and poultry. Local history horse-drawn cart tours and pony rides available. Also free pottery and dairy workshops. Toilets.

Hours
Tues-Sun 9am-6pm
Prices
Free (voluntary donation)
Travel
Whitechapel or Bethnal Green ⊖

Stepney Stepping Stones Farm 😊 🇪 ☼ ◐

Hours
Tues-Sun 9.30am-
5pm
Prices
Free (donations
invited)
Travel
⊖ Stepney

Stepney Way, E1 (0171 790 8204)

As well as the usual pigs, goats, cows, sheep, geese, ducks, rabbits and donkeys there is a wildlife pond and an attractive picnic garden. Shop sells farm produce. Toilets for disabled peole (no baby-changing facilities but staff are helpful).

Surrey Quays Farm 😊 🇪 ☼ ◐

Hours
Tues-Thurs, Sat &
Sun 10am-1pm,
2-5pm
Travel
DLR Surrey Quays

Rotherhithe Street, Rotherhithe, SE16 (0171 231 1010)

Our favourite city farm for under-5s, despite the fact the kid goats tried to eat Benjamin's shorts (he was wearing them at the time) it is very small but has a lovely atmosphere, very friendly staff and the café sells drinks and biscuits at amazingly low prices. Holiday activities include felt-making, egg-painting and farm activities. There is a small orchard, wild area, riverside walk and duck pond. Farm shop. Café. Toilets for disabled people (no baby-changing facilities).

Vauxhall City Farm 😊 🇪 ☼ ◖

Hours
Tues-Thurs, Sat &
Sun 10.30am-5pm
Prices
Free (except tours)
but donations
welcome
Travel
⊖ Vauxhall

Tyers Street (Off Kensington Lane), SE11 (0171 582 4204)

Goats, sheep, pigs, rabbits. Good riding facilities at reasonable rates (and pony and donkey rides for the very young). 'Spinning Club' and holiday play scheme. No café but reasonable picnic area. Toilets for disabled. Baby-changing area on request.

Crystal Palace Park Farm 😊 ☼ ◐

Hours
Daily 11am-5pm
Prices
Adults 70p,
children 35p
Travel
⇌ Crystal Palace

SE20 (0181 778 4487)

Farm with usual collection of pigs, cows, goats, rabbits, chickens, donkeys, otters and sheep. Animals roam free so limited access for buggies. Wheelchairs allowed. Picnic tables. Shire horse cart rides around the park, summer fair best for under-7s. The park itself is also worth a visit (see page 55 for details). Toilets for disabled people and baby-changing facilities.

Messing about in boats — whether you are cruising along Regent's Canal in a traditional narrow boat, rowing around the Serpentine or taking a pleasure boat along old Father Thames — is always a hit with the kids and not necessarily reliant on the weather being fine, although you will see more from the boats if it is not actually raining.

Waterways

Pleasure Trips

Prices
From £3, children
half-price
Travel
◔ Westminster,
Charing Cross

You can take trips up and down the Thames throughout the year (sailing times are irregular, from November–March), from Westminster and Charing Cross Piers. Day and half-day trips include Historic Greenwich, Tower of London, Thames Flood Barrier Cruise, Hampton Court, Disco Cruises and Lunch Cruises. For full details ring the London Tourist Board's Special Riverboat Information Service on 0839 123432 (calls cost 39p/49p per minute), or ring Catamaran Cruises on 0171 987 1185; London Launches on 0171 930 3373; Westminster Tower Boats on 0171 237 5134.

Also: from Richmond Pier to Hampton Court, Kew, Putney, Westminster, ring 0171 930 4721. From Richmond Pier take a circular 45-minute trip to Teddington Lock (operates April–September, adults £3, children and OAPs £2; ring Brian Parr on 0181 940 8505 for details).

Travel
◔⇌ Richmond

Boat Hire ☼

Richmond Bridge Motor and Rowing Boat Hire (0181 948 8270)

Rowing boats cost £2.50 per person per hour (under-14s are half-price if accompanied by an adult). Motor boats are £15 per hour for 3 people, £20 per hour for 4 people (under-14s free).

Prices
£15 per hour
Travel
⇌ Alperton

Canal Boat Trips ☺ ☼ ●

0181 810 9126.

Boat-hire and one-day and overnight trips on a narrow boat cruising up the Grand Union Canal. Ring for details of trips.

Hours
Daily every 30
mins from
10.30am-4pm
Prices
Adults £3-£5.90,
children £1.50-£3.
Return-trip family
ticket (2+3) £12.
Travel
◔⇌ Charing
Cross

Catamaran Cruises ☺ ☼ ◖

Charing Cross Pier, Victoria Embankment, WC2 (0171 987 1185)

A great, hassle-free way for children to see sights and get a real feel for London (as long as they're not seasick). Boats travel to the Tower of London and Greenwich.

Cutty Sark 😊 ☼ ◖

King William Walk, Greenwich Pier, SE10 (0181 858 3445)

The Cutty Sark was built as a tea clipper in 1869 and now stands in dry dock. Children love exploring the deck and can see where the sailors worked, slept and ate. In the summer you can also go aboard the Gypsy Moth IV, the boat in which Sir Francis Chichester sailed round the world single-handed in 1966. See also page 51.

Hours
Mon-Sat 10am-6pm, Sun 2.30-6pm, last tickets 5.30pm

Prices
Adults £3.25, concs £2.25, family ticket (2+3) £8

Travel
Greenwich or Maze Hill ⇥
DLR Island Gardens

HMS Belfast 😊 ☼ ◖

Symons Wharf, Vince Lane, SE1 (0171 407 6434)

Launched in 1938, this Royal Naval cruiser played an important role in the Battle of Northcape in December 1943. It is now a permanent museum and little has changed since it was in active service. The last tickets are sold 45 minutes before closing. See also page 66.

Hours
Apr-Oct daily 10am-6pm, Nov March daily 10am-4pm

Prices
Adults £4, children £2, under-5s free, family ticket £10

Travel
London Bridge ⊖ ⇥ or **River Boat** from Tower Pier

Jason's Canal Boat Trip 🌧 ◖

opposite 60 Blomfield Road, Little Venice, W9 (0171 286 3428)

A one-and-a-half-hour commentated round-trip narrow boat cruise from Little Venice, through the Maida Hill Tunnel, under Blow-up Bridge, past London Zoo, Primrose Hill and the Cumberland Basin to Camden Lock Market (too long for under-5s). Lunches and teas are available on board (to be ordered in advance). Children's birthday parties and some evening trips can be arranged. There is covered seating in case of rain and a canal-side restaurant.

Hours
April-Sept daily 10.30am, 12.30pm, 2.30pm. Oct daily 12.30pm and 2.30pm

Prices
Adult single £4.25, child £2.95. Under-4s free

Travel
Warwick Avenue ⊖ or **Bus** 6 or 46

Jenny Wren 🌧 ◖

250 Camden High Street, NW1 (0171 485 4433/6210)

The cruise is a one-and-a-half-hour round trip only from Camden Lock to Little Venice and back, which is too long for young children (one-way tickets are not available). Book privately to travel eastwards through the Islington Tunnel. Advanced booking is advisable. There is covered seating in case of rain.

Hours
March-Oct daily 11.30am, 2pm, 3.30pm (Nov-Feb weekend cruises subject to weather conditions)

Prices
Adult return £3.95, children £1.95

Travel
Camden Town ⊖

London Canal Museum

Hours
Open Tues-Sun
10am-4.30pm
(closed Dec 24-26,
Jan 1-2)

Prices
£2.50, concs £1.25

Travel
King's Cross

12-13 New Wharf Road, N1 (0171 713 0836)

Learn about cargoes and canal crafts, about the people who strove to make a living from the canals and the horses which pulled their boats. Housed in a warehouse built in the 1850s by the ice-cream manufacturer Carlo Gatti, the museum traces the story of London's canals from the early days as important trade routes to today's more leisurely activities.

London Waterbus Company

Hours
April-Oct daily.
Nov-March
weekends, every
2 hours

Prices
Adult single £3.30,
return £4.40
children single £2,
return £2.60,
under-3s free

Travel
Camden Town
and Warwick
Avenue

Blomfield Road, W9 (entrance at corner of Westbourne Terrace Road Bridge) and Camden Lock Place, NW1 (off Chalk Farm Road). (Details 0171 482 2550)

Boat rides between Camden Lock and Little Venice. If you want to get off to visit the zoo, tell the ticket master and you get a reduction on the price of admission included in your canal ride fare. Prices are subject to change. You can also hire a boat and crew for children's parties (£145 for two hours).

Puppet Theatre Barge

Prices
Adults £5.50,
children £5

Travel
Warwick Road

Little Venice, Blomfield Road, W9 (0171 249 6876 or mobile phone 0836 202 745)

Movingstage Marionettes company gives performances throughout the year on an old Thames barge converted into a delightful miniature auditorium, complete with proscenium arch and raked seating. Moored on Regent's Canal in Little Venice from November to June and sailing up the Thames with performances at Kingston and Richmond from June to September. Ring for details.

Thames Barrier and Visitor's Centre

Hours
Mon-Fri 10am-5pm,
Sat & Sun 10.30am-
5.30pm

Prices
Adult £2.50,
children £1.55.
Car park 50p

Travel
Charlton
Bus 177, 180
or **Riverbus**

Unity Way, Woolwich, SE18 (0181 854 1373)

Learn about the history of the river and why the barrier was built. There is a souvenir shop, cafeteria, picnic area, play area and riverside walk with view of barrier. To get a closer look at this remarkable piece of 20th-century engineering take a Barrier Cruise from Barrier Pier.

A puff of smoke, a whistle and you enter the bygone days of steam. No child can resist the excitement of steam travel, whether it is the funny face of Thomas the Tank Engine or the romantic charm of a Victorian paddle steamer. But it is not just railways and boats — impressive stationary engines which once powered heavy industry, textile mills and pumping stations are also put 'in steam' at many of Britain's steam and industrial museums and sites.

Steam Engines

LONDON
Brunel's Engine House

Railway Ave, Rotherhithe, SE16 (0181 318 2489)

The sole surviving example of a compound horizontal V-steam pumping engine, built in 1885, is housed here along with an exhibition entitled 'Brunel's Tunnel and Where It Led'. No toilets. Limited wheelchair and buggy access.

Hours
First Sun of every month noon-4pm, every Sun in Aug & Sept

Prices
Adults £1.50, children, OAPs 50p, family ticket £4.50

Travel
⊖ Rotherhithe East London Line

Kew Bridge Steam Museum

Green Dragon Lane, Brentford, Middx (0181 568 4757)

This 19th-century pumping station supplied London's water for over 100 years, powered by five enormous beam engines (three of which have been restored and are put in steam at weekends and on Bank Holidays). There is a miniature steam railway and a working forge. Special events are held throughout the year.

Hours
Daily 11am-5pm

Prices
Adults £2/£3.25, children & concs £1/£1.80

Travel
⇌ Kew Bridge, Gunnersbury Park then **Bus** 27, 237, 267/on-site parking

North Woolwich Old Station Museum

Pier Road, E16 (0171 474 7244)

The engines at this museum are put in steam on Easter Sunday and the first Sunday of the month in summer. See page 77, for further details.

Hours
Mon-Wed & Sat 10am-5pm, Sun 2-5pm

Travel
⇌ North Woolwich, ferry from ⇌ Woolwich, foot tunnel, **Bus** 69, 101, 276

Science Museum

Exhibition Road, South Kensington SW7 (0171 938 8000)

Here you'll find two Boulton and Watt engines (dating from 1788) which are sometimes put in steam, a 1903 Lancashire mill engine, Stephenson's Rocket, an Apollo space rocket, hands-on kids' activities and school holiday events. See page 81, for further details.

Hours
Mon-Sat 10am-6pm, Sun 11am-6pm

Prices
Adults £5, children (5-15) & concs £2.10, diasabled & under-5s free. Free after 4.30pm.

Travel
⊖ South Kensington

Southall Railway Centre

Glade Lane (entrance via footbridge linking Merrick Road and Park Avenue), Southall, Middx (0181 574 1529)

London's only independent live steam railway centre run by volunteers of the Great Western Railway Preservation Group. You can ride behind steam and diesel-hauled trains on 'Steaming Days' held on the last weekend of each month. On remaining weekends locos are on 'static' display.

OUT OF TOWN

Bluebell Railway

Sheffield Park Station, nr Uckfield, East Sussex 0182572 3777

The Bluebell Railway makes a memorable day out for anyone of any age. Small children versed in Thomas the Tank Engine thrill at the puffing, hissing locomotives while grandparents can journey back to the days of their youth. The locomotive sheds are at Sheffield Park and the station has been restored in the late Victorian style with signals, vintage advertisments and even an old trunk waiting to be loaded on to a train. The museum on Platform 2 is crammed with models, tickets, photographs and signs. The highlight is the train journey which takes you along a five-mile stretch of the old branch line between Sheffield Park and Horsted Keynes in historic coaches, meticulously restored in the elegant 1930s style of the Southern Railway. You can have lunch on the 1920s Golden Arrow Pullman (runs at weekends), or, less expensively, in the 1882 station buffet at Horsted Keynes. Crowded at weekends especially in May when the bluebells blossom in the woods through which the line passes. Special events like Thomas the Tank Engine weekends and Santa Specials (ring for details). Restaurant, gift shop, toilets, café and picnic area at both stations. Wheelchair access (ring in advance). Alongside the Bluebell Railway is Capability Brown's magestically landscaped Sheffield Park. Although the Gothic mansion is not open, visitors can wander round the 100-acre park (open April-November, Tuesday-Saturday 11am-6pm, Sunday 1-6pm or sunset £4/£2).

Hours
Apr to Oct, Sat, Sun & Bank Holiday Mon 11am-6pm

Prices
Steaming Day: adults £3.75, children £2, family ticket (2+3) £10. Static days: adults £2, children £1.

Travel
Southall ⇌
Bus 105, 120, 195

Hours
Talking timetable 01825 722370

Prices
Return fare, admission to museum and locomotive sheds: adult £7, child (3-15) £3.50, under-3s free, OAPs £6, family ticket £19. Single tickets available.

Travel
46 miles south of London. Haywards Heath, East Grinstead ⇌ on site parking

Nearby: Barnsgate Manor Vineyard, Herons Ghyll (A26, four miles north of Uckfield) has a vineyard, herd of llama, donkeys, museum, winery, wine-tasting, tearoom and restaurant.

Chuffa Trains Museum

82 High Street, Whitstable, Kent (01227 277339)

Hours
Mon-Fri 10am-3pm (5pm school and bank hols); Sat 10am-5pm

Prices
Adults £1, children and OAPs £75p, Family ticket (2 + 3) £3

Travel
Whitstable

A museum and model train shop which recalls the days of the 'Crab and Winkle Railway' opened in 1830. Children's activity area. Under-10s must be accompanied. No wheel chair or buggy access. Combine the visit with a trip to Whitstable beach (Herne Bay and Canterbury are both nearby).

Didcot Railway Centre

Didcot, Oxfordshire (01235 817200)

Hours
Mon-Fri Easter-Sept 25 and Oct 22-30 11am-5pm; Sat and Sun all year 11am-5pm (4pm winter)

Prices
Prices vary, adults £3-£5, children £2-£5 (under-5s usually free).

Travel
Didcot BR car park

Once a major maintenance post for Brunel's broad-gauge Great Western Railway, this is now a mecca for railway enthusiasts. The engine shed houses locomotives, some of which are still being restored, plus carriages and freight wagons. Train rides are available on the first and last Sunday in the month and Bank Holiday Mondays until the end of May, then every Sunday until the end of August. Special events are held, including Thomas the Tank Engine weekends (ring for details).

East Anglia Railway Museum

Chapel Station, Colchester (01206 242524)

Hours
Daily 10am-5pm (closed Dec 25)

Prices
Adults £2.25, children and OAPs £1.25, under-4s free, family ticket (2+4) £6.50 when steaming £4, £2, £11 respectively

Travel
Chapel Station

A working museum where visitors can watch the locomotives and coaches being restored as well as taking steam passenger rides. There is wheelchair access but no disabled toilets.

French Brothers Boat Trips 😊 ☼ ◑

The Runnymede Boathouse, Windsor Road, Old Windsor, Berkshire
(01753 851900/862933)

Regular 45-minute trips from Runnymede to Hampton Court,
Windsor and several stops in between, aboard the Lucy
Fisher, a replica paddle steamer. Tea rooms. Souvenirs.

Hours
Easter-Nov on the
hour, from 11am

Prices
Adults £2.40,
under-14s £1.20,
babes in arms free

Travel
Windsor ⇌

Kent and East Sussex 😊 ☼ ◑
Steam Railway

Tenterden, Kent (01580 765155)

The first of the rural lines introduced in 1898 steams through
the Wealden countryside from the re-furbished Edwardian
Ternterden Town Station to Northiam in Sussex. Railway
stock at Tenterden and Rolvenden includes an American
engine which was shipped over to Britain for the D-Day
landings and a Victorian passenger train complete with family and directors' saloon. There is a museum, railway shop
and children's playground. Special events in the summer.
Good venue for parties (ring for details). Wheelchair access.

Nearby: Sissinghurst Castle (5 miles).

Hours
Open March Sun
only; April-Oct
weekends only;
June & Sept Sat,
Sun, Tues-Thurs;
July & August
daily, Santa
Specials weekends
in Dec.

Prices
Adults £6, under-
15s £3, family
ticket (2+3) £16

Travel
Headcorn ⇌
then **Bus** (ring
01634 832 66 for
bus times)

North Downs Steam Railway 😊 ☼ ◔

London Road, Cotton Lane, Nr Dartford, Kent (01322 228260)

Steam and diesel locomotives run the half-mile line between
Cotton Lane and London Road. Events throughout the year
and a Santa Special in November and December. Right next
to Stone Lodge Farm (see also page 198).

Hours
All year Sunday
11am-5pm; Sat
and Sun Jun-Sept
2-5pm

Travel
By car just outside
Dartford on A226
London Road

Paddle Steamer 😊 ☼ ◔

Kingswear Castle, AQHM's House, The Historic Dockyard, Chatham,
Kent (01634 827648)

Trips from Chatham Historic Dockyard to Strood Pier on a
vintage river paddle steamer built in 1924 complete with
panelled saloons.

Hours
May-Jun and Sept
Wed and Sun
2.30-5pm, Jul-Aug
Wed-Fri and Sun
2.30-5pm

Prices
Adults £3.95-
£7.95, children (3-
16) £1.95, OAPs
£2.95-£5.95

Travel
Chatham ⇌

Hours
Summer daily
10am-5pm, win-
ter weekends only

Prices
Adults £3, children
£1.50, OAPs £2,
under-3s free

Travel
By car M25 then
A21

Quarry Farm Rural Experience

Bodiam, East Sussex (01580 830670)

Rural traction engines including road locomotives used by showmen to pull fairground equipment from village to village, and plough engines. Engines go round a former hop garden – at least one is in steam daily. Also young farm animals, birds of prey, tractor rides and miniature-train rides.

Nearby: Bodiam Castle. Special events include annual Easter egg hunt, Thomas and Friends (April and May), cross country car rally (July). See also page 202.

Hours
Trains run up to 12
times daily from
Easter-Sept 30 and
weekends in
March and Oct

Travel
➤ Hythe

Romney, Hythe and Dymchurch Railway

Hythe, Kent (01679 62353)

This 15-inch-gauge line which runs 14 miles from Hythe to Dungeness is – depending on how you look at it – the world's largest toy railway, or smallest public train service. The steam locomotives are one-third scale models of those used in the 1920s when the line was built as a tourist attraction linking the resorts along the coast. Stop off at New Romney station (three stops from Hythe) to see the model train and toy exhibition in the station before continuing on to Dungeness, a bleak, shingled expanse of wasteland where you can take a free guided tour round Dungeness nuclear power station (afternoons daily in summer; Thursday, Friday and Sunday in winter; safety helmets provided, wear sensible shoes, ring in advance) or climb the 168 steps up the old Dungeness lighthouse (01679 21300; daily March-September 30 10.30am-5pm and other times by arrangement) for some splendid views and an insight into how the lantern was worked and cleaned.

Travel
➤ Brighton

Volks Electric Railway

Madeira Drive, Brighton (01273 681061)

Britain's first public electric railway, opened in 1883, will be of interest to railway enthusiasts, despite the fact it is not steam. The track runs for about two miles along the seafront from the pier to the marina. Ring for times and prices.

Whether you are buying clothes, books and comics,
or indulging your child's new-found hobby for
making necklaces, this section provides all
the information you need.

Shopping

ARTS, CRAFTS AND HOBBIES

Bead Shop

Hours
Mon 1-6pm,
Tues-Fri
10.30am-6pm

Travel
Covent Garden

43 Neal Street, WC2 (0171 240 0931)

Beads of every imaginable shape, size and colour (often hand-carved or hand-painted) to make earrings, necklaces and bracelets, plus string, clasps, earring hooks, etc.

Covent Garden Candle Shop

Hours
Mon-Sat
10am-6pm, Sun
10.30am-7pm

Travel
Covent Garden

30 The Market, Covent Garden Market, WC2 (0171 836 9815)

Huge variety of candles, candle-making demonstrations and candle-making kits.

Janet Coles Bead Emporium

Hours
Mon-Sat
10am-6pm

Travel
Notting Hill

128 Notting Hill Gate, W11 (0171 727 8085)

A thousand types of beads from all over the world made from materials as diverse as amber, wood, ceramic and plastic.

Hobby Horse

Hours
Mon-Sat
10am-5.30pm

Travel
Earls Court
then **Bus** 28 or 31

15-17 Langton Street, SW10 (0171 351 1913)

Beads galore for jewellery-making as well as fittings, etc.

BOOKS, COMICS, MAPS

Books Etc

Hours
Mon-Sat
10am-10pm, Sun
noon-6pm

Travel
Bayswater or
Queensway

19 Whiteley's Shopping Centre, W2 (0171 229 3865) and branches

Good range of children's books.

Bookspread

Hours
Mon, Wed, Fri
10am-5pm, Tue &
Thurs 10am-7pm,
Sun 10am-3pm

Travel
Tooting Bec

58 Tooting Bec Road, SW17 (0181 767 6377/4551)

Reading advisory service and activities centre has daily activities including storytelling, rhymes, singing etc. Send

SAE for monthly news sheet listing time of activities. Catalogue, mail order and activity sheets.

Children's Book Centre

237 Kensington High Street, W8 (0171 937 7497)

Gigantic children's bookshop with over 30,000 titles including every type of children's book. Storytelling competitions and singing sessions in the holidays.

Hours
Mon, Wed, Fri
10am–5pm, Tue &
Thurs 10am–7pm
Travel
High Street
Kensington ⊖

Children's Bookshop

29 Fortis Green Road, N10 (0181 444 5500)

There are over 20,000 titles in this specialist children's book shop and helpful, well-informed staff will point you in the right direction for pre-school books or those on the National Curriculum. Summer storytelling sessions and other events throughout the year.

Hours
Mon–Sat
9.15am–5.45pm
Travel
Highgate ⊖
Bus 134, 43

Forbidden Planet

71 New Oxford Street, WC1 (0171 836 4179)

Large bookshop stuffed full of comics, sci-fi, fantasy and horror.

Hours
Mon–Wed & Sat
10am–6pm, Thurs
& Fri 10am–7pm
Travel
Tottenham Court
Road ⊖

Hatchards

187 Piccadilly, W1 (0171 439 9921)

Good children's section upstairs as well as a useful search department.

Hours
Mon–Sat
9am–6pm, Sun
11am–5pm
Travel
Piccadilly
Circus ⊖

Marchpane

16 Cecil Court, WC2 (0171 836 8661)

Wonderful collection of illustrated children's books, rare first and second editions for collectors young and old.

Hours
Mon–Sat
10.30am–6.30pm,
Sun noon–5pm
Travel
Leicester
Square ⊖

Tin Tin Shop

Hours
Mon–Sat
10.30am–6.30pm,
Sun noon–5pm
Travel
◉ Covent Garden

34 Floral Street, WC2 (0171 836 1131)

Tin Tin books, post cards, T-shirts, key rings, slippers and clothes. Prices range from fairly expensive to outrageous.

Waterstones

Hours
Mon–Fri
9.30am–9pm, Sat
9.30am–7pm, Sun
noon–6pm
Travel
◉ High Street
Kensington

193 Kensington High Street, W8 (0171 937 8432) and other branches

Good children's book section in this well-stocked chain.

BUGGY REPAIRS

Cottams Baby Carriages

Hours
Ring for details
Travel
⇌ Mitcham
Bus 127

3 Bramcote Parade, Cricket Green, Mitcham, Surrey (0181 648 4397)

Repair all makes including old ones (usually takes one week).

The Pram Centre

Hours
Ring for details
Travel
◉ Goldhawk Road

182 Railway Approach, W12 (0181 743 4126)

Service and repair all makes except Mothercare. Also re-cover hoods and supply new aprons.

CLOTHES AND SHOES

0–12 Benetton

Hours
Mon–Sat
10am–6.30pm
(Thurs until 8pm)
Travel
◉ Oxford Circus

255-259 Regent's Street, W1 (0171 355 4881) and other branches

This Italian store sells expensive but bright and attractive separates for children up to 12 years. Good value for jumpers.

Adams

Hours
Mon–Wed, Fri
9.30am–7pm,
Thurs
9.30am–8pm, Sat
9.30am–6.30pm
Travel
◉ Marble Arch

475 Oxford Street, W1 (0171 355 3435)

The mix-and-match clothes are amazingly good value for money and wash-and-wear through several hand-me-downs. Tough-wearing cool shirts, simple pinafore dresses, brightly coloured leggings and denim jackets. Also good for pyjamas, hats, coats, belts, socks and tights. Good-quality shoes from the Birthday range.

Asda Superstore

Clapham Junction, 204 Lavender Hill, SW11 (0171 223 0101)

Well-designed value-for-money range of clothes and shoes for children from birth onwards.

Hours
Mon–Thurs
9am–10pm, Fri &
Sat 8.30am–10pm

Travel
Clapham
Junction ⇌

Baby Gap, Gap Kids

144-146 Regent Street, W1 (0171 287 5095) and other branches

Children from toddlers upwards look gorgeous in Gap's trendy, hard-wearing, good-value American sweatshirts, denims, dresses and jumpers. The new-born-and-baby-range is delightful, practical and survives several hand-me-downs.

Hours
Mon–Wed & Fri
9am–7pm, Thurs
9am–8pm, Sat
9.30am–6.30pm

Travel
Oxford Circus or
Piccadilly
Circus ⊖

Buckle My Shoe

19 St Christopher's Place, W1 (0171 935 5589)

Fashionable and fun shoes for babies and children up to eight years old from patent party shoes to flip-flops at a price. Expect to pay around £30 for a pair of toddler's shoes. Also sells clothes.

Hours
Mon–Sat
10am–6pm, Thurs
10am–7pm

Travel
Bond Street ⊖

C&A

501-509 Oxford Street, W1 (0171 629 7272) and other branches

Inexpensive, if sometimes naff, range of clothes for babies and children up to 16 years old. Best for baby clothes and accessories and excellent street-cred sports wear.

Hours
Mon–Sat
9.30am–6pm,
Thurs 9.30am–7pm

Travel
Marble Arch ⊖

Children's World

Purley Way (A23), Croydon (0181 760 0484) and other branches

Large warehouse with rows and rows of children's clothes (jumpers that look hand-knitted and basic jeans from £8.99), as well as toys, games, nursery equipment. Shoe department

Hours
Mon–Fri
10am–8pm, Sat
9am–6pm, Sun
11am–5pm

Travel
Waddon ⇌
Bus 289

149

and a hairdresser. Children like the giant slide down which they enter the 'world'. Café with high chairs and kids' food. Catalogue, children's toilets, father-and-baby room, mother-and-baby room, play area.

Circus Circus

Hours
9am–6pm, Sat
9am–6pm, Sun
10am–5pm
Travel
✆ Fulham
Broadway
Bus 28

176 Wandsworth Bridge Road, SW6 (0171 731 4128)

Well-stocked shop with labels like Osh Kosh often cheaper than other shops. Kickers shoes. Tasteful nursery furnishings, hand-painted items and bedding and soft furnishings to match.

Clark's

Hours
Mon–Sat
9.30am–6.30pm,
Thurs 9.30am–6pm
Travel
✆ Marble Arch

437 Oxford Street, W1 (0171 629 9609) and other branches

Proper foot measurement and shoes to fit narrow and extra-wide feet. Members of TAMBA, the twins' club get a 10% discount. The Clarks Factory shop sells end-of-range shoes and seconds up to half-price. If you know what you want they will send shoes direct to you.

Hennes

Hours
Mon–Fri
10am–6.30pm,
Thurs 10am–8pm,
Sat 9.30am–6pm
Travel
✆ Oxford Circus

Oxford Circus, W1 (0171 493 4004) and other branches

Huge range of fashionable and fun clothes in natural fibres at budget prices (many jeans and shirts under £9) from birth onwards. Sizes very generous. Best place for sensible no-frills girls' clothes.

Humla

Hours
Mon–Sat
10am–6pm, Sun
noon–6pm
Travel
✆ Hampstead

9 Flask Walk, NW3 (0171 794 8449)

Original, jolly knitwear for 0-12s which can be made to order and a colourful range of mix-and-match clothes at reasonable prices. Also traditional wooden toys and mobiles. Play area.

Laura Ashley

256-258 Regent Street, W1 (0171 437 9760) and other branches

Sailor suits, pretty pinafores, floral printed skirts and shirts and fancy party dresses.

Hours
Mon & Tues
10am–6.30pm,
Wed 10am–7pm,
Sat 9.30am–7pm
Travel
Oxford Circus ⊖

Marks & Spencer

458 Oxford Street, W1 (0171 935 7954) and other branches

Excellent-value children's clothes and shoes.

Hours
Thurs & Fri
9am–8pm, Sun
noon–6pm, rest of
week 9am–7pm
Travel
Marble Arch ⊖

Mothercare

461 Oxford Street, W1 (0171 629 6621) and other branches

As a parent you cannot avoid going to Mothercare at some point and for basics (stretch suits, vests, socks) it is great value. Good-quality, hard-wearing co-ordinated tops, bottoms and accessories, as well as wellies, jellies, overalls and aprons. A good selection of co-ordinated nursery equipment. Mail order available. Nappy-delivery service. Mother-and-baby-room.

Hours
Mon–Wed & Sat
9am–7pm, Thurs &
Fri 9am–8pm
Travel
Marble Arch ⊖

Next

54-60 Kensington High Street, W8 (0171 938 4211) and other branches

Trendy kids' clothes, some good shoes, beautiful but expensive duffle coats. Best value are their wonderful, wool-mix jumpers and thick cotton track suits.

Hours
Mon–Sat
10am–6.30pm,
Thurs 10am–8pm,
Sun noon–6pm
Travel
High Street
Kensington ⊖

Trotters

34 King's Road, SW3 (0171 259 9620) and other branches

A lovely shop for browsing – full of beautiful clothes, imaginative toys and good shoes, but expensive. Popular for haircuts (from £8.50).

Hours
Mon–Sat
9am–6.30pm,
Thurs 9am–7pm
Travel
Sloane Square ⊖

EQUIPMENT HIRE

Nappy Express (Baby Equipment Hire)

(0181 361 4040)

Long and short-term hire of everything you might need for a baby (travel cot for 2 weeks £20.50, double buggy for 6 months £78). Will deliver and collect in central and south-west London. Members of the Baby Equipment Hirers Association.

The Nursery Hire Company

(0181 995 5332)

Baby equipment to hire for holidays, etc. Can deliver.

HAIRCUTS

Hours
Mon–Fri
9.30am–5.30pm,
Sat 10am–5.30pm

Travel
✪ Ladbroke Grove

Cheeky Monkey

202 Kensington Park Road, W11 (0171 792 9022)

Good toy shop and no-nonsense hairdresser. Cut £7 (appointment necessary).

Hours
Mon, Tues & Sat
10am–6pm,
Wed–Fri
10am–7pm

Travel
✪ Knightsbridge

Harrods

Knightsbridge, SW1 (0171 730 1234)

A popular hairdressers in children's clothes section so book at least a week in advance. You receive a certificate and lock of hair of your child's first haircut. Trim £10, cut £12.

Hours
Mon–Wed
10am–5.45pm,
Thurs & Fri
10am–7pm, Sat
9am–5pm

Travel
≠ Waddon

Snips at Children's World

Purley Way, Croydon (0181 681 3141)

Cut for 3-10-year-olds £6.25, 11-14-year-olds £7.95.

Hours
Mon–Sat
10am–5.30pm

Travel
✪ Sloane Square

Swallows & Amazons

91 Nightingale Lane, SW12 (0181 673 0275)

Cut £5 (appointment necessary). Also second-hand toys, clothes, books and equipment for children up to 13. Play area.

Trotters

34 Kings Road, SW3 (0171 259 9620)

Under-3s £8.50, over-3s £9.50 for a cut (first-hair-cut certificate included in price).

Hours
Mon–Sat
10am–6.30pm,
Thurs 10am–8pm,
Sun noon–6pm

Travel
Sloane Square

MARKETS

Markets can be great fun for children of all ages but you need to keep a tight rein on younger ones as the markets can get very crowded.

Billingsgate (wholesale fish market)

North Quay, West India Docks Road, Isle of Dogs, E14

An amazing sight of tons of fish changing hands each week.

Hours
Mon–Sat 5–8am

Travel
DLR West India
Quay

Brick Lane Market

Brick Lane, E1

Wonderful East End market full of everything you could possibly want, and a whole lot more you wouldn't.

Hours
Sun 5am–2pm

Travel
Whitechapel

Brixton Market

Brixton Station Road and Electric Avenue, SW9

Every kind of fruit, veg, meat and fish you could want. Especially good for Afro-Caribbean fare.

Hours
Mon, Tues,
Thurs–Sat
8.30am–5.30pm;
Wed 8am–1pm

Travel
Brixton

Camden Lock

Chalk Farm Road (at crossing of Regent's Canal), NW1

Hotch-potch of items from antiques to ethnic clothing. Good food stalls. Gets very crowded by 1pm.

Hours
Sat & Sun
9.30am–6pm

Travel
Camden Town or
Chalk Farm

Camden Passage

off Islington Green, N1

Alleyway market reminiscent of Dickensian London.

Hours
Sat & Wed am

Travel
Angel

Covent Garden Market

Travel
⊖ Covent Garden

The Piazza, Covent Garden, WC2

Toys, hats, hand-knitted jumpers, jewellery, wooden toys, mobiles and games to catch the eye.

Deptford Market

Hours
Best on Wed, Fri and Sat am
Travel
⊖⇌ New Cross

Douglas Way, SE8

Good cheap new children's clothes and piles of second-hand clothes, toys, bric-a-brac and junk.

East Street Market

Hours
Tues–Thurs & Sun 8am–3pm, Fri & Sat 8am–5pm
Travel
⊖ Kennington or Elephant & Castle

East Street, SE17

One of London's best fruit and vegetable markets but there are plenty of stalls selling clothes, toys, material, household goods and other market wares.

Greenwich Arts and Craft Market

Hours
Sat & Sun 10am–5pm
Travel
⇌ Greenwich

Covered Market Square, SE10

General arts and crafts and good wooden toys to be found here. Prices are reasonable but standards are high. Excellent shop called Women and Children First. Not very buggy friendly unless you arrive before 11.30am. Parking restrictions are now fierce in Greenwich so go by train.

Petticoat Lane Market

Hours
Sun 9am–2pm
Travel
⊖ Aldgate
⊖⇌ Liverpool Street

Middlesex Street, E1

The most famous of London's Sunday markets, it is best for fashion (teenagers love it here).

Portobello Market

Hours
General market Fri 8am–3pm, Sat 8am–5pm
Travel
⊖ Notting Hill

Portobello Road, W11

Fruit and vegetables, second-hand goods and antiques.

Old Spitalfields Market

Brushfield Street, E1 (0171 247 6590)

England's first and largest organic-food market as well as a general market with jewellery, wooden toys and crafts.

Hours
Fri & Sat
Travel
Liverpool
Street

Riverside Walk Market

under Waterloo Bridge, SE1

Book market with a good stock of children's books.

Hours
Sun 10am–5pm
Travel
Waterloo

MISCELLANEOUS

The Doll's Hospital

16 Dawes Rd, SW6 (0171 385 2081)

As well as being a casualty ward for teddies and dolls this shop has an excellent range of inexpensive toys, puzzles and jokes. Postal repair service available. Also antique restoration.

Hours
Mon, Tues & Fri
9.30am–5pm, Sat
10am–4pm
Travel
Fulham
Broadway

Anything Left-Handed

57 Brewer Street, W1R 3LF (0171 437 3910)

Nearly one in 10 people are left-handed. But be warned – if your left-handed children are used to using right-handed implements they might not grasp the joys of this shop immediately. Jake got to grips with the scissors (£3.95) with ease but found the pencil sharpener (£3.25) difficult because 'you have to twist the other way'. The older kids we asked soon got used to both scissors and sharpener and were particularly keen on the ruler (£2.95). Mail-order service available.

Hours
Mon–Fri
9.30am–5pm, Sat
10am–5pm
Travel
Fulham
Broadway

The Back Shop

24 New Cavendish Street, W1 (0171 935 9120)

Sells children's chairs and desks designed to encourage good posture (also good for mums whose backs have never been the same since pregnancy, birth or carrying kids and shopping round all day).

Hours
Mon–Fri
10am–5.45pm, Sat
10am–2pm

Travel
Regents Park

Hours
Mon–Fri 9am–5pm

Travel
⊖ Marble Arch

Safe & Sound

8 Porchester Place, W2 (0171 402 5943)

A shop selling and fitting child safety products for the car with a back-up advice service by co-owners John Handman and Michael Hall. Handman had been so shocked by the lack of available information when he tried to buy a car seat for his own baby that he set up Safe & Sound to offer parents essential information (eg: it is not safe to use a rear-facing baby seat in the front seat if your car is fitted with a passenger airbag). Matches seat to car make.

MODELS AND TOYS

Hours
Mon–Fri
9am–6pm, Sat
9am–5.30pm

Travel
⊖ Holborn

Beatties

202 High Holborn, WC1 (0171 405 6285) and other branches

Hornby, Lima and Marklin models, train sets, railway landscapes etc., as well as a good range of radio-controlled and general toys. Plenty of old-fashioned politically incorrect toys like plastic guns and swords.

Hours
Mon–Fri
10am–8pm, Sat
9am–6pm, Sun
11am–5pm

Travel
≥ Waddon
Bus 289

Children's World

Trafalgar Way, Purley Way, Croydon, Surrey (0181 760 0484). Branches

Nursery furniture, toys, books, baby and toddlers clothes. Also has Dash and Benetton shops, a hairdressers and party shop. Snack bar, toilets and mother-and-baby room. Ample parking. Pick-up point for large items. Home delivery service and nappy-delivery service available.

Hours
Mon–Fri
9.30am–5.30pm,
Sat 10.15am–4pm

Travel
⊖ ≥ Charing
Cross

Davenport's Magic Shop

7 Charing Cross Underground Concourse, Strand, WC2 (0171 836 0408)

London's most famous magic shop has complex tricks for the serious magician and pocket-money jokes, tricks and puzzles. Mail order.

Early Learning Centre

225 Kensington High Street, W8 (0171 937 0419). Branches

Good sturdy toys suitable for babies and children up to 10, always fun, often educational, mostly stimulating, usually good quality and reasonably priced, never racist or sexist (children can try out toys before purchase). Some branches have community notice board. Direct mail catalogue.

Hours
Mon–Sat
9am–6pm, Sun
11am–5pm

Travel
High Street
Kensington ⊖

Hamleys

188 Regent Street, W1 (0171 734 3161)

The largest toy shop in the world with everything from traditional nursery toys to all the latest fads squeezed into six floors. As you are likely to lose anyone under 12 who is not literally tied to you, avoid the chaos of Saturdays or any festive countdowns. People do come here for a day out, and have lunch in the café.

Hours
Mon, Wed & Fri
10am–7pm, Thurs
10am–8pm, Sat
9.30am–7pm

Travel
Oxford Circus or
Piccadilly
Circus ⊖

Just Games

71 Brewer St, W1 (0171 437 0761)

Chess, snakes and ladders, snap, mouse trap and other tried-and-tested favourites and a range of more unusual games.

Hours
Mon–Wed, Fri &
Sat 10am–6pm,
Thurs 10am–7pm

Travel
Piccadilly
Circus ⊖

Benjamin Pollock's Toy Shop

44 Covent Garden Market, WC2 (0171 379 7866)

Exquisite antique dolls for lucky children and collectors as well as the more affordable Victorian cut-out model theatres.

Hours
Mon–Sat
10am–6pm, Thurs
10am–7pm

Travel
Covent Garden ⊖

Singing Tree

69 New King's Rd, SW6 (0171 736 4527)

This wonderful shop full of new and antique dolls' houses and everything imaginable to go in them is as popular with adults as children. Good-quality 4-room dolls' house in kit form for £118. Lots of collectors' items in miniature. Catalogue available.

Hours
Mon–Sat
10am–5.30pm

Travel
Parsons Green ⊖

Hours
Mon–Thurs
9am–8pm, Fri
9am–9pm, Sat
9am–8pm, Sun
11am–5pm

Travel
⇌ Waddon
or East Croydon
then **Bus 289**

Toys 'R' Us

Trojan Way, off Purley Way, Croydon, Surrey (0181 686 3133). Branches

The enormous warehouse has toys and games piled up from floor to ceiling (fine if you know what you want, but my kids hate it because everything is packaged and can't be tried out). They do, however like the kids' restaurant. Good value clothes and baby equipment. Toilets, mother-and-baby room.

Travel
⊕ Oxford Circus
or Piccadilly Circus

Warner Bros. Studio Store

178-182 Regent Street, W1 (0171 434 3334)

Two floors of Warner Bros merchandise and toys from both their animated and live-action films. Interactive paint station where children can computer-colour animated scenes. Original cartoons from the animation gallery.

NURSERY FURNISHING

Hours
Mon–Fri
9.30am–5.30pm,
Sat 10am–5pm

Travel
⊕⇌ Victoria

Dragons of Walton Street

23 Walton Street, SW3 (0171 589 3795)

Traditional, nostalgic, classic, expensive – a Rosie Fisher nursery is a status symbol. Prices for individual pieces start from £54 for a hand-painted chair to a hefty £2,600 for a child's double four-poster bed. A complete room costs from £3,000 to upwards of £20,000 for one like that bought for King Hussein's twin granddaughters.

Hours
Mon–Sat
10am–5.30pm

Travel
⊕⇌ Victoria

The Nursery Window

83 Walton Street, SW3 (0171 581 3358)

Excellent range of fabric and wallpaper designs from bright but tasteful trains, boats and planes, or pastel bunnies to tartan prints and interesting stripes. Designs include 'Blackfoot Star', 'India Stripe' and 'Hat Shop'. Wallpaper £14.75 a roll; fabric from £16.95 a metre. Also matching accessories from a basinette and cover (£350) to a bathcap (£11.75).

This chapter aims to take the stress out of eating out with young children. There are child-friendly cafés, themed fast-food outlets, restaurants that entertain children leaving adults to eat in peace, those with children's menus, reduced-price children's portions, highchairs, booster seats and baby-changing facilities. Call the Locator Hotline (01737 770074) for a choice of up to three restaurants to suit all your requirements.

Eating Out

RESTAURANTS WITH CHILDREN'S ENTERTAINERS

Chicago Pizza Pie Factory

Hours
Mon–Thurs
11.45am–11.30pm,
Fri 11.45am–1am,
Sat 11.45am–
midnight,
Sun noon–
10.30pm

Prices
Adult's menu £10.
Children's menu
(burger or pizza,
ice-cream and soft
drink) £6

Travel
Oxford Circus

17 Hanover Square, W1 (0171 629 2552)

Weekly Sunday Funday programme noon–5pm for 3–10-year-olds and accompanying adults: children's disco, face painting, stories and party games with Smarty Arty (1pm, 2pm & 3pm) and sketches performed by The Arts Theatre Workshop. You can join in with the kids or eat in peace while your offspring enjoy the activities. As well as a wide selection of pizzas there are hamburgers, salads and some great puddings. Children are actively welcome and treated in a friendly way by very patient staff. Good value and exhausting enough to get an afternoon sleep out of the whole family. Crayons and paper, highchairs, booster seats, baby-changing facilities. A family of four can be well fed and entertained for around £32. Booking is essential on Sundays.

Deals

Hours
Mon–Wed
noon–11pm,
Thurs–Sat
noon–11.30pm,
Sun noon–10pm

Travel
Bus 11 or 22; Car,
parking in under-
ground car park

Chelsea Harbour, SW3 (0171 352 5887) Also Deals West, 14–16 Foubert's Place, W1, (0171 287 1001), and Deals, Bradmore House, Hammersmith Broadway, W6 (0181 563 1001)

Sunday is family day in this friendly restaurant. It has a children's menu with fish fingers (£3.95), burgers and fries (£4.25). Magician and face painting noon–3pm. Booking essential. High chairs.

Newtons

Hours
Mon–Fri 12.30pm–
2.30pm and 7pm–
11.30pm, Sat
12.30pm-3pm and
7pm-11.30pm, Sun
12.30pm-11.30pm

Travel
Clapham South

35 Abbeville Road, SW4 (0181 673 0977)

Excellent restaurant with a clown on Saturdays, reduced-price portions at weekends, and highchairs. There is a two-course set lunch for adults on weekdays (£6.95), otherwise the average price is £8.50 per adult. Service is friendly and the often strange-sounding food – such as potato, herring and bacon salad is very palatable. The Saturday Club Menu (kids' menu with sausages, chips and beans and a drink for £2.80, ice-cream 95p) offers the best value.

PJ's Grill

30 Wellington Street, WC2 (0171 240 7529)

The additive-free children's menu (£3.95), with wholesome options like carrot and cucumber sticks, people-shaped peanut butter sandwiches and a muesli bar are popular with parents and kids alike. The New York Grill-style set menu for adults at £9.95 is fairly imaginative and you can eat in peace knowing your offspring are in safe hands. There's an unsupervised 'multi-sensory' play area for small babies, a supervised play area for toddlers with an indoor slide. Regular entertainers. High chairs, booster seats, nappy-changing and feeding room.

Hours
Mon–Sat noon–midnight; Sun noon–4.30pm Uncle PJ's Fun Club when a clown does balloon-bending and face-painting (£1.50)

Travel
Covent Garden ⊖

Signor Zilli

41 Dean Street, W1 (0171 734 3924)

You can eat here any day of the week with kids but family Sunday lunch is the thing to go for (either Italian food or traditional roast, adults £12.50, children £4.50 – which is not just the usual kids' fare but pasta, etc). There's also good and extensive à la carte options for parents. There is a table-side magician, then, while the parents finish their meal in peace, the kids are invited downstairs for a children's party with puppets, Punch and Judy shows, a disco, ice-cream, and other delights which change each week (Sunday 1–3pm).

Hours
Daily noon–3pm & 6–11.30pm (closed Sat lunch). Children's entertainment Sun 1–3pm

Travel
Tottenham Court Road ⊖

Smollensky's Balloon

1 Dover Street, W1 (0171 491 1199)

It is absolutely essential to book well in advance for this popular American-style child-friendly watering hole, especially for the weekend family lunches. The kiddies' menu has burgers, junior steaks and amazing desserts (try the peanut butter cheesecake). To make your offspring feel really grown-up there are Kids Koktails, too. There is a puppet show from 2.30–3pm, balloons, and magic tricks at your table.

Hours
Mon–Sat noon–11.45pm; Sun noon–10.30pm; family lunches Sat & Sun noon–3pm. Average adult £14, children £7

Travel
Green Park ⊖

Smollensky's on the Strand

Hours
Sat, Sun & Bank
Holiday Mon
noon–3pm

Travel
Charing
Cross

105 The Strand, WC2 (0171 497 2101)

This is an exceptional restaurant that bends over backwards to accommodate and entertain children of all ages, especially under–5s. There is a supervised play area, video games, a raffle, and a kids' magic show (2.30pm). With plenty of high-chairs, booster seats, and a decent nappy-changing area in the toilet, nobody seems to mind how much mess the kids (or adults) make with the food, which is very popular even with fussy children. Children's main courses (bangers and mash, chicken nuggets, fish fingers, hamburgers, hot dogs, steak) are around £3.95; desserts are around £1.95. The adults' fixed-price menu included starter or salad, steak, fries and a drink for £10.95. There's a wide choice a la carte selection. The steaks for which Smollensky's is famous are varied and delicious. Booking advised.

Sol e Luna

Hours
Daily noon-
midnight
Travel
Covent Garden

22 Shorts Garden, WC2 (0171 379 3336)

A popular pizzeria where Spotty Dotty will entertain your children on Sundays between 1–3pm while they eat pizza, pasta and ice-cream for around £3.75, leaving parents to choose from a more imaginative menu.

FAMILY RESTAURANTS

Benihana

Hours
Lunch
12.30pm–3pm
Travel
Swiss Cottage

100 Avenue Road, NW3 (0171 586 7118)

Sunday lunch is cheerful, though not especially cheap at this impressive American-style Japanese restaurant where an average lunch is around £20. At least it's unusual, and children are kept amused by a magician (and their own menu for around £7, plus very popular alcohol-free cocktails). Parents can marvel at the chef's knife-wielding feats.

Blue Elephant

4–6 Fulham Broadway, SW6 (0171 385 6595)

For a real treat this very expensive, very good and wonder-fully atmospheric Thai restaurant is great on Sundays when they do a splendid brunch offering adults all-you-can-eat for £14.50. For children there's a novel pricing system where those under 4ft tall are measured and charged £2.50 per foot (£4–£6). Clowns entertain while you eat. Dress smart.

Hours
Mon–Fri & Sun noon–2.30pm and 7pm–12.30am, Sat 7pm–12.30am, Sun noon-2.30pm & 7-10.30pm

Travel
Fulham Broadway

Calabash

The Africa Centre, 38 King Street, WC2 (0171 836 1976)

Babies and children are welcome at this large restaurant in the basement of the Africa Centre. It's a fun place to try dishes from every corner of Africa, and there's lots to choose from (and helpful staff and an explanatory menu make choices easier for newcomers). Main courses are around £6 with reduced-price children's portions available.

Hours
Mon–Fri 12.30pm-3pm and 5pm-8pm, Sat 5pm-8pm, closed Sun

Travel
Covent Garden

Chiarascuro

24 Coptic Street, WC1 (0171 636 2731)

After a Sunday morning stroll around the nearby British Museum, this friendly family run restaurant is the perfect antidote to burgers and chips. The kids can eat in a separate playroom if the grown-ups want to enjoy their choice of modern European food in peace. For every adult eating, one child eats free on Sunday.

Hours
Mon–Fri noon-3pm & 7pm-late. Sun closed evenings

Travel
Holborn, Tottenham Court Road

Chuen Cheng Ku

17 Wardour Street, W1 (0171 437 1398)

Lunchtime dim sum (about £10 per person) comes on a trol-ley loaded with small baskets of goodies from which to choose. This large, busy restaurant is very baby-and-child friendly, provides highchairs and boasts the longest menu in Chinatown. There are reduced-price children's portions.

Hours
Mon–Sat 11am–midnight, Sun 11am-11.15pm

Travel
Leicester Square or Piccadilly Circus

Hours
Mon–Fri noon–
3pm and 7.30pm–
11.30pm, Sat
12.30-4pm and
7.30-11.30pm, Sun
12.30-4pm and
7.30-10.30pm
Travel
⊖ Fulham
Broadway

Glaister's Garden Bistro

4 Hollywood Road, SW10 (0171 352 0352)

Half portions at half-price are available for children. You can leave kids at Nipper Snippers, a registered crèche next door, while you enjoy a quiet bistro lunch (crèche open 12.30–4.30pm Sundays and summer holidays; £2.50). Children will be fed peanut butter and jelly sandwiches, fruit, biscuits and fruit juice and can play Nintendo, watch videos and run riot with the other kids. No highchairs or changing facilities.

Hours
Mon–Fri
10am–10pm, Sat
10am–9pm, closed
Sun
Travel
⊖ Goodge Street

Greenhouse Vegetarian Restaurant

16 Chenies Street, W1 (0171 637 8038)

A relaxed, informal vegetarian restaurant beneath the Drill Hall Arts Centre with a continually changing menu of hot vegetarian dishes and various salads plus a wide range of home-baked desserts and cakes. Prices are reasonable. It's unlicensed so bring your own booze (no corkage), and there are occasional art exhibitions. Full take-away service. Monday nights 6–10pm is for women only. No smoking. Children and babies welcome.

Hours
Daily 10am-3pm
(evening bookings
only)
Travel
⇌ Acton Central

Honey For the Bear

167 The Vale, W3 (0181 749 9581)

A good lunchtime family restaurant with bear-themed burgers (Rupert Burger, Boo Boo etc) to go with the stuffed toys and bear pictures. Prices are reasonable with burgers at £3 and starters around the £2 mark.

Hours
Mon-Sat 7pm til
late, Sun 12.30pm
til late
Travel
Forest Hill or
⇌ Sydenham

Hornimans

124 Kirkdale, SE26 (0181 291 2901)

Not to be confused with the museum of the same name, this restaurant is ideal for a lunchtime treat (three-course set lunch for £9.95) and children under ten get a free main course on Sundays. There are also reduced-price children's portions and babies are welcome (no high chairs though). The international menu is divided into set meals (grill, seafood or vegetarian) and the food is good, if a little unambitious.

The Inebriated Newt

172 Northcote Road (nr Broomwood Road), SW11 (0171 223 1637)

Great bistro-style restaurant especially good for brunch and traditional Sunday roast. Crayons are provided for children to draw on the paper tablecloths, and a guitarist plays tunes from children's favourites to jazz. The kids' menu (main course £4.50, pudding £1) includes burgers, pasta, milkshakes and of course Mrs Newt's bangers and mash. Highchairs.

Hours
Sat & Sun lunch; evenings from 7.30pm

Travel
Clapham Junction ⇌

Joanna's

56 Westow Hill, SE19 (0181 670 4052)

Joanna's stands out for its imaginative cooking, fast, friendly service and atmosphere. Although the specialities are burgers which you can have every-which-way, this is no ordinary diner. Try the Thai Red Curry Mussels or the Supreme of Chicken with Ginger Mint Butter. Good for Sunday roast and all the trimmings. Lunchtime and early-evening children's menu, high-chairs, booster-seats and crayons for table-cloth drawing.

Hours
Daily 10am-late

Travel
Gypsy Hill ⇌

Kleftiko

163 Chiswick High Road, W4 (0181 994 0305)

A lovely, airy Greek restaurant which provides a change from American burgers or British beef. Children of all ages are wel-comed especially at lunchtimes and at weekends, and there's a children's buffet on Sundays (noon–3pm). There's a good vari-ety of food from meze to metaxa. The Meze (which comes in three different sizes £4.40-£7) are an excellent way to get kids to try different foods and each dish is very tasty. Recommended. Highchairs. Branches in Holland Park and Kew Green.

Hours
Café daily 8am-6pm, restaurant daily noon-midnight

Travel
Turnham Green ⊖

Le Shop

329 King's Road, SW3 (0171 352 3891)

This is a friendly, busy creperie with lots of combinations to choose and mix for their deliciously, light crepes. From noon to 5pm you can have a one-course set lunch with a glass of wine for £5 . Otherwise a meal will set you back around £8. Reduced-price children's portions. Highchairs and books for kids.

Hours
Daily noon-midnight

Travel
Sloane Square ⊖ then **Bus** 11, 19, 22

Sweeney Todd's

Hours
Mon 10am-10pm,
Tues-Fri 10am-
11pm, Sat 10am-
9.30pm, Sun
10am-9pm

Travel
⊖ ⇌ London
Bridge

35 Tooley Street, SE1 (0171 407 5267)

Conveniently near the London Dungeon, this friendly restaurant serves burgers, ribs, chicken, pizzas and pasta. The children's set meal of a drink, a main course and a pudding is £3.95. Adult main courses are £4.95–£8.95.

AMERICAN-STYLE RESTAURANTS

The Chicago Rib Shack

Hours
Mon-Sat noon-
11.45pm, Sun
noon-11pm

Travel
⊖ Knightsbridge

1 Raphael Street, SW7 (0171 581 5595)

The children's menu is £5.95, with colour-in menus, competitions and balloons. They also do good children's parties. Staff friendly. It's a popular haunt for the likes of Princess Di and sons. Baby-changing facilities, highchairs and booster seats.

Hard Rock Café

Hours
Mon-Thurs
11.30am-midnight,
Fri & Sat 11.30am-
1pm, Sun
11.30am-12.30am

Travel
⊖ Hyde Park
Corner

150 Old Park Lane, W1 (0171 629 0382)

Called The Smithsonian of Rock 'n' Roll, this legendary burger bar has what it claims to be the world's greatest collection of pop memorabilia (which is rotated around the London, Dallas, New York, Tokyo and Stockholm restaurants) and includes Elvis Presley's last will and testament. The ubiquitous T-shirts and sweat shirts are available. Bookings are not accepted so expect to join long queues.

Henry J Bean's Bar and Grill

Hours
Daily 11.45-11pm

Travel
⊖ Sloane Square
then **Bus** 11, 14,
19, 22, 49

195–7 King's Road, SW3 (0171 352 9255), 490 Fulham Road, SW6 (0171 381 5005) and 54 Abingdon Road, W8 (0171 937 3339)

Its huge garden and play area boasts a mulberry tree dating back to the reign of Queen Elizabeth I. In the equally enormous American bar you can get burgers and hot dogs with fries. The children's menu consists of chicken, burgers, salad and ice-cream. The Abingdon Road branch has pin-ball tables.

McDonald's

108 Kensington High Street, W8 0171 937 3705). Other branches.)

Let's face it, you can't fault McDonald's as far as children are concerned – food they are guaranteed to eat, fast and friendly service, kiddies' balloons, and other bits and bobs especially at weekends (see also page 180). Your child can drop food all over the floor and they don't bat an eyelid, spill a drink and another one miraculously appears at no extra charge. Highchairs, booster seats, uniform hamburgers and great milkshakes. Birthdays – entertained with games and activities by trained hostesses, special present for the birthday child and party gifts for others. Invitations and birthday cake available.

Hours
Most branches open daily 7am–11pm

Travel
High Street Kensington ⊖

Pizza Express

30 Coptic Street, WC1 (0171 636 3232)

Numerous other branches listed in telephone directory. One of the best pizza chains serving consistently excellent, thin, crispy pizzas with a variety of good toppings (Benja's favourite is the Veneziana with sultanas, capers, pine kernels, onions and olives; £3.75). Kids can 'share-a-pizza'. Highchairs and booster seats. Very friendly attitude to children.

Hours
Daily 11.30am–midnight (Sun closes 11.30pm)

Travel
Holborn, or Tottenham Court Road ⊖

Planet Hollywood

Trocadero, Piccadilly, W1 (0171 287 1000)

Over-priced and over-hyped restaurant of cardboard-cut-out stars. No booking, long queues (often over 40 minutes) and it'll set you back about £20 for three courses. But children and teenagers love the loud music, garish decor and fabulous collection of film memorabilia. There's also a sci-fi room, alien grotto and 75-seater preview theatre. Huge portions are a big advantage and there are highchairs and baby-changing facilities.

Hours
Daily 11am–1am (Sun closes 12.30am)

Travel
Piccadilly Circus ⊖

Rock Island Diner

Plaza Centre, London Pavilion, Piccadilly W1 (0171 287 5500)

Hours
Mon–Thurs
11am–11.30pm; Fri
& Sat 11am–1am;
Sun 11am–11pm.
Sat & Sun
12noon–5pm.

Travel
↔ Piccadilly
Circus

For that all-American drive-in feeling you can't beat the Rock Island Diner, where your senses are bombarded with the sights and sounds of '50s America – rock 'n' roll, chrome, waiters jiving on the tables, dancing waitresses and even the restaurant's own radio station. Portions are generous and there's all the usual diner delights. Kids just love it (especially at weekends when there are '50s dance routines, games and competitions, DJs). Children choose from the Diner 'Mites' Menu with a choice of hamburger, hotdog or chicken nuggets, served with fries and followed by chocolate or vanilla ice-cream (until 5pm; £3.50). Under-10s get free meal noon–5pm Saturday & Sunday if accompanied by an adult who buys a main course And don't miss the chocolate brownies with hot fudge sauce and ice-cream. High chairs. No bookings.

Roxy Café Cantina

297 Upper Street, N1 (0171 226 5746)

Hours
Mon–Sat
noon–midnight,
Sun 12.30–
11.30pm

Travel
↔ Angel
or Highbury &
Islington

Good, reasonably priced Tex-Mex restaurant with tacos, tostadas and enchiladas which can be served as side orders for kids. They can also choose from the children's menu of burgers, chips and a drink. High chairs.

Sticky Fingers

1a Phillimore Gardens, W8 (0171 938 5338)

Hours
Daily noon–
11.30pm

Travel
↔ High Street
Kensington

Rolling Stones ex–bass player Bill Wyman's American-style restaurant is popular with celebrities like Eric Clapton, Jerry Hall and Jason Donovan, as well as the kids. Surrounded by rock 'n' roll memorabilia you can choose from a menu of burgers, sandwiches, barbecue chicken wings, chilli dogs and a range of sticky puddings. Children are given colouring books and crayons and invited to enter a 'draw your waiter' competition. On Sundays there's a magician on hand to entertain from 1–3pm.

Texas Lone Star Saloon

154 Gloucester Road, SW7 (0171 370 5625), 58 Turnham Green Terrace, W4 (0181 994 3000) and 117a Queensway, W2 (0171 221 9235)

I've been going to this Tex-Mex restaurant since I was 17 and I still love it. The ribs and pecan pie (not usually together) are adored by Jake and Benja and the burgers are a rare treat. Decked out like a saloon, with Wild West videos to keep the restless, fast eaters happy, there's lots of cowboy paraphernalia to look out for. There's a children's menu and the average price for adults is £10.

Hours
Mon–Wed noon–11.30pm, Thurs–Sat noon–12.15am, Sun noon–11.15pm

Prices
Average adults £10

Travel
Gloucester Road ⊖

Thank God It's Friday

6 Bedford Street, W2 (0171 379 0585)

Branches of this American import have popped up all over the place in recent years (see telephone directory). This noisy, lively, very big diner is not to everyone's taste (and it's not cheap) but the Tex-Mex food is good, the choice extensive and the portions large. There's a hamburger menu for children or smaller portions of the regular menu available. Highchairs and booster seats. Excellent for children's parties but you cannot book.

Hours
Daily noon–midnight

Travel
Charing Cross ⊖ ≥

CAFES

Alfredo's

4–6 Essex Road, N1 (0171 226 3496)

At this popular budget café with it's art deco features you would be hard pushed to spend more than £4 a head and that's not counting the reduced-price children's portions.

Hours
Mon–Fri 7am–2.30pm, Sat 7am–noon

Travel
Angel ⊖

Café in the Crypt

St Martin-in-the-Fields Church, Duncannon Street, WC2 (0171 839 4342)

This a healthy alternative to burgers and coke with a central location, next to the London Brass Rubbing Centre. All the food is made on the premises with a choice of hot meat or

Hours
Daily, coffee & snacks 10am–8pm, hot food noon–3.15pm and 5–8pm

Travel
Charing Cross ⊖

vegetarian dishes as well as salads, sandwiches and hot puddings. There's a kid's menu, but half adult portions are half price (average three-course full meal £10; children £5).

Café Laville

Hours
Daily 10am–7pm
Travel
⊖ Warwick
Avenue or
Edgware Road
Bus 6

453 Edgware Road, W2 (0171 706 2620)

Straddling the canal at Maida Vale this small, friendly place is a good pit-stop if you're taking a boat trip or canal walk. The balcony at the back is suspended over the canal and gives a good waterway view. Brunch dishes such as eggs Benedict or scrambled eggs on toast are available all day, as well as more substantial dishes such as spag bol or bangers and mash. The usual range of salads, pasta and cakes are on offer. Advisable to book on Sundays. There are pavement tables but if you have small children go for one of the 12 balcony tables. Takeaway service, vegetarian dishes.

Fatboy's Diner

Hours
Mon–Sat
11am–midnight,
Sun 11am–
10.30pm
Travel
⊖ Covent Garden
⊖ ⇌ Charing
Cross

21-22 Maiden Lane, WC2 (0171 240 1902)

A taste of the States with loads of atmosphere and burgers in this tiny, original American trailer diner with bench seating on the Astroturf forecourt for sunny days. Cheap, cheerful and good (made-to-order burger £3.95–£7.35; fries £1.30) but best for children over six.

Fat Sam's

Hours
Take-away service
Sun–Thurs 10am–
midnight, Fri & Sat
10am–2am
Travel
⊖ Hampstead

57-61 Heath Street, NW3 (0171 431 3064) and 78 High Street, Barnet, Herts (0181 441 4171)

More of the traditional American-style, this diner is red, white and blue with a long menu, and enormous portions. Good salt beef and pastrami on rye as well as the usual range of burgers and hot dogs.

Free Range

159 Lordship Lane, SE22 (0181 693 5008

On a summer day in the patio garden full of flowers, regulars at this charming café enjoy ample portions of bangers-and-mash style food. We rarely waver from the superb breakfast served all day which, as well as the usual bacon, beans and sausages, often includes kedgeree and poached eggs done to perfection. High chairs and reduced-price children's portions.

Hours
Wed-Sun 10am-5pm

Travel
Bus 185, 176

Holland Park Café

Holland Park, W8 (0171 602 2216)

This is a perfect setting with lots of outside seating. The food is home-made Italian – soup, pasta, pizza, ice-cream – with good-sized, reasonably priced child portions. Average prices for adults are £5, children £2.

Hours
Daily 10am-30 mins before sunset (closed January)

Travel
Holland Park ⊖

Lauderdale House

Waterlow Park, Highgate Hill, N6 (0181 341 4807)

The café at the back of this community arts centre overlooks the beautiful park, and has its own terrace for summer lunches. The food is good, plain and family orientated (fish fingers, lasagna and salads are all under £5). See also pages 33 and 34.

Hours
Tues-Sun 9am-6pm

Travel
Archway ⊖

Marine Ices

8 Haverstock Hill, NW3 (0171 485 3132)

Delicious fresh, home-made pastas and pizzas and wonderful ice-creams and sorbets are made on the premises without additives (see also pages 36 and 37).

Hours
Ice-cream parlour open Mon-Sat 10.30am-10.15pm, Sun noon-8pm

Travel
Chalk Farm ⊖

Photographer's Gallery Cafe

5-8 Great Newport Street, WC2 (0171 831 1772)

A spacious, airy and relaxing café with budget-priced snacks (from £1.50), good cakes (under £1) and teas (from 45p) and a friendly attitude to children. Reduced-price children's portions.

Hours
Tues-Sat 11am-5.30pm

Travel
Leicester Square ⊖

Hours
Mon–Sat
8am–midnight,
Sun 10.30am–
10.30pm

Travel
⊖ Leicester
Square

Swiss Centre (Marché)

Swiss Centre, Leicester Square, W1 (0171 734 1291)

This excellent self-service-style café is very popular with children who can choose exactly what they want from the colourful display of hot and cold food, and watch bread being made when they get bored. Reduced-price children's portions, highchair and nappy-changing facilities. Prices average around £6.50.

BUDGET CAFÉS

Hours
Daily 9.30am–
6.30pm (later in
summer)

Travel
⊖ St James' Park
⊖≠ Charing
Cross

The Cake House

St James's Park, SW1 (0171 839 5179)

A self-service park cafeteria with plenty of tables on its grass terrace. There is a help-yourself pasta bar for £3.50 per plate, or fish and chips, grilled meats and salad from the counter.

Hours
Mon–Sat
7am–11.30pm, Sun
9.30am–11.30pm

Travel
⊖ Sloane Square
Bus 11, 19, 31

Chelsea Bun Diner

9a Limerstone Street, SW10 (0171 352 3635)

With main courses in the £3 region this is an excellent, if busy, budget café offering pastas, fish and chips, moussaka, sandwiches and old favourites like bread-and-butter pudding. Breakfast is served all day and there's an excellent-value fry-up at £2.95. There are reduced-price children's portions, vegetarian dishes and a take-away service. Tables on the first-floor balcony add the al fresco touch without losing toddlers to the traffic.

Hours
Daily 8am–
11.45pm

Travel
⊖ Sloane Square

Chelsea Kitchen

98 King's Road, SW3 (0171 589 1330)

Not strictly a kids' joint but this popular haunt is great value, with most dishes under a fiver. Kids love the spag bol and sponge pudding and you can keep the little terrors in check by taking one of the cosy pine booths (discreet for breast feeding). Fare includes stews, omelettes, savoury pancakes, moussaka, lasagna and puddings like apple crumble. You can ask for reduced-price children's portions if you phone ahead. A useful bolt-hole from the rigours of the King's Road. The average price for a three-course meal is £7.

Golders Hill Park Refreshment House

North End Way, NW3 (0181 455 8010)

Hours
April–Sept daily
10.30am–sunset
Travel
Golders Green ●

This wonderful park café is run by an Italian family whose home-made food is heavenly. A main course will set you back around £3 (£4.95 if you have poached salmon) and there are plenty of snack options such as sandwiches and soups as well as delicious puddings. Ice-creams can also be bought from a hatch at the side of the café. Children are most welcome and highchairs are available. No smoking inside (there are tables on the terrace).

The Stockpot

6 Basil Street, SW3 (0171 589 8627) and branches.

Hours
Daily 9.30am–
11pm
Travel
Knightsbridge ●

Although not especially geared to children (no highchairs, reduced-price portions on request) its reasonable food at very low prices in an expensive area makes it an ideal venue for families on a budget. Hot main courses around £3, puddings £1. There's a minimum charge of £2.20 and the average price is about £6.50.

The Well

2 Eccleston Place, SW1 (0171 730 7303)

Hours
Daily 9am–6pm
(Sat to 5pm)
Travel
Victoria ● ⇌

A bit of a find if you are in the area. Budget meals of the home-made variety include quiches, casseroles and baked potatoes (all around £3.50) and delicious cakes. Highchairs.

FISH 'N' CHIPS

Geales Fish Restaurant

Hours
Tues–Sat
noon–3pm &
6–11pm (closed
Sun & Mon)
Travel
⊖ Notting Hill
Gate

2 Farmer Street, W8 (0171 727 7969)

There is no better way to introduce your small fry to real fish and chips than this delightful, homely up-market chippie. Prices, however, are not cheap – cod £6.50 plus £1 for chips. Reduced-price children's portions. Highchairs and booster seats.

Rock and Sole Plaice

Hours
Mon-Sat 11.30am-
11.30pm, Sun
11.30am-8.30pm
Travel
⊖ Covent Garden

47 Endell Street, WC2 (0171 836 3785)

When faced with the daunting choice of restaurants in the area it's refreshing to find a down-to-earth fish 'n' chip eating place which serves first-rate fodder at second-rate prices (cod and chips £4.50; minimum charge £1). Highchairs.

AFTERNOON TEA

Harrods' Georgian Restaurant

Hours
Tea from 4pm
(£11.50 per person)
Travel
⊖ Knightsbridge

Knightsbridge, SW1 (0171 730 1234)

Tea here is a very special treat for older children.

Maids of Honour

Hours
Tues–Sat lunch
served 12.30 and
1.30pm
Tea served 2.30-
5.30pm

Travel
⊖ ≠ Kew Gardens

288 Kew Road, Richmond (0181 940 2752)

Named after the Maids of Honour which is curd tart in puff-pastry, of which Henry VIII was so fond and which are still served, this is a tea-time favourite for all the family. Teas come with a choice of delicious scones and cakes as well as more substantial fare like sausage rolls and chicken pies. Babies and children are welcome and highchairs available. Must book for lunch (two sittings). Get there early for tea to avoid queues.

ICE-CREAM PARLOURS

Baskin Robbins

Leicester Square, WC1 and branches

Their 31-flavour tradition, one for every day of the month, includes low-fat and fat-free flavours, but the full-fat are best! Cones and cups from 90p per scoop, toppings 25–50p.

Hours
11am–9pm

Travel
Leicester Square ⊖

Criterion Ices

118 Sydenham Road, SE26 (0181 778 7945)

With such scrumptious flavours as Lemon Meringue, White Chocolate and Toffee Nut Crunch, this wonderful, old-fashioned gelateria, which has been making its own ice–creams since 1920, is hard to beat. Kids also tea, coffee and snacks. Not especially child–friendly but kids love the ice-cream.

Hours
Mon–Fri
10.30am–5.30pm,
Sat & Sun
10.30am–6pm

Travel
Sydenham ⇌
Bus 75, 108, 194

The Fountain Tea Room

Fortnum & Mason, 181 Piccadilly, W1 (0171 734 8040)

Definitely not suitable for young, boisterous children, although they do have a babies-and-children-welcome policy and provide highchairs. This elegant tea room, with its uniformed waitresses and pretty décor, is best kept for the celebration treat. The ice–creams, made specially for Fortnums come in a dozen varieties of sorbets, sundaes, sodas and frappés. The list of high teas is long: there are seven varieties of tea alone. Not cheap but very charming. Dress smart. The minimum charge is £4.50.

Hours
Mon–Sat
7.30am–11pm

Prices
Minimum charge
£4.50

Travel
Green Park or
Piccadilly
Circus ⊖

Golders Hill Park Refreshment House

North End Way, NW3 (0181 455 8010)

The Italian owners of this exceptional park café make ice-cream every day. Inside you can have banana splits, gondolas and knickerbocker glories from £2.75, or take-away ices at 70p small, £1 medium or £1.40 double.

Hours
April–Sep daily
10.30am–sunset

Travel
Golders Green ⊖

Hours
Sun-Thurs 10am-
midnight, Fri & Sat
10am-1am
Travel
Leicester
Square

Haagen–Dazs

14 Leicester Square, WC2 (0171 287 9577) and branches

Incredibly expensive ice-cream but once you've tried a Haagen-Dazs you won't care. The venues look a bit clinical but the tastes and textures of the various ices, shakes, sundaes, cakes and creams are unbelievable. My kids will do anything for a lick of Belgian chocolate or a bite of Macadamia Nut Brittle. Highchairs. £1.95 for a scoop of frozen yoghurt, £3.25 for three ice-cream scoops, £4.25 for a praline basket.

Hours
Mon, Tues & Sat
9am-6pm, Wed,
Thur, Fri 10am-
7pm
Travel
Knightsbridge

Harrods' Ice–Cream Parlour

4th Floor, Harrods, SW1 (0171 730 1234)

Conveniently near the toy department this newish parlour seats 100 in an English country garden with wrought Italian-iron furniture, umbrellas, hedges and a mural. Home-made American-style ice-cream comes in nine flavours including Mint and Chocolate Chip, Macadamia Nut Brittle and Maple Walnut, and Kumquat Sorbet (from £2.95 for 2 scoops). Specialities £4.95–£9.50.

Hours
Mon-Sat 10.30am-
10.15pm, Sun
noon-8pm
Travel
Chalk Farm

Marine Ices

8 Haverstock Hill, NW3 (0171 485 3132)

The Italian ice-creams and sorbets are made on the premises without additives by the Mansi family, who have run this gelateria since 1913. With 15 flavours of ice-cream and seven flavours of sorbet it's not easy to choose, but at 85p per scoop at the hatch (or £1 inside) you can always go back for more. Give into the hedonistic delights of a blissful bombe or sumptuous sundae which will make the eyes of even the jaded ice-cream junkie pop out in wonder. The lemon, orange and melon sorbets are to die for. The venue also doubles up as an Italian restaurant which is cheap and cheerful.

From a traditional tea party for toddlers to an
overnight stay in a museum, there are a host of
ideas to ensure your child's birthday goes with a
bang whatever your budget. If you don't want cake
on your carpet and chocolate on your chairs there
are plenty of suitable venues for hire in London.
Whether you're hiring bouncy castles,
buying balloons, booking a magician or
borrowing a marquee, it's all here.

Children's Parties

VENUES

A good starting point is your local leisure or sports centre for Sports Parties (to hire football, netball, tennis, cricket pitches, etc), Swimming Parties, or Trampolining Party. Football clubs will usually arrange birthday parties to include football coaching, food, tour of the ground, a signed football and even a surprise guest (Chelsea Football Club on 0171 385 0710 and Fulham Football Club on 0171 736 6561 charge from £6 per head including food). To make it an extra special day you could hire a limo and be chauffeur-driven to the venue of your choice, or even make the limo the centrepiece and be driven round for an hour or so. All Stretched Out (0171 837 0793) stretch limos with 7-10 seats will take kids (and adults) anywhere from £35 per hour. Each chauffeur-driven limo has tv, video, stereo, ice boxes and mini–bars. For £47 per hour a white limo from American Stretch Limousines (0181 889 4848) will transport up to 8 children in total luxury – tv, video, intercom, telephone and bar.

Travel
⇌ Battersea Park

Battersea Park Children's Zoo

Albert Bridge Road, SW11 (0181 871 7540)

You can hire anything from a self-catering package to an all-inclusive party with catering, decoration, entertainers and zoo tours. See also page 108.

Travel
⇌ Clapham
Junction

Discovery Zone

The Junction Shopping Centre, Clapham Junction, SW11 (0171 223 1717)

Over an hour of moonwalking, ball ponds, giant mazes, climbing, bouncing and crawling in this popular indoor adventure playground followed by burgers, chips and present for the birthday child; £5.99 per head for 2 hours.

Travel
⊕ Loughton

Epping Forest Field Centre

High Beach, Loughton, Essex (0181 508 7714)

Environmental birthday parties with activities including pond-dipping, treasure hunt, mini-beast search, forest survival and tree detectives all of which can be tailored to individual needs. Provide tables, chairs and food if required; £30 for use of room and tutor to supervise activities for up to 12 children (additional children £2.50 per head).

Fantasy Island Playcentre

Vale Farm, Watford Road, Wembley (0181 904 9044)

Adventure playground with ball ponds, scramble nets, slides and trained staff. Two-hour party costs £7 per head (£7.95 weekends and school holidays).

Travel
North
Wembley ⊖

Grasshoppers

Horewell Farm, Baynards Green, Bicester, Oxfordshire (01869 345902)

Five to 15-year-olds can spend the day on quad-bikes (four-wheeled motorbikes) and have a barbecue (or you can bring your own picnic or even retire to a nearby McDonald's). On Thursdays throughout the summer holidays children can camp out overnight; £8 per head for 20 mins or £25 per head for an overnight camp and quad–biking (children must bring their own tents).

Travel
Bicester ⇌

HMS Belfast

Morgan's Lane, off Tooley Street, SE1 (0171 407 6434)

You can hire a room on the ship for children's parties for no extra cost. Bring your own food, drink and, if you wish, decorations. If the party is on a weekday the children will get a guided tour. Also quiz trail, badges and cards signed by the Commander. Admission on to the ship is £1.60 per child; £3.20 per adult.

Travel
London
Bridge ⊖ ⇌

London Toy and Model Museum

21 Craven Hill, W2 (0171 402 5222/706 8000)

An excellent place to hold a child's dream birthday party. They have free rides on the mini-railway (steam on Sundays) and carousel, and the run of the museum and garden. There

Hours
Mon–Sat
10am–5.30pm,
Sun 11am–5.30pm
Travel
Paddington ⊖ ⇌

are three set menus aimed at different age groups from £5.75 to £6.50 per head (excluding VAT; adults £2.95 per head). Maximum 25 children. See also page 71.

London Waterbus Company

Travel
⊖ Warwick
Avenue or
Camden Town

Blomfield Road, W9 (0171 482 2550)

You can hire one of the canal boats that go between Camden Lock and Little Venice for a children's party (stop off at London Zoo optional) for £145 for two hours.

London Zoo

Travel
⊖ Camden Town

Regent's Park, NW1 (0171 586 3339)

Private room available for birthday tea, then tour of zoo with special animal encounters, face-painting and masks. From £12 per child, minimum 10 children.

McDonald's

Hours
Daily 7am–11pm;
parties Thurs-Sun
4–6pm

(0181 700 7000 and other branches)

Usually has an area set aside especially for kids. A hostess organises games (if desired), balloons, hats, token gifts and a present for the birthday child. The restaurant can also supply a birthday cake (£5.99) for 10 children; 50p per child plus cost of food (which works out at approximately £3.99 per head).

Pippa Pop-Ins

Travel
⊖ Fulham
Broadway

430 Fulham Road, SW6 (0171 385 2457)

Children's hotel and venue for any kind of party you can think of, from adventure parties (complete with camp fires) to more traditional tea parties, dinner parties and theme weekends. An average party of 25 children will set you back about £250. Open every day, 24 hours a day.

Playscape Pro-Racing

Triangle Place, Clapham, SW4 or Hester Road, Battersea, SW11 (0171 498 0916)

The excitement of the track with indoor go–karting for 8–16-year-olds. Up to 10 drivers for 1 hour costs £125 (including overalls, helmets, gloves and tuition). Ring for times.

Travel
Clapham Common ⊖
Clapham Junction ⇌

Polka Children's Theatre

240 The Broadway, SW19 (0181 543 4888/0363)

You can hold a party in the pantry at any time without actually watching the show (maximum 30 children, minimum 4). Set menu for £4 per head includes hats, balloons and novelty chocolates.

Travel
South
Wimbledon ⊖
Wimbledon ⇌

Quasar

Trocadero, Piccadilly, W1 (0171 734 8151) see phone book for other Quasar centres

Exclusive use of a room for up to 40 children costs £200. Otherwise £10 per child (on–site McDonald's £3.50 per head). Games last 20 minutes for children over 5. Ring for times.

Travel
Piccadilly Circus ⊖

Science Museum

Exhibition Road, SW7 (0171 938 9785)

Science nights offer children of 8–11 years the chance to camp overnight in the Museum, go on spooky torchlit tours and listen to late–night story-telling while snuggled up in sleeping bags (for 6 or more children accompanied by an adult); £18 per head including breakfast. Ring for times.

Travel
South
Kensington ⊖

Unicorn Theatre

6 Great Newport Street, WC2 (0171 836 3334 or 0171 240 6338)

Up to 15 children can put on a short play in a real theatre. Workshop based on child's favourite film followed by tea in the café downstairs. Members £75 for children, non-members £90 (includes the £15 membership fee).

Travel
Leicester Square ⊖

Travel
🔵 Wembley Park

Wembley Stadium

Wembley, Middx HA9 0DW (0181 902 8833)

Fun-filled children's party packages available. Ring for details.

ENTERTAINERS AND PARTY PLANNERS

Annie Fryer Catering

134 Lots Road, SW10 (0171 351 4333)

Very popular up-market theme parties for small children to teenagers. Menus designed to the children's taste with shaped sandwiches, meringue mice, knickerbocker glories, etc. You can have as much or as little as you wish from food only to entertainment for the whole party (magicians, clowns, game organisers, waitresses from £70–£100). One client had real miniature ponies brought up from the country for her daughter and friends to ride! Homemade birthday cakes to any theme or design cost £20–£70. A standard tea for 3–5-year-olds is, on average, £6 per head. They will also provide smoked salmon and champagne for the adults.

Barney the Clown

(David Barnes 0181 452 9505)

Clowning, magic, games, balloon-modelling and competitions. Average £70 for a 1-hour show and party of up to 30 children (no food). Any age from three to 90.

Billy Banjo

(0181 542 1599)

Will provide 45 minutes of music and magic for under-5s. Ring for details; £70.

Carolyn's Puppets

12 York Road, Richmond (0181 940 8407)

For £155 Carolyn James and Cindy Peters will do a theme party show — anything from traditional fairy-tale puppets behind a booth, plus some magic, and games (2–8-year-olds), to Camelot, Peter Pan or Star Wars (5–7-year-old boys) and Cinderella or Aladdin (for girls). Or invite 'Queen Victoria' to your party and play Victorian games (6–10-year-olds).

Creschendo Party

(0171 259 2727)

Well-established party service – Chendo the Clown, a 'Lion Hunt', mini–magic, bouncy castle, bubbles, and party games all tailored to the age and needs of the children. Also provides food, party bags, decoration, hall hire and searches. Gym or disco parties for older children. Creschendo equipment used. Prices start at £80 per hour, cakes average £135, children's theme menus average £5.95 per head.

Diane's Puppets

(0171 820 9466)

Bobby Bunny Show for 2–8-year-olds or Red Riding Hood and Punch and Judy for over-5s. Puppet show and face-painting from £65.

Hippopartymus

(0181 940 6880)

Children's parties are done around a theme of your choice and the food is shaped to match.

Kid–A–Gram

(0171 376 0418)

Will send your child's favourite film or cartoon character to the party for half an hour; £65.

Lydie's Children's Entertainment

(0171 622 2540)

From £60 Lydie will set up a mini-theatre in your home with plenty of props. The story can be based on any character.

Len Belmont

(0171 254 8300)

Popular ex–holiday camp entertainer with magic, ventriloquist acts and balloon-modelling.

Marmaduke

(01992 446211)

A very popular children's entertainer who uses live animals such as owls, chinchillas, snakes and bats. Best for over-4s (and very good with shy children). Book early; £100 for 1 hour.

Melissa Dee

(also known as Bumble the female clown; 0181 399 6007)

For £60 an hour or £95 for 2 hours (including prizes but no sweets), Melissa will organise jugglers, clowns, magicians and other children's entertainers as well as games for children's bashes. Bumble herself specialises in under-6s with magic, puppets and sculpting anything from balloons (from a Harley Davidson to a teddy bear). Kidigrams of any characters from Mr Blobby to Postman Pat (£45 for half an hour).

Non–Stop Party Shop Puddleduck Party

(0171 351 0432)

Organises theme parties including venue, invitations, food, party bags, etc. Prices start at £100.

Norman Myers

(0181 458 4295)

Has been doing children's parties for 30 years and will provide a little bit of everything – puppets, Punch and Judy, magic, games, films and food for 3–13-year-olds. From £120 for two hours.

Patchy Peter and Snowy the Dog

(01442 61767)

Two hours of traditional entertainment with a real white rabbit and Peter's mischievous dog; £100.

Pekko's Puppets

28 Dorset Road, Ealing W5 (0181 579 7651)

Traditional tales from all over the world using rod, glove or giant puppets. Shows last for one hour including songs and clowning. For under-5s two short stories and a few nursery rhymes. Over-5s usually have one play (*Dracula*, *The Three Pigs* or *Clever Polly and the Stupid Wolf*) and a little something at the end. Book three months in advance for weekends and holidays; £80.

Peter Pinner Entertainments

(0181 863 1528)

Ring for detailed information pack from these versatile children's entertainers for all events – clowns, balloon animals, magic, Punch and Judy, ventriloquism, games, junior discos. Bouncy castles to hire. Entertainers from £75 for a show; whole two-hour party from £130.

Piccolo Puppet Company

(Angela Passmore: 0181 898 9247)

Specialises in shows for children aged three to eight. Suitable for large living room or hall.

Prof Alexander's Punch and Judy

(0171 254 0416)

Traditional Punch and Judy show performed in theatres as well as private parties. Also magic shows.

Rhubarb the Clown

(Martin Solity 0181 800 5009)

A silent clown who does a wonderful 45-minute show of mime, juggling and magic. He also plays the nose flute. THe act requires some space (either a high-ceilinged living room, a garden or local hall). From £75.

Smartie Artie

(01582 461588)

Magic, clowning and party games for 3–7-year-olds. A whole party with 45 minutes before tea and 45 minutes after tea costs from £90 and includes balloon-modelling, comedy magic, puppetry, games and competitions, depending on the age of the child. Also disco parties. There are several Smartie Arties, so if your kids have seen a particular one they like, make sure you ask for the same one.

Storytime with Maxine and her Puppets

(0181 809 1284)

Forty-five minute show for under-5s with hand puppets, animals and nursery rhymes or full two-hour party with break for tea, for up to seven years. Reasonable prices.

Strawberry Fool

(0171 622 0277)

Kate Bagnall does a wonderful puppet show as well as the usual clowning, magic, face painting, games and storytelling for children from two to eight. Reasonable prices.

The Wonderland Puppet Theatre

(01932 784467)

Over 20 years experience in shows for children from two to nine. Games before tea, prizes provided. Will do complete party. Ring for details.

Tiddleywinks

(0171 736 1842)

Actress Gabrielle Lister and a team of actresses do drama-based party workshops for 2–12-year-olds with plenty of audience participation. Three to 7-year-olds have a theme party with drama games, dressing up, story-telling and simple performances over two hours. Eight to 12-year-olds produce a play in their own home, helping to make the costumes, props and make-up, rehearsing and finally performing to parents at the end of the party (three to four hours). From £100 (drama parties £155).

Twizzle the Clown

(0181 748 3138)

Very popular entertainer with parents of children aged 2–8 – games, magic, balloon modelling, stories and a Punch and Judy show. Also stilt-walkers, craft parties, magic shows, go-karting for older children and a pony in your garden. Party bags and food can be provided and tables and chairs hired, as well as a special visit from Father Christmas or Mr Mouse. It is a very caring and personalised service (one boy had a cowboy party with the world gun-slinging champion in attendance). One-hour show £75, two hours £125.

CAKES, PARTY SHOPS, FANCY DRESS AND EQUIPMENT HIRE

American Party Store

Hours
Mon–Sat
10am–7pm, Thurs
10am–8pm
Travel
⊖ Bond Street or
Oxford Circus

16 Woodstock Street, W1 (0171 493 2678)

So-called because most of their stock comes from America, this excellent party shop can provide anything from balloons, banners, bags, napkins, hats, table wear, invitations, etc and what they don't stock they will get for you. Children's costumes to buy cost anything from £15. Allow three to four weeks for costumes. Masks from £1.99. Cake-making and balloon delivery services and a list of entertainers.

Carnival Store

Hours
Tues–Sat
2.30–6pm, Sat
10am–6pm
Travel
⊖ Hammersmith

95 Hammersmith Rd, W14 (0171 603 7824)

Huge variety of costumes to hire for all occasions.

Circus Circus

Hours
Mon–Sat
9am–6pm
Travel
⊖ Fulham
Broadway

176 Wandsworth Bridge Road, SW6 (0171 731 4128)

As well as having a good selection of novelties they offer a full party service (caterers, balloons, tableware, etc).

City Dress Arcade

Hours
Mon–Sat
11am–4.30pm,
closed Thurs
Travel
⊖ Bethnal Green

437 Bethnal Green Road, E2 (0171 739 2645)

Excellent value costume hire for children aged two to 11 – anything from Andy Pandy and clowns to Cavaliers and Cinderellas; £20 refundable deposit.

Escapade

Hours
Mon–Fri
10am–7pm, Sat
10am–6pm, Sun
noon–6pm
Travel
⊖ Camden Town

150 Camden High Street, NW1 (07 485 7384)

Everything you could want for a party – costumes, masks, wigs, hats, tricks, jokes and novelties. Four to 10-year-olds can hire costumes ranging from monkeys and clowns to cowboys and Cinderellas from £12–£18 plus £20 refundable deposit.

It's My Party

23 Webbs Road, SW11 (0171 350 2763)

In addition to kids' theme party plates, mats, masks, cutlery and napkins featuring anything from Batman to Thomas the Tank Engine, princesses to pirates, they can rent you tables, chairs, cake tins and bouncy castles (£35–£55). They also have a list of reliable entertainers.

Hours
Mon–Sat
9.30am–5pm,
closed daily
1–2pm

Travel
Clapham
South ⊖

Juke Box Junction

12 Toneborough, Abbey Road, NW8 (0171 328 6206)

With over 3,000 rock 'n' roll tunes to get a party swinging this is the place to hire (or buy) a juke box; from £95.

Hours
Mon–Sat
9am–5pm

Travel
Kilburn High
Road ⇌

Just Balloons

127 Wilton Road, SW1 (0171 434 3039)

All kinds of balloons for sale here. If you can't find the design you want they will make them for you. Balloons start at 10p for one and 25 personalised printed balloons cost £20 plus VAT. Also stocks paper tableware.

Hours
Mon–Sat
9.30am–6pm

Travel
Victoria ⊖⇌

Kiddywinks – Children's Party Hire

(0181 876 6149)

The usual tables (£1.50), chairs (50p), bouncy castle (£30–£35), tunnels and ball ponds plus very popular Orient Express and Santa Fe ride-on electric trains for use indoors and out (14ftx18ft track). Can deliver.

Kite and Balloon Emporium

613 Garratt Lane, SW18 (0181 946 5962)

They will print balloons with a message of your choice (£32 for 100), decorate halls with them, and organise balloon releases. You can hire heligas cylinders by the week or personalise a single foil balloon (£2.50 plus 25p per letter).

Hours
Mon–Sat
9am–5.30pm

Travel
Earlsfield ⇌

Louise Holland

(0171 736 2747)

Will undertake any kind of cake from a fairy castle to a Ferrari. Prices start from £30. Two weeks' notice is needed.

Minimarkee

45 Larkhall Rise, SW4 (0171 720 5283)

Free-standing marquees – canopies start at £40.

Hours
Mon–Sat
9.30am–5.30pm
Travel
⊖High Street
Kensington

Non–Stop Party Shop

214–16 Kensington High Street, W8 (0171 937 7200) or 694 Fulham Road, SW6 (0171 384 1491) and other branches

Ten partyware ranges, fancy dress accessories, hats, masks, balloons, helium balloons, decorations and a good selection of novelties for party bags and prizes. Fancy dress to buy. Bouncy castle hire and cake tin hire.

Hours
Mon–Sat
9.30am–5.30pm
Travel
⊖ Belsize Park

Oscar's Den

127–129 Abbey Road, NW6 (0171 328 6683)

Novelties, paper tableware, balloons, jokes, masks, toys. Will prepare party gift bags to any value. Hire bouncy castles (from £30) and tables and chairs. Also organise parties (day trips to Alton Towers with party bags and food boxes are popular) and find entertainers.

Hours
Mon–Sat
9.30am–5.30pm
Travel
⊖ Chalk Farm

Party Party

11 Southampton Road, NW5 (0171 267 9084)

Best known for its customised novelty cakes which start at £30 for Thomas or Postman Pat. Table and chair hire. Novelties, masks, streamers and party bags.

Take a break from the city and spend the day in the country. Follow a woodland trail in Sevenoaks, lose the kids in a maze near Maidstone, climb a Norman keep in Kent, tickle a skate in Sussex, adopt a donkey at Lockwood or take a day-trip to France. Castles, country houses, farms, zoos, wildlife parks, museums and monuments — whatever the weather there is something to suit everyone.

Out of Town

BEDFORDSHIRE

The Shuttleworth Collection

Old Warden Aerodrome, Biggleswade (01767 627288)

Hours
April-Oct daily
10am-5pm (last
admission 4pm),
Nov-March daily
10am-4pm (last
admission 3pm)
Prices
Adults £5, children
£2.50, under-5s
free. Flying Display
Days extra
Travel
⇒ Biggleswade
By car 45 miles
north of London,
on-site parking

Flying Days are only held during the summer in good weather but the collection is on permanent display under cover throughout the year. Recalling the history of aviation with the 1912 Blackburn monoplane, the oldest British aeroplane still flying, a Bleriot 1909 plane, WWI fighters and a WWII Spitfire. In addition, there is a large collection of vehicles from steam cars to fire engines, horse-drawn carriages to tricycles, all in perfect working order. Look out for the 1898 Panhard Levassor in which Richard Ormonde Shuttleworth, the collection's founder, won the London to Brighton run in 1928. There is an adventure playground and restaurant with children's menu of Skyliners, Spitfire Sandwiches and Flying Hot Dogs. Disabled facilities.

Whipsnade Wild Animal Park

Whipsnade, nr Dunstable, Beds (01582 872 171)

Hours
May-Sept daily
10am-6pm (Sun
and Bank Hols to
7pm), Oct-April
daily 10am-sunset
Prices
Adults £7.30,
children 3-15
£5.50,
OAPs, students £6,
under-3s free
Travel
⇒ St Pancras
to Luton, then Bus
43 from
Bus station
By car off the M1
at junction 9 or 12
32 miles north of
London

A large, open-air conservation park houses 3,000 animals including cheetahs, lions, tigers, rhinos, elephants and reptiles and many endangered species. Animal Encounters sessions where you can meet the animals and talk to the keepers. Birds of prey demonstrations. Discovery Centre with hands-on displays, a miniature desert and a rainforest. Large adventure play area. Café and picnic area. Take binoculars or use telescopes provided. You can drive round in your own car or take the free bus. There is also a train which goes around the park. Baby-changing facilities. Pushchairs for hire.

Woburn Wild Animal Kingdom

Woburn, Beds (01525 290407)

Hours
Mid-Mar-Oct daily
10am-5pm, Nov-
mid-March Sat &
Sun 11am-3pm
Prices
Adults £7, Children
£4.50, under-4s
free

Britain's largest drive-through wildlife park takes you on a safari trail past tigers, wolves, bears, rhinos and monkeys (watch out for your wipers where the monkeys are concerned). A good place to visit in winter when there are fewer cars. You have to stay in the car with windows closed and you can get a good view of the animals even if it is raining, as they often come right up to the car (this sometimes frightens very young children). There is an adventure playground, boating lake, pets corner and parrot and sealion shows in the leisure park and a 15 minute cabin-lift 'Sky Ride' above a section of the park. Picnic area, toilets, gift shop, restaurant.

BERKSHIRE

Windsor Castle

Windsor, Berkshire (01753 868286)

Originally built by William the Conqueror, this is the oldest, largest inhabited castle in the world and, despite the terrible fire in 1992, it is a splendid royal residence. It is rather formal and staff do not take kindly to tear-away toddlers or boisterous children running around playing knights in shining armour inside the castle. The highlight of the trip is the enormous Queen Mary Dolls' House, an exquisite miniature palace complete with running water, real leather-bound books and a working vacuum cleaner. No buggies in State Apartments. Changing of the Guard can be seen outside free of charge on most days at 11am (see page 14, 43). The State Apartments are closed when the Royal Family is in residence. Toilets but no baby-changing facilities.

Hours
Mid-Mar–Oct daily, 10am–5pm; Nov–mid-March, Sat & Sun, 11am–3pm

Prices
Adults £7, children £4.50, under-4s free

Travel
By car M1 exit junction 12 or 13; 44 miles north-west of London; 50 mins from North London

KENT

Badsell Park Farm

Crittenden Road, Matfield, Tonbridge, Kent (01892 837228)

A working fruit and arable farm which has turned the clocks back, offering a glimpse into rural culture between the wars. Watch the daily farming activities, visit the pet area, see rare

Hours
April–Nov daily 10am-5.30pm

Prices
Adults £4, children (3-16 yrs) and OAPs £2.50, under-3s free

Travel
44 miles from
central London
by car A228, off
A21.
By train to
⇌ Paddock Wood
then taxi 2 miles:
£3.50

breeds of cows, goats, sheep, bantams and pigs, pick your own fruit and visit the Butterfly House. Good outdoor play area and large indoor playbarn for under-9s. Open-air and covered picnic areas. Café. Baby-changing facilities, high chairs, accessible by buggy.

Chatham Historic Dock Yard

Dock Road, Chatham, Kent (01634 812551)

Hours
Easter-Oct Wed-
Sun and Bank Hol
Mons 10am-6pm;
Nov-March Wed,
Sat and Sun
10am-4.30pm.

Prices
Adults £5.60,
children £3.60,
concs £4.60,
under-5s free,
family ticket (2+4)
£15

Travel
⇌ Chatham
then bus to
dockyard's
Alexandra Gate, by
car off A25,
free on site
parking)

The Chatham Naval Dockyard, which served the Royal Navy for over four hundred years, has now been turned into the most complete and perfectly preserved Georgian river dock-yard with eight museum galleries. You can see rope-making in the traditional working ropery and guess the strength of a finished rope as it is stretched to breaking point. The most popular gallery is the award-winning Wooden Walls, a multi-media 'living history' attraction showing how HMS Valient, a wooden warship, was built. This is a wonderful site for older children or those who don't mind walking and climbing. Wheelwrights Cafeteria, Tea Shop, open and covered picnic areas, wheelchair access, baby-changing facilities and children's play area. Events include Model Railway exhibitions, Dockyard in Steam days, Easter Madhatter's Tea Party.

Chiselhurst Caves

Old Hill, Chiselhurst, Kent (0181 467 3264)

Hours
Wed-Sun 11am-
4.30pm (closed
Christmas Day)

Prices
Adults £3,
under-15s £1.50,
under-5s free
(short trip only,
there are longer
tours visiting parts
not otherwise
seen at 2.30pm on
Suns and Bank
Holidays)

Travel
⇌ Chiselhurst
Free parking

Wonderfully eerie lantern tours of the caves leave on the hour and take 45 minutes. They pass through a network of man-made caves, enhanced by chilling tales, amusing anec-dotes and historical detail from the superb guide. Jake, who was allowed to hold a lantern, was intrigued by the loos, the pool and the stage, while Benja occupied himself searching for bats. Not suitable for children afraid of the dark. Wear sensible shoes. Café, shop, picnic area, surrounding woods to explore. No buggy or wheelchair access.

Great Hollanden Farm Park

Mill Lane, Hildenborough, nr Sevenoaks, Kent (01732 832276)

With visions of Jake and Benjamin communing with nature as they at last got the chance to pet the animals they had hitherto only seen from the other side of a fence we drove into Hollanden Farm Park. Instead, the kids rampaged round the recreated iron age settlement, while the adults were more interested in the rare and traditional farm breeds and the old farming equipment. But the children did show greater interest in the animals when it was suggested they could feed them (35p per bag from the kiosk). If you haven't a picnic there is a reasonable coffee shop. There is a woodland walk, adventure playground, tractor and trailor rides and guided tours available by prior arrangement. Farm shop, tearoom, picnic area. Wheelchair and buggy access.

Hours
End March-end Sept daily 10.30am-5pm. Pick your own fruit from May-October

Prices
Adults £3.95, children (3-17) £2.60

Travel
Hildenborough ⇌ by car off the A225

Hever Castle

Edenbridge, Kent (01732 865224)

Inside the enchanting 13th-century double-moated castle, complete with huge gatehouse, arrow slits and portcullis drawbridge stands the 15th-century manor house, childhood home of Anne Boleyn and scene of her courtship with King Henry VIII. You will need plenty of time to explore the beautiful grounds, discover the grotto, get lost in the maze, examine the strange and beautiful statues and sculptures in the formal Italian Garden, wander round the rose garden, and roll down the hill from which you can overlook the castle and maze. Take a picnic (food in the restaurant is expensive). We went on a sunny day in April when the daffodils carpeted the grounds and the tourists hadn't arrived. There is a small but popular mini-adventure playground near the exit. There are baby-changing facilities in restaurant toilets., toilets for disabled and a gift shop.

Hours
Castle open daily noon-6pm, Gardens from 11am

Prices
Adults £5.70, children 5-16 years £2.90, family ticket (2+2) £14.30 (less for gardens only)

Travel
Hever ⇌ then 1 mile walk, or Edenbridge and 3 mile taxi ride. Free on-site parking

Howletts Wild Animal Park

Bekesbourne, nr Canterbury, Kent (01303 264646/7)

Dedicated to the breeding of rare species, the animals in John Aspinall's park enjoy conditions as close to the wild as is possible in captivity. This does mean that the animals are rather more difficult to see than in a conventional zoo, so

Hours
Daily summer 10am-7pm (last admission 5pm), winter 10am-5pm (last admission 3.30pm), closed Dec 25

Prices
Adults £6.99,
children (4-14 yrs)
and OAPs £4.99,
under-4s free

Travel
Off A2 south of
Canterbury

you have to be patient and look carefully. As well as the largest collection of tigers in the world and a massive breeding colony of gorillas, there are deer, antelope, chimps, cheetahs, African elephants, wolves, bongos and bison. Plan your day carefully especially with small children who tire easily. There is a cafeteria, kiosks, picnic sites, toilets and baby changing facilities in the café. Children's Parties available.

Hours
Open all year daily
11am-5pm (closed
Dec 25, June 26,
July 3, Aug 29 and
Nov 6). Special
events include an
International Hot
Air Balloon festival
in June, a grand
firework display in
November, and
open-air concerts
in summer.

Prices
Adults £7.50,
children 5-15
years £5, under-5s
free, family ticket
(2 adults, 2
children) £22 (less
for grounds only)

Travel
40 miles east, M20
junction 8

Leeds Castle

Maidstone, Kent ME17 1PL (01622 765400)

A real fairytale medieval castle built spectacularly upon two islands in the lake. Dating from the ninth century, it is one of the oldest castles in the country. Apart from Les Chambres de la Reine, the two rooms recreated as they might have looked in the 15th century, the inside of the castle is rather a disappointment and much to the relief of most children, it takes as little as 15 minutes to go round. The extensive gardens and parklands, however, are splendid and you will need to spend the whole day here. Ideal for older children unless you take a buggy (there is a lot of walking involved for toddlers and the car park is some distance from the castle for scenic reasons). Everyone loved the Maze-Grotto which has a delightful underground fairy grotto complete with tunnels, caves and falling water. The Dog Collar Museum was also very popular. There are lovely woodland walks, a duckery (where the birds have right of way and the public must keep to the path), aviaries and an ancient vineyard. Restaurant, cream teas, barbeques. Picnic area by car park, toilets. Limited wheelchair access, leave buggies at the entrance.

Hours
March-Oct daily
10am-5pm

Prices
Adults £2.50,
children £1.50,
concs £2

Travel
on A25 between
Maidstone and
Sevenoaks

Nepicar Farm

Wrotham Heath, Sevenoaks, Kent (01732 883040)

This is a marvellous place for children who think milk only comes from cows (or worse still, bottles). They can watch sheep being milked at close range and in spring help bottle-feed the lambs. There are sheep-shearing and cheese-making demonstrations and a large well-stocked children's play area with bicycles, footballs, rounders and cricket equipment. Toilets for the disabled, mother-and-baby room. Wheelchair and buggy access.

Penshurt Place and Gardens

Penshurst, nr Tonbridge, Kent (01892 870307)

Medieval manor house whose state rooms are full of wonderful furniture, tapestries and portraits. The huge and splendid Baron's Hall dates back to 1341. For children there is a toy museum with lead soldiers, dolls, dolls' houses and games. Imaginative adventure playground, Tudor Garden, lake, nature and farm trails, toy museum, restaurant and shop. Wheelchair and buggy access, disabled toilets.

Hours
Daily April-Sept
(March and Oct
weekends only)
house noon-
5.30pm, grounds
11am-6pm

Prices
Adults £5.50
(grounds only £4),
under-16s £3
(grounds only
£2.75)

Travel
By car off M25,
6 miles from
Tonbrige Wells

Port Lympne Wild Animal Park

Lympne, nr Hythe, Kent (01303 264646/7)

In summer the best way to see the animals here is to take a Safari trailer ride (pre-book as it is very popular). Alternatively you can take the two-mile Trek around the park to see the rhinos, elephants, tigers, wolves, monkeys, deer and antelope. There is a lot of walking to do but it is all accessible by double buggy. Shop with animal-related toys and books from pocket money prices up. Cafeteria, kiosks, picnic sites, baby-changing facilities in the café, toilets. Children's Birthday Parties available.

Hours
All year daily from
10am-5pm or dusk
(closed.Dec 25)

Prices
Adults £6.99,
children 4-14 and-
concs £4.99,
under-4s free

Travel
Exit 11, M20 south
of Ashford, off the
B2067

Sea Life Centre

Rock-a-Nore Road, Hastings, Kent (01424 718776)

The Sea Life Centre, at the western end of the beach, has octopus, lobster, sharks, rays and hundreds of other sea creatures from Britain's deep waters. The large glass tanks are accessible even to small children. Some tanks have concave bubbles so you can stick your head right in, and the dappled lighting in others is magical. The highlight of the centre is the underwater viewing tunnel with a carpeted step running along one side. There are no reflections here and looking up can make you feel quite dizzy. There are outdoor pools where the children can pick up crabs – if they dare – and picnic tables providing a good place for biscuits and a drink (bring your own). If you don't have a picnic there is a Breakers

Hours
All year daily
10am-6pm (until
9pm summer hols)

Prices
Adults £4.50,
children (4-14
years) £3.25, OAPs
£3.45, under-4s
free

Travel
Charing Cross
or Victoria ⇌
to Hastings.
National Express
coach from
Victoria.
By car A21

Restaurant. We took the double buggy round with ease but there are 12 steps down to the tunnel. There is an alternative wheelchair route which misses the tunnel but stops by a huge floor-to-ceiling concave wall, making you feel as if you are standing inside the tank with the sharks, sting-rays and other sea beasties. **Nearby:** The Fisherman's Museum, the Shipwreck Heritage Centre, the East Hill Cliff Railway and Hastings Castle and the 1066 Story.

Hours
Apr-Sep daily
10.30am-5.30pm,
Oct-March Tues-
Sun 10.30am-
4.30pm

Prices
Adults £3.25,
children (3-15)
£1.50, OAPs £2.75

Travel
By car off M20 at
junction 10, A2070
to Hamstreet then
B2067 for 3 miles

South of England Rare Breeds Centre

Highlands Farm, Woodchurch, nr Ashford, Kent (01233 861494)

Apart from the 65 rare farm breeds to see on this working farm, there's a kids corner where children are encouraged to touch the pigs, sheep, goats, rabbits and cattle, and watch milking, grooming and shearing demonstrations. There is a lovely woodland walk, and nature trails to follow or you can save your energy and take a farm trailer ride. There is a good picnic area, well-stocked farm and gift shop and a tea room. Disabled toilets. Wheelchair and buggy access.

Hours
March 1-Oct 31
daily 10am-5pm

Prices
Adults £3.25,
children £2.25

Travel
on the A226
London Road
opposite the
hospital

Stone Lodge Farm Park

London Rd, Stone, nr Dartford, Kent (01322 292211)

Any farm that can cope with 73 kids from Jake's school visiting for the whole day deserves a medal, and Stone Lodge Farm not only coped, but did it with a smile. The children watched the cows being milked and had a go at milking a cut-out cow, watched a bird of prey demonstration, learnt about the horses, had a tractor ride round the whole farm and met the animals in the Children's Corner. Throughout the year there are milking and spinning demonstrations and tractor and wagon rides. Tea Room, picnic site and souvenir shop. Disabled and buggy access. Toilets for the disabled. Baby-changing facilities. **Nearby:** Right next door is the North Downs Steam Railway (see page 143) which runs for half a mile between London Road and Cotton Lane. Park in the field beside the station, ride the train, then make your way to the farm down the hill (or drive round if you have a buggy with you).

Whitbread Hop Farm

Beltring, Paddock Wood, Kent (01622 872 068)

A working farm that provides hops for the Whitbread Brewery and trains the Whitbread Shire horses that pull the barrel-laden drays through the City of London. It is also the retirement home for the older horses. It has the largest collection of Victorian oast houses in the world and two museums. You can watch horse-driving demonstrations and see the horses being groomed and harnessed. There is an Animal Village with free Animal Activity Packs, owl and birds of prey flying displays, a farm trail and adventure play area. Take a picnic and spend the day here, especially if you choose one of the event-days. Nature trails, craft workshops, picnic area, toilets for the disabled, baby-changing facilities, gift shop, café and restaurant.

Hours
Mar-Oct daily
10am-6pm,
Nov-Feb daily
10am-4pm
Prices
Adults £2.95, over
5s & concs £2
Travel
Beltring ⇌
or Paddock Wood
then bus, free
on-site parking

SURREY

Birdworld and Underwater World

Farnham, Surrey (01420 22140)

Birdworld is home to a large variety of birds from the tiny wren to the giant ostrich all housed in beautifully tended landscape gardens. Find out about owls, parrots, vultures, cockatoos, spoonbills, flamingos and many more from the strategically located information plaques. Aim to arrive at Penguin Island for feeding time (daily 11.30am and 3.30pm), watch the pelicans catching fish in their beaks or feed the parrots (buy macaw fruit feed from the gift shop). Follow the Seashore trail, a recreated seashore complete with waves, a boat wreck and sea birds. Next door Underwater World has a large indoor aquarium full of meat-eating piranhas, blind cave fish, gaint pacu and other colourful tropical fish. Birdworld and Underwater World make a very good combined day trip. Café. Unlimited wheelchair and buggy access to both worlds. Nappy-changing facilities, highchairs in restaurant.

Hours
Apr-Aug daily
9.30am-6pm, Sept
daily 9.30am-5pm,
Oct-March daily
9.30am-4.30pm
(closed Dec 25).
Prices
Birdworld: Adults
£3.95; children
£2.25, OAPs £3,
under-3s free,
Family Ticket (2+2)
£11.50.
Underwater World
adults £1.20, children 60p.
Travel
Waterloo ⇌
to Aldershot then
bus ride to Birdworld Green Line
Coach from Victoria April-Sept Sat
and Sun only, by
car 35 miles south
west of London, 3
miles south of
Farnham on A325

Bockett Farm

Hours
Daily 10am-6pm

Prices
Adults £2.50, children (3-17) £2, children (2-3) £1.35, under-2s free, concs £2.25 (weekdays reductions))

Travel
By car 5 mins from M25, junction 9 from A3 on to A246 Leatherhead by-pass

Young Street (off Fetcham Roundabout), Fetcham, Leatherhead, Surrey (01372 363764)

Set in beautiful Norbury Park you can easily spend a day at this excellent family-run farm where children can feed the animals in the large open barn full of rabbits, rare breeds of sheep, pigs and a dray horse. There are agricultural equipment displays and demonstrations, farm walks and pony rides. Watch lambing in the large undercover area and learn how the farm operates year round. Adventure playground, huge sandpit and picnic area. The Old Barn tea rooms do excellent home made lunches, cakes and cream teas. Toilets with baby changing facilities. Disabled access.

Gatwick Zoo, Aviaries and Butterfly Tropical Gardens

Hours
March-Oct daily 10.30am-6pm, Dec-Feb Sat and-Sun, (daily during school holidays) 10.30am-4pm or dusk (closed Dec 25-26)

Prices
Adults £3.75, children (3-14) £2.75, under-3s free

Travel
By car off A23

Russ Hill, Charlwood (01293 862312)

There is a varied collection of birds and free-flying butterflies in the tropical garden. Animals include otters, penguins, wallabies, Vietnamese pigs, eagle owls and cranes. The 'Monkey Island' is very popular. Excellent play area and a new log cabin adventure playground. Café, outdoor and undercover picnic tables and burger and chips stall (summer only). Wheelchair and buggy access, full disabled facilities.

Godstone Farm

Hours
Daily Mid Feb-Oct 10am-6pm (5pm in winter), Oct-Feb weekends only

Prices
Adults £2.95, children over 2 years £2.95 (one accompanying adult free with each paying child)

Travel
By car near A22 and Junction 6 M25, free on-site parking

Tilburstow Hill Road, Godstone (01883 742546)

For a perfect family outing with lots of kids who want to run off steam while parents sit back and relax, you cannot fault Godstone Farm. Children are positively encouraged to handle the farm animals and invited to climb into the pens with the sheep, lambs and calves, as well as petting the rabbits, guinea pigs, and hens. There are plenty of information pannels and everything is meticulously labelled. Staff are friendly and helpful. There are several covered picnic areas, places to shelter, and a covered under-5s play area so rain cannot spoil your day. However, the highlight is the adventure play area, spread over two enormous fields (and still growing) which is by far the best we have ever visited. There are ropes to climb, bridges to cross, several wooden forts, mazes, well-equipped sand pits, old tractors, climbing frames, bridges, slides, pullies, tobogganing on Astroturf, and so on. It doesn't matter how many people there are, it never feels crowded, the toilets are always clean and never run out of loo paper, and there is plenty of room to spread out on the grass for a picnic while the kids exhaust themselves. The only problem is how to get the children to leave. Wheelchair and buggy access, baby-changing facilities, shop and refreshment kiosks.

Hampton Court Palace

East Molesey, Surrey, KT8 9AU (0181 781 9500/977 8441)

Built to be the largest palace in Europe in the 1500s by Cardinal Wolsey, Henry VIII's chief minister, Henry decided he'd like to live there himself, moved in in 1525 and spent five of his six honeymoons at the Palace. Pause a moment in the Haunted Gallery on dark winter afternoons and you might hear the screams of the ghost of Catherine Howard, Henry VIII's fifth wife whom he accused of adultery and had executed. The children enjoyed the Tudor Kitchens best – their eyes stood out on stalks at the amount of food that would be prepared for feasts. The gardens, designed to rival those of Versailles, house the famous maze whose yew hedge walls are over seven foot high.

Hours
Mid-March–mid-Oct Mon 10.15am–6pm, Tues–Sun 9.30am–6pm; mid-Oct–mid-March closes at 4.15pm (closed Dec 24-26, Jan 1)

Prices
Adults £7.50, children (5-15) £4.90, under-5s free, OAPs £5.60, family ticket (2+3) £19.30

Travel
Hampton Court ⇌ 15 miles west of central London, on site parking

Lockwood Donkey Sanctuary

Farm Cottage, Sandhills, Wormley, Godalming, Surrey (01428 682409)

Old and sick donkeys from all over the world who have outlived their usefulness find their way here to this wonderful, privately-run sanctuary. In addition to the 164 donkeys the sanctuary houses horses, cows, sheep, goats, hundreds of cats, deer, wallabies, dogs, geese, ducks, cockerels and a white llama. If you forget to take carrots, biscuits or sugar lumps you can buy a bucket of food for them (don't bring apples for donkeys – they cause colic which can be fatal). Full facilities for the disabled.

Hours
All year daily 9am–5.30pm or dusk

Travel
Off the A283 Godalming-Chiddingfold Road)

Painshill Park

Hours
Open mid-Apr-
mid-Oct
Sun 11am-6pm
(last admission
5pm)

Prices
Adults £3, children
(5-16) £2.50,
family ticket
(2+5) £10

Travel
Off the A245

Portsmouth Road, Cobham, Surrey KT11 1JE (01932 868133)

This delightful 18th-century landscape garden with lake, islands, a Gothic Temple, Turkish Tent, Chinese Bridge and Grotto really appeals to children's imaginations. Learn about water power with the 19th-century Waterwheel and animal engine, conjure up the mysteries of the east in the Turkish Temple or explore the Ruined Abbey. It is a great venue for children's birthday parties with themes such as Survival, Technology, Happy Earthday, Pirate, Costume, and Treasure Hunt Parties (up to 3 hrs, 25 children £80-£95, suitable for 6–12 year olds). Excellent holiday activities include survival days, treasure hunts, pond-dipping, craker-making, earth-days, and Easter egg hunts. Shop, picnic site, light refreshments. Wheelchair and buggy access, full disabled facilities.

EAST SUSSEX

Bentley Wildfowl and Motor Museum

Hours
Open daily April-
Oct 10.30am-
4.30pm and house
opens from noon
daily. Nov-Dec &
Feb-March Sat &
Suns 10.30am-
4.30pm (Closed
Jan) and house
closed all winter

Prices
Adults £3.80,
children 4-15
years £2.20, OAPs
£2.90, family
ticket (2+4) £10.50

Travel
Free on-site
parking

Bentley, Halland, nr Lewes, East Sussex (01825 840573)

The late Gerald Askew build up the largest private collection of rare wildfowl in the UK amidst the lakes, ponds, shrubs and trees which surround Bentley House. You can see every kind of swan in the world and over 115 species of waterfowl all roaming freely in the parkland setting. There is a small animal section with tame farm animals, an adventure playground and on summer Sundays (April-Sept) a miniature steam railway. There is also a gleaming collection of Veteran, Edwardian and Vintage cars and bikes in the motor museum. Tea room. Picnic area. Facilities for the disabled.

Bodiam Castle

Hours
Open April 1-Oct
31 daily 10am-
6pm (last
admission
5.30pm), Nov 1-
March Tues-Sun
10am-dusk

Bodiam, Robertsbridge, East Sussex TN32 5UA (01580 830436)

This is one of the most popular castles in Britain for children – it looks just like a story-book castle, complete with huge, water filled moat. You can let your imagination run riot round the turrets, towers and gateways which look just the same as the day it was built. Climb the spiral staircase up to battlements and spooky turrets (steps are quite high for toddlers and young children) and spend the day exploring nooks and cranies. Older children can clamber round the ramparts to their heart's content while younger ones explore the nooks and crannies of lower levels. Plenty of space for playing ball games, flying kites and having picnics. If you forget your picnic there is an excellent Egon Ronay listed restaurant, Knolly's, with a garden abutting the castle grounds. Tea room and burger bar (summer only). Picnic areas. Wheelchair and buggy access. Dogs on leads in ground only. National Trust shop. Baby-changing facilities.

Hours cont...
Events include Dragon Egg Hunt April 1, Medieval Fair May 1-2, Family Day in July.

Prices
National Trust members free, adults £2.50, children £1.30, under-5s free

Travel
Robertsbridge ⇌ 5 miles then bus Hastings-Tunbridge Wells or Eastbourne-Rye, on-site parking 50p

Brighton Sea-Life Centre

Marine Parade, Brighton, East Sussex (01273 60422334/3)

The oldest public aquarium in England has four dozen tanks of sea- and fresh-water fish and a unique whale and dolphin exhibition. Children's favourite is the underwater Shark Tunnel. Sea Life shop. Coffee shop.

Hours
Open daily 10am-5pm (closed Dec 25)

Prices
Adults £4.75, children £3.25, under 3s free, OAPs £3.95

Travel
Brighton ⇌

Drusilla's Zoo Park

Alfriston, East Sussex (01323 870234)

Get here early and stay all day. This is a truly wonderful small zoo whose main aim is to delight small children (especially those frightened by the larger animals in traditional zoos). The park is laid out in themed areas and designed so that you can get really close to the animals and watch the family groups in their natural settings. Children can have a go at milking a (plastic) cow and follow the journey of a pint of milk from farm to shop. Everything is accessible by wheelchair and buggies with doors and windows at just the right height for tiny tots. You can feel the weight of an elephant's tooth, measure the length of a python, and take part in the popular Zoolypics. Exhasted adults might find some peace from the squeal of delighted children in the formal Japanese and Rose Gardens before venturing into the village which is full of craft shops or

Hours
Open daily 10am-dusk (4.30pm in winter; closed Dec 25-26; some attractions closed in winter - phone for details).

Prices
Zoo, train and play land: adults £5.20, children (3-13) £4.50, concs £3.50, under-3s free

Travel
From Victoria ⇌ to Berwick (one and a half hours) then taxi or walk; by car off the A27, free on-site parking)

heading for the Thatched Barn where cream teas and snacks are served. Even if it rains you can enjoy a day here as half the zoo is under cover. The large adventure playground is well-equipped and there is an indoor play barn. Bring a picnic or try the excellent, extremely child-friendly Toucans Restaurant (Egon Ronay's Family Restaurant of the Year 1991). It has a good children's menu and the popular 'kiddies cocktails', play area, baby food, bottle-warming facilities, high chairs and nursing and changing areas (open weekends and school holidays). Wheelchair and buggy access. Disabled toilets and baby-changing facilities.

WEST SUSSEX

Fishers Farm Park

Hours
Open daily 10am-5pm (Closed Dec 25 & 26)

Prices
Adults £2.50, children over 1 year £2.20

Travel
⇥ Billingshurst

Newpound Lane, Wisborough Green, West Sussex, (01403 700063)

This is a particularly good farm to visit for the whole family when you are at a loss on a wet winter's day (there is a heated indoor playbarn with fort and sandpit, and lots of the animals are under cover). Children are encouraged to go into the pens to stroke the animals, and even sulky teenage siblings can join in the fun with go-karting (£1 extra). Look out for Casper – one of the biggest horses in the world, and Jacko, one of the smallest. There are woodland trails, trailer rides and home-made cakes at tea time. The restaurant does family lunch noon-2pm. There is also an adventure playground with old tractors, a combine harvester and the usual play equpipment. Wheelchair access limited. Baby-changing facilties. Camping in summer.

DAY TRIPS & WEEKEND BREAKS

Day trip to France

A day trip to Boulogne for a family of six with a full tank of petrol for under £60

We left South East London at 6.30am, caught the 8 o'clock ferry from Dover to Calais (£18 for our car, two adults, two boys and two babies), changed our remaining £42 into francs, bought three croissants, several teas and a coffee and sat back while our children played in the soft play area. Leaving the ferry, Calais and the map behind us, we headed straight for Boulogne along the well-signposted coastal road which took about 25 minutes. You can't miss the signs to **Nausicaa** (Centre Nationale de la Mer) which you come to just before **Boulogne**. There is a car park which stretches along the seafront up to the Sea Life Centre so you can walk along the beach watching the boats, wind surfers and a few very brave swimmers, and have a quick play on the slide, swing and climbing frame in the sand next to the Centre. **Nausicaa** is one the largest, newest and most high-tech Ocean Centres in the world. Quite apart from the astonishing array of sea creatures, the interior design, the clever use of ultra-violet light and weird New Age music combine to create a marvellously eerie underwater, other-worldly experience. There are plenty of buttons to push, telephones to listen to and a touch-tank to amuse and delight the kids while you step back and enjoy the atmosphere. We spent over two hours in here and went round twice.

Boulogne is one of the prettiest of the cross-Channel ports with its attractive medieval quarter, the Ville Haute, and its impressive fortress with grassy ramparts. In the lower, new town are some excellent patesseries and good fish restaurants (to which our budget sadly didn't stretch). Newcomers shouldn't miss visiting Philippe Olivier's famous cheese shop in rue Thiers which displays over 200 different cheeses lovingly gathered from all over Europe, and if you are here on a Wednesday or Saturday the produce market in place Dalton is excellent (7am-1pm). If we hadn't forgotten that French shops shut between 12noon-2pm we would have bought a picnic to have on the grassy slopes by the Cathedral (you can buy French bread, pate, olives, cheese, fresh fruit, juice and even a bottle of wine for less than £10). As it was we ate at a little café, just beyond the gateway (2 croque-monsieurs, a large plate of French Fries, hot chocolates all round and some French bread) and still had some coins spare to buy lollipops from the nextdoor candy shop. There was just time for a wander along the 13th-century ramparts for the splendid views of the town and port below before heading back for the 9pm with £5.50 spare to buy supper for the children.

Hours

Nausica, Boulogne (Tel 21.30.98.98): open all year daily 10am-6pm (7pm at weekends) Office de Tourisme Pont Marguet (Tel 21.31.68.38): open daily 10am-noon & 2-7pm.

Prices

Nausicaa: Adults 45F, children (3-12) 30F

Travel

We travelled on P&O Ferries (Tel 01304 203388) on one of their special offer day-returns for £15 per car and £1 per person over the age of 5. Ferry offers are usually advertised in the national press.

Prices
One week in a two-bedroomed villa from £282-£691 (excluding food and most activities). Week-end or mid-week breaks available

Travel
Ring for details of different holiday villages

Center Parcs UK 😊 🌧

Longleat, Sherwood Forest and Elvedon Forest (Tel 01272 244744)

This is quite possibly the most relaxing break with children available in the UK. Center Parcs have holiday villages at Longleat, Sherwood Forest and Elveden Forest, where even in mid-winter you can shoot the rapids of Jungle River or wander among lemon groves without freezing to death. In their huge glass domes which make the weather redundant, the temperature is always tropical, the surroundings are rural and the individual villas are dotted among the trees in a traffic free environment. There are kids clubs and activities for all ages. But the major pleasure factor is derived from villa life in the forest – biking through pines with not a car in site, swans tapping on the windows, walks round the lake, superb chalets, excellent facilities in every department. Children thrive in this environment – even the most boisterous little devils turn into angels here and a good night's sleep for parents is guarenteed by the kids' sheer exhaustion. A family could easily spend days in the poolside paradise of well-run shallow-ends and spine-tingling flume rides, if it weren't for the many other activities available. You can do almost anything from archery to aromatherapy and there is a full children's programme to suit all ages, a kindergarten and discos. There is plenty of scope for children to go off on bikes on their own without parents constantly worrying about their safety. There are also fully trained nannies and baby sitters should you want to pamper yourselves in the sauna or have a round of golf away from young children. For those wanting a night out but not wishing to venture beyond the boundaries an evening in the superb Le Caprice restaurant is highly recommended – the food, which is exquisite, can hold its own with the best in Soho. The dome area food is not so good – mostly unambitious, stodgy and pricey. But the chalets are well equipped for self-catering and there is a competitively priced supermarket in the dome. You should books as many activities as possible as soon as you arrive because they get booked out very quickly (they all cost extra except the pool).

Disneyland Parks

Marne-la-Vallée Cedex 4 (Tel 64.74.30.00). For information in the UK Tel 0171 753 2900 or from Disney Travel Centre, 140 Regent St, W1 (Tel 0171 287 1819).

After a rocky start the renamed EuroDisney is now a major European attraction. A Russian journalist once remarked that it fondly reminded him of Moscow, because you have to queue for everything. This is indeed still the case, although if you are clever and take the major rides (Space Mountain, Big Thunder Mountain, Indiana Jones and the Temple of Peril) at the beginning or very end of the day you can fill the rest of your time with some of the quieter attractions. In fact these ones are the most beguiling – the Small World and Fairytale rides, both taking you on little boats through narrative treats, are amongst the best entertainment experiences for young children anywhere in Europe. On-site shows such as Mickey and His Friends provide lots more fun and the well-known street parades are another dependable attraction. The park is divided into areas, the centre of which is Main Street USA with arcades of Victorian shops, vintage cars and street parades. We spent most of our time in Fantasyland exploring Sleeping Beauty's Castle, topsy-turvy cottages, a flying Dumbo ride, and the Small World canal cruise which we went round three times. Adventureland, Frontierland and Discoveryland are worlds of film-set adventure with rocky mountains, deserts, croc-infested swamps, pirate ships and space stations. There are plenty of self-service themed restaurants as well as snacks and ice-creams from food carts. The highlight of the trip was the *Buffalo Bill Wild West Show* – a stunning evening of cowboys and Indians, horses, stage coaches, wagons, stampeding buffalo, long horn cattle and delicious finger-lickin' western food eaten at ringside tables. We stayed at the pink-and-white, fairytale Disneyland Hotel, a luxury hotel right over the park's main entrance, which has excellent facilities for babies and children of any age. Travelling by Eurostar is now a real attraction for London families – it takes you from London Waterloo to Paris Gare du Nord from where the connection to Disney's own station at Marne-la-Vallée is easy even with double buggies, babies and loads of luggage (about 50 minutes).

Hours
Open daily but times vary. Ideal time to go mid-week off-peak, otherwise week-ends off-peak when queues are not so long.

Prices
Prices vary according to season with one- and two-day passes as well as reduced price passports for those staying longer. Adults 225F, children 3-11 150F

Travel
Eurostar (tel 0345 881 881 – calls charged at local rate), prices, if booked in advance start from adults £76, children (4-11) £62.50, under-4s free if a seat is not reserved. The high-speed intercity passenger service from Waterloo to Paris takes 3 hours. Wheelchair access, disabled toilets and baby-changing facilities.

Hours
Denmark (open
April-Oct) daily,
times vary.

Prices
Adults Dkr100, 3-
13-year-olds
Dkr90, OAPs Dkr60
(prices include all
rides except the
Traffic School.
Legoland® Hotel:
single room
Dkr650, double
room Dkr875, suite
for 5 people Dkr
1600 (if you stay
in the hotel admis-
sion to Legoland®
is Dkr50 per per-
son and is valid for
the entire stay).

Travel
Scandinavian
Seaways (tel
01255 241234):
overnight ferry
crossing (approx.
18 hours) from
Harwich to
Esjberg.

Legoland® Denmark

Billund, Denmark (0045 7533133)

Having stepped on numerous corners of Lego and extracted at least three sets from the vacuum cleaner, the idea of going all the way to Denmark just to see a giant model village was not all that appealing. But this is far more than its (rather impressive) model village. Like other theme parks it is divided into themed sections such as the Wild West and Pirate Land, an amazing proportion of which are made out of Lego, but great care has been taken to ensure that both adults and children have a thoroughly enjoyable time and you do not have to spend money at every turn. Of all the themed areas Oscar never really wanted to come out of the Wild West where among other things he could become a sheriff, have his name printed on a WANTED poster and pan for real 'gold' nuggets, while Felix yo-ho-ho-ed his way round Pirate Land on a boat ride through a pirate cave to find Lego treasure and life-size pirates. We had over 75 goes on the various different rides but by far the most popular was the Indian canoe ride which took us up hill past prairie animals (squawking eagle, hissing rattlesnake – all made of Lego) before hurtling down a waterslide at the other end. Queuing is not a problem here – even in the height of the summer, queues on the best rides rarely last more than 20 minutes. For smaller children there is Duploland with larger than life Duplo helicopters and aeroplanes to ride and a Duplo train. We did Legoland in one day but you could eas-ily find enough to do in two. A lot of thought and care has gone into the layout, the facilities are all of a high standard, the staff are helpful and all speak English. On a short break the popular safari park Givskud Lionpark is an excellent antidote to the Lego lions but you do need your own car. You drive through the giraffes and ostriches, leave your car and walk through the monkey enclosure, returning to your car to drive through the lion area, and so on. There is a restaurant and a wonderful adventure play area set in the woods. See also Legoland® Windsor, page 124. For further information on Legoland® and Givskud Lionpark, contact the Danish Tourist Board, 55 Sloane Street, London SW1X 9SY (tel 0171 259 5958).

Football, fencing, roller-skating and riding are all sports available for children in London. This section covers these activities and many more, whether spectator or participatory, formal or informal.

Most local councils lay on sports facilities for children in the summer and during other holidays. These are usually for 6–18 year olds (with separate programmes and entertainment for under-5s) and can be anything from riding, shooting, archery and fencing to nature days, golf, canoeing, football, tennis and sailing. Your local library and leisure services department will have details.

Useful addresses:

British Sports Association for the Disabled, Solecast House, 13-27 Brunswick Place, N1 6DX (0171 490 4919). Monday-Friday 9am-5.30pm. For information on sports clubs with special facilities and related advice.

The Sports Council, 16 Upper Woburn Place, WC1 (0171 388 1277). Monday-Friday 9am-5pm. Information on all sport in and around London and on various governing bodies.

Sportsline (0171 222 8000). Mon-Fri 10am-6pm. Operators give information on sports clubs and venues in London.

Adventure Playgrounds

Although 'adventure playground' has become a loose term for all army-style wood-and-rope assault courses designed for children, the official ones, which are run either by charities or by London boroughs, are areas fully supervised at all times by trained playworkers. They are run all over London, are extremely successful, absolutely free and children from about 5–14 love them. For information on adventure playgrounds near you phone 0171 820 3800.

Climbing

British Mountaineering Council, 177–179 Burton Road, West Didsbury, Manchester M20 2BB (0161 445 4747). To find out about introductory summer courses in rock climbing and mountaineering for children aged 12-16.

Brixton Recreation Centre, Brixton Station Road, SW9 (0171 926 9779). Inside wall for climbing without ropes. Wednesday evening coaching. For aged seven and over.

Cricket

Lords Cricket Ground, St John's Wood Road, NW8 (0171 289 1611). To watch county and international cricket and for behind-the-scene tours; **Oval Cricket Ground,** Kennington Oval SE11 (0171 582 6660).

Cricket coaching is usually for children over 8 – get in touch with your local cricket ground in the Yellow Pages. Also see Parks for practice nets which are bookable during the summer.

MCC Indoor Cricket School, Lords Cricket Ground, St John's Wood Road, NW8 (0171 432 1014). Coaching for children of 8 and over.

Cycling

Bike 1: Country Bike Rides (details 01252 624022) a cycle tour company which arranges one-day country bike rides. Set up from local village halls where refreshments and maps are provided, there is also a bike mechanic and ambulance on hand plus a telephone helpline. £9.95 registration fee (under-16s £3.50).

Bike hire shops: Most bike shops don't hire out kids' bikes, but if your children already have bikes you can hire one for yourself for a country bike ride.

On Yer Bike (retail and hire shop), 52-54 Tooley Street, SE1 (0171 378 6669). Open Mon-Fri 9am-6pm; Sat 9.30am-5.30pm. A good place to hire a bike.

Fencing

Amateur Fencing Association, 1 Baron Gate, 33 Rothschild Road, W4 (0181 742 3032). Phone for a full list of clubs and events in London. Minimum age usually seven years.

Football

Sunday Youth League Football. For information on your local youth football clubs contact Alan Clarke (01959 57018), the London Youth Football Association Secretary, who will put you in touch with your nearest clubs.

Football in the Community: professional clubs run soccer courses for girls and boys of all ages and abilities with schemes ranging from weekly after-school or Saturday morning clinics run by trained coaches, to work with ethnic minorities, under-privileged children and disabled people. Some are free, while others charge up to £1 an hour. The following is a list of Football in the Community phone numbers:

Arsenal Football Club 0171 226 2150

Charlton Athletic 0181 850 2866

Chelsea Football Club 0171 385 01710

Crystal Palace Football Club 0181 771 5886

Millwall Football Club 0171 231 0379

West Ham United Football Club 0181 548 2707

Queen's Park Rangers Football Club 0181 743 0262

Fulham Football Club 0171 736 6561

Brentford Football Club 0181 560 2021

Wimbledon Football Club 0181 771 1772

Go-Karts

Karts and karting were invented in America and brought over during the Second World War. For details on fixtures, safety, etc contact the British Motor Sports Council (01753 681736).

Playscape, Old London Transport Bus Garage, off Triangle Place, Clapham Common, SW4 (0181 986 7116). Open daily 9.30am–10pm. Admission £37.50 per 4-hour session; £18 tester session for anyone of eight years and over. Exhilarating fun, but don't take under-8s as it's not a children's spectator sport. Weekends are group bookings only.

Ice-Skating

Outdoor rinks: Broadgate Ice Rink, Eldon Street, EC2 (0171 588 6565). Open Nov-March; sessions Mon-Fri noon-3pm; Tues-Thurs 4-7.30pm; Fri 4-8pm; Sat & Sun 11am-1pm, 2-4pm, 5-7pm. Adults £7; under-12s & OAPs £4. London's only outdoor rink. Children's ice-skating courses (four half-hour lessons £24 plus £1 skate hire). Ice Christmas Gala event in December. Smallest skate hire, children's size 6.

Indoor rinks: Alexandra Palace Ice Rink, Alexandra Palace Way, N22 (0181 365 2121). Good place for beginners and potterers. Adult £3.50, children £2.80. Skate hire free.

Lee Valley Ice Centre, Lea Bridge Road, E10 (0181 533 3151). Open Tues-Fri 1.30-10.30pm; Sat & Sun 10am-10.30pm (phone for exact times). Adults £3.70; under-16s £2.70; under-5s 70p. This vast rink is excellent value for money, and strict supervision on the ice means troublemakers are soon sorted out.

Michael Sobell Ice Rink, Hornsey Road, N7 (0171 609 2166). Adults £2, children 50p including skate hire. Small but good value ice rink.

Queens Ice-Skating Club, 17 Queensway, W2 (0171 229 0172). Mon-Fri 11am-4.30pm & 7.30pm-10pm; Sat 10am-noon, 2-5pm & 7-10.30pm; Sun 10am-noon, 2-5pm & 7-10pm. Adults £3.50-£5; under-15s £2.30-£5, OAPs free. Skate hire £1.20. Children's classes £18 for a four-week course. Family hours Monday and Tuesday 5-6pm. If you want to see serious skaters, as well as wobble about yourself, then central London's most famous rink is well worth a visit – it might tempt you to some personal tuition from one of the 16 full-time instructors. Smallest skates for hire are size eight. Minimum age to skate is three years.

Romford Ice Rink, Rom Valley Way, Romford, Essex (01708 724731). Adults and children from £4.70 including skate hire.

Streatham Ice Rink, 386 Streatham High Road, SW16 (0181 769 7771). Mon-Fri 10am-4.30pm, 7.30-10.30pm; Sat 11am-4.45pm, 8-11pm; Sun 11am-4.45pm, 7.30-10.30pm. Adults £4.50-£5, children £3.50. Includes skate hire. Instruction courses available for under-8s. After school sessions for under-12s. Good for kids' birthday parties. Minimum age for skaters is three years.

Shops: Queen's Ice-Skating Shop: see above.

Skate Attack, 95 Highgate Road, NW5 (0171 267 6961). Large selection of ice and roller skates, protective gear, clothing and accessories.

Judo

Contact the **British Judo Association**, 7a Rutland Street, Leicester LE1 (0116 2559669).

Riding

The British Horse Society, British Equestrian Centre, Stoneleigh, Kenilworth, Warks (01203 696697). Will supply a list of riding clubs near you and deal with all Pony Club enquiries. Otherwise the following list will cater for children:

Belmont Riding Centre, The Ridgeway, Mill Hill, NW7 (0181 906 1255). Open Tues-Fri 9am-5.30pm & 7pm-9pm; Sat & Sun 9am-5pm. Lessons: groups £13.50 per hour; private £21 per hour; £11.50 per half hour. Book well in advance.

Ealing Common Riding School, 17-19 Gunnersbury Avenue, Ealing Common, W5 (0181 992 3808). Lessons for beginners to intermediate for children over 5. Under-5s do pony rides. Hacks to Osterley Park on Mondays. Book well in advance.

Hyde Park Riding Stables, 63 Bathurst Mews, W2 (0171 723 2813). Riding in Hyde Park. Lessons or ponies for hire. Minimum age 5 years.

Mudchute Farm Riding School, The Mudchute Park and Farm, Pier Street, E14 (0171 515 5901). All-weather menage for lessons or you can ride and jump in the 32-acre park. One-day courses in equitation and stable management during the school holidays as well as gymkhana, show jumping and Cross-Country events.

Ross Nye, 8 Bathhurst Mews, W2 (0171 262 3791). Open Tues-Fri 7am-4.30pm; Sat & Sun 10am-3.30pm. Group lessons £16 per hour; private £24 per hour. Early morning rides in Hyde Park are especially popular at this 16 horse school. Minimum age 7 years.

Roehampton Riding Stables, Priory Lane, SW15 (0181 876 7089). Riding takes place in Richmond Park and there are lessons on Tues-Fri. Minimum age 7 years.

Trent Park Equestrian Centre, Bramley Road, Southgate N14 (0181 363 8630/9005). The centre runs "own a pony" weeks where you visit the stable daily to look after and ride the pony allocated to you. Also 4-day holidays where you look after a pony and ride twice a day.

Wimbledon Village Stables, 24a High Street, SW19 (0181 946 8579). Open daily 8am-5pm. Group lessons Tues-Fri £19 per hour; Sat & Sun £25 per hour. The great two-hour park and common rides, lots of calm horses for timid first-timers, and the fact that they take children from two and a half years make this otherwise expensive school very popular and good value for money. Book well in advance.

Roller-Skating

Hornsey School, Sports Hall, Hornsey School, Inderwick Road, N8 (0181 292 0362). Every Mon 6-7.15pm. £1.50. Roller skating instruction and games for children aged 4 and over and family groups.

Meadowside Leisure Centre, Tudway Road, Kidbrooke, SE3 (0181 856 0101). Saturdays roller hockey for over-12s and under-12s. Sundays family roller skating open sessions. Mondays tuition and grading. Also holiday programmes, speed skating and beginner sessions. Times vary. £1.60 (skate hire 50p).

Roehampton Recreation Centre, Laverstoke Gardens, SW15 (0181 871 7672).

Roller City, Campus West, The Campus, Welwyn Garden City, AL8 6BX (01707 339211). Weekdays noon-5pm; Wed 6-9pm; Fri 7-10pm; Sat & Sun 9.15-11.15am & 2-6pm. £2.50-£3.50 (includes skate hire).

Roller Express, Unit 16, Lea Valley Trading Estate, Angel Road, N18 (0181 807 7345). Regular family sessions (£3.50 pp inc skate hire). Light & sound shows, video games, burger bar, bouncy castle, ball pond, skate games, competitions, face painting.

SKATE HIRE:

Ellis Brigham Mountain Sports, 30-32 Southampton Street, WC2 (0171 240 9577). Ring for details.

Road Runner, Unit 002, Lancaster Road, W11 (0171 792 0584). Ring for details.

Skiing (dry ski slopes)

Alexandra Palace Ski Centre, Alexandra Park, N22 (0181 888 2284). Open Mon-Fri 2-10pm; Sat & Sun 10am-6pm. Four-lane slope and nursery slope. Private and group lessons available.

Beckton Dry Ski Slope, Alpine Way, E6 (0171 511 0351; near Royal Docks Waterski Club, Woolwich ferry and Thames Barrier). Open daily 10am-11pm. Lessons adults from £18, children from £12. Snowboard hire. Shop, bar, restaurant. All equipment hire included in the price.

Bromley Ski Centre, Sandy Lane, St Paul's Cray, Orpington, Kent (016898 76812). Instructor Olly Jeffrey gives 1-hour 'taster' lessons for £9 while a full course of six 1-hour lessons spread over 3 weeks costs £36 for children (adults £50). Smallest shoe size 5.

Crystal Palace Ski Slope, Ledrington Road, SE19 (0181 778 0131). Open Mon-Fri 9am-10pm, Saturday till 8pm, Sunday till 6pm. Nursery slope, courses from Oct-March. Saturdays and school hols Junior Ski Club. Children's boots from size 3.

Ski Club of Great Britain, 118 Eaton Square, SW1 (0171 245 1033). Send stamped addressed envelope for list of dry ski schools in London area.

Snowboarding

The British Snowboarding Association (01494 462225). Information on competitions, trips, clubs, camps.

Swimming

Water temperature for under-5s should be 82-84°F/28-29°C. Most indoor pools have mother-and toddler-sessions, special holiday programmes and lessons so phone your local pool or leisure centre for details. For kids who are really serious about swimming contact the **Amateur Swimming Association,** Harold Fern House, Derby Centre, Loughborough (01509 230431). **Royal Life Saving Society,** Mountbatten House, Studley, Warwickshire (01527 853943). **North London Rescue Commando** (0181 980 0289).

Central Swimming Club, Palace Pool, Fulham Palace Road, W6 (0171 359 1570). Sun 2-5pm for children of all ages. Individual tuition £160 for ten half-hour sessions, £80 for pairs. There are too many pools to list but the following are particularly interesting or good ones.

INDOOR POOLS

The Arches, Trafalgar Road, SE10 (0181 317 5000). Beach area, water flume, water cannon, volcanic eruptions, bubbling spring. Excellent for even small children (also good soft play gym for under-5s). Café. Creche and playpens. Family sessions Friday evenings.

Archway Leisure Centre, 14 Macdonald Road, Archway, N19 (0171 281 4105). Mon-Fri 3.30-6.30pm, Sat 11am-4pm, Sun 8.30am-4.30pm. School holiday weekdays 10am-7pm. Adults £2.80, children £1.40. Water jets, wave machine, water slide, river run, spa pool.

Baltham Leisure Centre, Elmfield Road, SW17 (0181 871 7196). Tues 2-4pm; mother-and-baby or toddler swimming sessions, £1.70. You can leave babies at the pool side in their buggies or swim with them. Baby-changing facilities. Good café provides high chairs. No creche.

Britannia Leisure Centre, 40 Hyde Road, N1 (0171 729 4485). Open Mon-Fri 9am-8.45pm, Sat & Sun 9am-5.45pm. Adults £2.50, children £1.25. Tropical setting with beach-style pool, wave machines, fountain and large slide. Summer holiday sessions with inflatables and floats. Wed 6-8.45pm women-only sessions.

Brixton Recreation Centre, Station Road, SW9 (0171 926 9779). Under-8s learner pool (parental supervision). Creche noon-8pm Mon-Fri, Sat & Sun 9am-8pm can also be used as play area for as long as you wish if you stay with your child. Very popular place with very reasonable prices.

Dolphin Swimming Club at JFS Pool, Camden Road, NW1 (0181 349 1844). Sunday swimming classes for children of all ages, up to Gold standard. 9.15am-12.15pm. Eleven individual half-hour lessons for £199; two in a group cost £99, five in a group £60.50. Ring for details.

Elephant and Castle Leisure Centre, 22 Elephant & Castle, SE1 (0171 582 5505). Adults £2.20, children 80p. Main pool with sloping edge, wave machine and enormous pink elephant slide. Very shallow toddlers' training pool. Inflatables in the pool in the afternoon. Good baby-changing facilities. Mother-and-baby sessions include instructor.

Fulham Pools, Normand Park, Lillie Road, SW6 (0171 385 7628; West Brompton BR). Parent-and-toddler sessions Mon-Fri 9.30am-noon. £1.80, children and concs £1. Sloping sides, wave machine, fountain, water slide into separate pool, water toys. Teaching pool. The water is very warm. High chairs and café/refreshments. Sessions for disabled children and adults some Sundays 3-5pm. Wave pool for parents and toddlers only, Mon-Fri 9.30am-noon. Children under 9 must be accompanied by an adult. Ring to check times of pool openings.

Jubilee Sports Centre, Caird Street, W10 (0181 960 9629). Mon-Fri 7am-8pm; Sat & Sun 8am-4pm. Weekend afternoons mother-and-baby sessions and family sessions. Creche.

Latchmere Leisure Centre, Latchmere Road, SW11 (0181 871 7470). Seashore slope into pool, wave machine, toddlers pool, slide and lots of greenery make this clean, modern pool very popular especially for the baby and toddler classes in the training pool on Mon, Tues & Fri. Playpens and changing mats available. Other clubs and activities available to children from tennis and fencing to judo and gymnastics.

Water Palace, 619 Purley Way, Croydon (0181 688 2090). Adults £5, 3–15-year-olds £4, under-3s free, family ticket (2+2 or 1+3) £16 (less during the week off peak). Tropical family 'paradise' built round a beach-style, tree-lined setting with a huge variety of water attractions in an indoor complex kept at 84°F/29°C. Six flume rides, geysers, gushers, water cannon, a Lazy River Trip, wave pool and rapids, kiddies harbour with frog slide. Shop, bar, soda bar, café, poolside tables and chairs, baby-changing facilities etc. Best for children over 4 (no creche or playpens) but kiddies harbour suitable for babies and toddlers. Children's Party Pack includes party meal, ice-cream, drinks, party bag and an inflatable birthday cake and card for the birthday child.

Waterfront Leisure Centre, High Street, Woolwich, SE18 (0181 317 5000). Mon-Sun 10am-1.30pm, 2-8pm. Adults

£3.50, children £2.50. Wave machines, waterfalls and 80m flume. Fun sessions.

OUTDOOR SWIMMING POOLS

Brockwell Lido, Brockwell Park, Dulwich Road, SE24 (0171 274 3088). Daily 10am-7pm. Recently reopened outdoor pool with toddlers' paddling area, café, therapy rooms and fitness complex.

The Oasis, 32 Endell Street, WC2 (0171 831 1804). Open all year Mon-Fri 7.30am-8pm; Sat & Sun 9.30am-5pm. Adults £2.50, children 85p. Central London's only heated outdoor pool, surrounded by a sundeck.

Parliament Hill Lido, (off Gordon House Rd), Parliament Hill, NW5 (0171 485 3873). Open daily 7-9.30am free, 10am-6.30pm adults £1.50, children 25p. Until late September.

Pools on the Park, Old Deer Park, Twickenham Road, Richmond (0181 940 0561). Outdoor pool open, weather permitting, until September. Mon-Fri 6.30am-8pm (Wed to 9pm); Sat & Sun 7am-7pm. Adults £2.50, 5–16-year-olds £2, under-5s free (various concs and season tickets). Also toddlers' and indoor pools.

Serpentine Lido, Hyde Park, W2 (0171 724 3104). Open until end of September daily 9-5pm. Adults £3, children £1.50. Lido is chlorinated.

Tooting Bec Lido, Tooting Bec Road, SW16 (0181 871 7198). Open daily 10am-7.30pm. Adults £2, children £1.50 (extra 60p at weekends). Huge unheated and often crowded pool, kid's play area with sandpit, grassy area for picnics and sunbathing and café.

Valentine's Open Air Pool, Brisbane Road, Illford, Essex (0181 554 3794). Open Tues-Sun noon-7pm until September. Adults £1.65, children 90p.

Tennis

Parks, recreation grounds and leisure centres usually have tennis courts (see relevant sections) and tennis clubs usually start coaching children over 7 years. Look out for short tennis courses for 6–10-year-olds. For more information contact **The Lawn Tennis Association,** Palliser Road, W14 (0171 385 2366).

Watersports

Docklands Sailing and Water Sports Centre, Kingsbridge, Westferry Road, Millwall Dock, E14 (0171 537 2626). Summer courses in July and August in sailing, windsurfing, dragon-boat racing, canoeing and rowing. Children from 9-18 years £1. Sailing every afternoon. Requirements: ability to swim 50 metres, parental/guardian permission, change of clothing, towel and suitable shoes. Special theme days such as Pirates Day and Beach Party.

Pirates Castle Watersports Centre, Oval Road, Camden, NW1 (0171 267 6605). Boat Club where over-8s can try canoeing.

Peter Chivers Windsurfing Centre, Gate 5, Tidal Basin Road, west end of Victoria Docks, E16 (0171 474 2500). Open April-Oct Tues-Sun dawn-dusk; Nov-March Sat & Sun dawn-dusk. Board Hire £5 per hour (children 7+ free). Very friendly venue which runs informal sessions for children to get them into the water. Recommended age 7 and over (depending on size) are given a board for a day or two to get them used to it, then the sail is put on.

Royal Docks Waterski Club, Gate No 16, King George V Dock, Woolwich, Manor Way, E16 (0171 511 2000). Open daily 10am-dusk (closed in January and February). Non-member fees, including equipment hire: 4 lessons £52; single lesson £15; day course (five tows) £50; half-day course (three tows) £35 (ring for membership prices). The most flexible waterski club as far as children are concerned. There is no age limit as long as the child is fairly confident about water. Ring in advance for one of the instructors to ski with the child (who in this case can be as young as 3 or 4 depending on size and temperament).

Thames Young Mariners, Ham Fields, Riverside Drive, Richmond (0181 940 5550). Dinghy training offered at all levels with courses especially for children (also orienteering and mountain biking).

Westminster Boating Base, Dinorvic Wharf, 136 Grosvenor Road, SW1 (0171 821 7389). Canoeing and sailing etc for 10-23-year-olds.

Learn to juggle, make a film, speak French, improve your maths and try your hand at mask-making, pottery or archaeology (see also Museums and Galleries, pages 57–86, for half-term and holiday activities).

Workshops

Arts and Craft

Battersea Arts Centre, Old Town Hall, Lavender Hill, SW11 (0171 223 2223). Saturday art-and-craft workshops and summer school with extensive workshops for under-5s and under-21-year-olds. Saturdays and 4 weeks in August; daily £5, weekly £22.50 (concs £20).

Bethnal Green Museum of Childhood, Cambridge Heath Road, E2 (0181 980 2415). Open workshops in the art room where work leaders offer activities for children of 3 and over. Saturdays 10am–5.50pm; free.

Busy Bees, Albercorn Place School, 28 Albercorn Place, NW8 (0171 286 0923). Activity weeks for 3–7-year-olds – cooking, art, craft, music, drama, outdoor games and a party on the last day; £95 per week.

Camden Arts Centre Arkwright Road, NW3 (0171 435 2643) Courses for 7–16-year-olds include painting, drawing, sculpture, print-making and ceramics. Saturday workshops and holiday courses; 10-week half-day workshop, £65.

Creative Wiz Kids (0171 794 6797 for details). A year-round programme of painting, movement and music for children from 6 months to 4 years based in St John's Wood and Fulham. Also customised parties for under-7s. Twelve one-hour sessions £72–£91; parties £70.

Lauderdale House, Waterlow Park, Highgate Hill, N6 (0181 348 8716). Art for 7–11-year-olds on Tuesdays and for 9–15-year-olds on Thursdays, covering still-life, portraiture and landscape; £45–£55 per term (various concessions).

Paint Pots (Montessori), Chelsea Christian Centre, Edith Grove (entrance Slaidburn Street), SW10 (info 0171 792 0433). July summer school with 3 weeks of arts, crafts, music and drama for children of 18 months–2 years, 2–3 and 3–6 years. Weekly classes for the same age ranges as summer school; £5–£35 per session, classes £96–£193 per term.

YMCA Youth Arts Centre, Drake House, 44 St George's Road, SW19 (0181 944 6974). Activities for 12–16-year-olds throughout the year with art and drama, circus skills, dancing, music, jewellery-making, day trips, etc. Weekly tickets £33, (single parents £23, DHS parents £14); daily rate £10, individual workshops £3.

Brass Rubbing

All Hallows-by-the-Tower, Byward Street, EC3 (0171 481 2928). A choice of 30 brasses. Price includes materials and tuition. Daily 11am–4pm; 75p–£4 per brass.

London Brass Rubbing Centre, St Martin-in-the-Fields, WC2 (0171 930 9306). Dozens of replica brasses to rub including a 7ft-tall knight, various animals, merchants and children. Monday–Saturday, 10am–6pm, Sunday noon–6pm; £1.50 to £12 per brass, depending on size.

Circus

Albert and Friends Instant Circus, St Paul's Church, Queen Caroline Street, Hammersmith, W6 (0181 741 5471). Circus workshops for children aged 3–8 and 9–16, including unicycling, stilt-walking and juggling, working towards end-of-term productions. After-school on Monday, Tuesday and Wednesday. Saturday morning drop-in sessions and summer holiday courses. Drop-in session £3.50–£4; £35–£40 per term, one-week course £65.

Circus UK Summer School, c/o Alternative Arts, 202b Brushfield Street, E1 (0171 375 0441), Children from 11–14 years can learn the art of juggling, stilt-walking, acrobatics, body-balancing and trapeze. Book early. Ring for details of venue; free.

Jackson's Lane Circus Skills Workshop, Jackson's Lane Community Centre, 269a Archway Road, N6 (0181 341 4421). Weekly classes in unicycling, stilt-walking and tightrope walking for 5–8-year-olds. £17.50 for 5 weeks – book early.

Computer Courses

Computer Workshops, 4 St John's Hill, SW11 (0171 585 2067). Imaginative and educational computer courses for children from 7 years. Simple reading, writing and problem solving for 5–6-year-olds. Courses usually last for one week; £50–£80.

Cooking

Le Cordon Bleu Culinary Institute, 114 Marylebone Lane, W1 (0171 935 3503). Les Petits Cordons Bleus is a series of 10 Saturday morning workshops for 8–14-year-olds. Long waiting list; £250 plus £16.40 for hat and apron.

Dance

For a list of teachers and local dance schools send a stamped, addressed envelope to Imperial Society of Teachers of Dancing, Euston Hall, Birkenhead Street, WC1 (0171 837 9967).

Battersea Arts Centre, Lower Hall, Old Town Hall, Lavender Hill, SW11 (0171 223 2223; 0181 679 1794). Christina Ross Dance. Creative movement for 3-year-olds, and fun ballet and tap for 4-year-olds. Formal ballet, modern dance and tap dance grade exams from 5 years to adults. Daily, £47–£56 for a £12-week term.

Carousel, Brompton Oratory, Knightsbridge (Sue Knowles on 0171 731 7921). Drama club for 3–10-year-olds. Saturday morning, half-term and holiday workshops. Saturday 10am–3pm, holidays 9.30am–4.30pm; £4 per hour.

Capoiera Workshops, Studio 3a, 22 Highbury Grove, N5 (0171 354 2084). Lessons for 6–12-year-olds in Capoeira, an Afro-Brazilian art form mixing dance, music, play and self-defence. Friday 4.30–6pm; £5 per class, £45 for 10 weeks.

Chisenhale Dance Space, 64–84 Chisenhale Road, E3 (0181 981 6617). Creative dance classes for children aged 2–15-years-old, divided into groups. Long waiting list. Tuesday morning and Saturday afternoon; £1.

Crazee Kids (ring Lisa on 0181 444 5333). Weekly classes in NW3 and N6, including creative movement, dance, drama and music through a wide range of activities for 3–5-year-olds; £5.25 per 45-minute class or £63 per term.

Dance Classes (0171 289 1869). Susan Zalcman's classes (pre-ballet for under-3s, ballet for over-3s, tap for over-5s) at Covent Garden, Marble Arch and Maida Vale.

Donald McAlpine Dance Studio, The Parish House, 330 Clapham Road, SW9 (0181 673 4992). Very good, friendly music and movement classes for under-5s (not really suitable for under-3s). Thursday at 2pm and 3pm, Friday at 4.15pm; £22 per term.

English Folk Song and Dance Society, Cecil Sharp House, 2 Regent's Park Road, NW1 (0171 485 2206). Members of the children's section, The Hobby Horse Club, receive newsletters, a badge, birthday card and list of festivals. Children's dance day once a month.

Greenwich Dance Agency, The Borough Hall, Royal Hill, SE10 (0181 293 9741). Dance Play for under-5s. Creative dance workshops with contemporary and African dance for 5–8-year-olds. Under-5s Wednesday 10.15–11am, 5–8-year-olds Saturday 10–11am; £2.50–£2.75.

Highbury Roundhouse, 71 Ronalds Road, N5 (0171 359 5916). Weekly term-time children's classes include under-5s creative dance, ballet, tap, drama, painting, karate and French; £1.75–£3.50 per class.

Islington Dance and Arts Factory, 2 Parkhurst Road, N7 (0171 607 0561). Classes for children from 12–16 including kit drumming, contemporary dance, band workshop, visual art workshop and ballet Grades 3 and 4. Ballet for 5–11-year-olds and dance theatre workshops for 8–13s and over-13s. Saturday and after school £20 per term.

Laban Centre, Laurie Grove, SE14 (0181 692 4070). Creative dance classes for 4–6-year-olds and 7–10-year-olds. Saturday; £18.20 per term.

Lauderdale House, Waterlow Park, Highgate Hill, N6 (0181 348 8716). Parent-and-toddler dance and creative dance for 3–4s, 4–5s, 5–6s with work towards an end-of-term performance for 7–11-year-olds; £30 per term.

Mini Movers, Rosslyn Hall, Willoughby Road, NW3 (01728 452253). Based on classical Greek dance, these classes are performed in bare feet and are suitable for 5–14-year-olds. Ring for times; £40 per term.

The Young Place, 17 Duke's Road, WC1 (0171 388 8956; details Julia Buckley). Classes in contemporary, jazz and dance composition for 5–18-year-olds. Youth Dance group for 10–16-year-olds. Saturday; from £45.

Royal Academy of Dancing, Vicarage Crescent SW11 (0171

223 0091). Classical ballet classes for 5–17-year-olds. Residential and non-residential summer schools for 8–12s and 10–14s. Entry to classes is by audition. Times by arrangement; prices vary.

Union Dance Summer School, Dance Works, 16 Balderton Street, W1 (0171 734 3262). Dance workshops in jazz, contemporary, ballet and tap classes, for 7–11s and 12–18s, working with professional dancers. There is also a choreographic workshop where participants create their own dance to be performed at the end of the week. No previous dance experience necessary. Book early. August; £10 (£5 for Westminster residents).

Vacani School of Dancing, Broomwood Hall, Kyrle Road, SW11 (0171 589 6110). Traditional ballet and dancing for over-4s, nursery rhymes and games to music for 2–4s. Branches all over London.

Drama

Anna Scher Children's Theatre, 70-72 Barnsbury Road, N1 (0171 278 2101). Excellent, imaginative after-school classes for over-5s in improvisation, poetry, production, stage technique and theatre production. Summer school acting courses. after-school and summer holidays, 10.30am–12.30pm (6–11s), 3–5pm (12–16s); £5 per session or £20 for 5 sessions if paid in advance.

Battersea Arts Centre Acting Factory and Summer School, Old Town Hall, Lavender Hill, SW11 (0171 223 2223). 'Acting Up' for 5–7s, 'Acting Around' for 8–11s, 'Acting Out' for 12–15s, Saturday and Wednesday throughout the year. Also summer school for 4 weeks in August for under-5s and under-21s, with extensive classes and workshops. Half-term workshops; from £20–£30 per term.

Drama Drama (0181 560 9893). Weekly term-time drama workshops for children aged 3–15 held at various venues in south and west London. Ring for times. Under-8s £3.50, over-8s £4.50 per session. Free trial, second child half-price.

Greenwich and Lewisham Young People's Theatre, Burrage Road, SE18 (0181 854 1316). Term-time workshops for 11–14,

14–17 and 16–25-year-olds covering drama and visual arts. Monday–Friday, evenings; £12 per term.

Group '64 Youth Theatre, 203b Upper Richmond Road, SW15 (0181 788 6943). Drama and improvisation games for 8–11, 12–14-year-olds and over 14s. Saturday morning and Wednesday evening; £2 per session.

Hampstead Performing Arts, 402 Finchley Road, NW2 (0171 431 9726). Regular music, dance and theatre workshops for children of all ages. From £3.00 per class.

Highbury Roundhouse, 71 Ronalds Road, N5 (0171 359 5916). Weekly term-time children's classes include creative dance, ballet, tap, drama, painting, karate and French for under-5s; £1.75-£3.50 per class. Singing for over-7s on Saturday morning.

Hot Tin Roof Theatre School (0171 485 3722) Union Chapel Project, Compton Avenue, N1 and Highbury Roundhouse, 71 Ronalds Road, N5. Drama sessions for ages 4-6, 7-10, 11-14 and 15-18-year-olds. Weekly after-school and Saturday mornings. Fun with improvisation, theatre games, theatre skills, self-expression; £3.50 per session (Saturday 3-hr session £6) or £42 per term (various concessions).

Islington Arts Factory, 2 Parkhurst Road, N7 (0171 833 4843). Summer courses for 7–12 and 13–17-year-olds culminating in a performance. Ring for details.

Mountview Theatre School, Ralph Richardson Memorial Studios, Clarendon Road, Wood Green, N22 (0181 889 8110). Saturday-morning activities for 6–12-year-olds, stage dance sessions for over-5s; £40-£50 per 11-week term.

National Youth Theatre, Holloway Road, N7 (0171 281 3863). Auditions held in February and March to select cast for plays to be rehearsed and performed during the summer holidays. Applications by December. For 14–21-year-olds.

Polka Theatre, 240 The Broadway, SW19 (0181 543 4888). Six- to 10-week courses for children from 18 months to 12 years. Workshops based on current production (£6-£25).

Questor's Theatre, Mattock Lane, W5 (0181 567 0011). High-standard amateur theatre. Drama playgroups for ages 5–9 with emphasis on imaginative play and role-playing activities (Saturday 11am; £1 per class). Junior drama workshops for ages 10-14: improvisation and acting exercises (weekday evenings, £5 per term). Older children's plays are performed for parents and friends. Long waiting list.

Stagetalk, 120 Heath Street, NW3 (0181 518 5657/531 5211). Holiday drama club for 6–11-year-olds. Games, improvisations, rehearsals for end-of-week production in New End Theatre; £65 per week with 10 per cent discount for siblings.

The Tree House, 18 Furley Road, SE15 (0171 252 8712). Every Saturday drama and performance workshops for 5–7-year-olds (2pm) and 8–14s (3.30pm). Under-5s arts nursery daily £15. Also weekly evening instrument and voice tuition.

Tricycle Theatre, 269 Kilburn High Road, NW6 (box office 0171 328 1000). Term-time drama workshops for children from 18 months to 16 years; £17 per term. Booking essential.

Unicorn Theatre, 6-7 Great Newport Street, WC2 (0171 836 3334/membership 0171 379 3280). Term-time and holiday theatre workshops. One-week summer school in August for children of 8 and over to learn stage-fighting, clowning, improvisation, script work, mask and mime, make-up, etc. A chance to perform on this West End stage for 8–14-year-olds. Good facilities and workshops for the disabled. From £6.50 per 2-hour workshop.

Watermans Arts Centre, 40 High Street, Brentford, Middlesex (0181 568 1176). Theatre Club including drama, improvisation and theatre games. School holidays workshops on a wide range of activities. Ring for times and prices.

Film

Children's Film Unit, 9 Hamilton House, 66 Upper Richmond Road, SW15 (0181 871 2006). Film-making for 8–16-year-olds including acting, camera skills, make-up, script-writing, sound, etc. Saturday; £10 membership, £2 per workshop.

Music Workshops

Fun with Music, 2 Queensmead, St John's Wood Park, NW8 (0171 722 9828). Musical appreciation through colouring books and instruments for three-and-a-half to 5-year-olds. Musical story sessions for 5–6 and 7–11-year-olds. Waiting list. From £110 (+VAT) for 9-week term.

Honeywell School, Honeywell Road, SW11 (0171 223 6369). Daily after-school classical piano working towards jazz piano for 4-12-year-olds (and over-12s). Individual lessons £6 per half hour.

Janet Sodring Spectrum Singers, 19 Combe Road, W4 (0181 994 8149). Beginners' singing for 6–8s and soloists aged 9–14. Teens in harmony for 11–14-year-olds. Ring for times and prices.

Lewisham Academy of Music, 77 Watson's Street, SE8 (0181 691 0307). Workshops for 5–14-year-olds in guitar, bass, drums, piano, keyboard and instrument-making; free.

London College of Music, Thames Valley University, St Mary's Road, Ealing, W5 (0181 231 2304). Junior music school for children 4–17 where they can learn one or two instruments, speech, drama, theory and oral work. Range from average to highly talented. Times and prices vary.

London School of Singing, 18 Cranhurst Road, NW2 (0181 452 5502). Sets very high standards and progress is rapid for children over nine wanting to sing seriously or for pleasure. Four private lessons for £80.

Tafelmusik (Chelsea and St John's Wood 0171 376 5201; Wimbledon 0181 874 3670). Creative music workshops for 1–8-year-olds. 'Starter' sessions for 3–8-year-olds in guitar, recorder, piano and violin. Ring for details.

Under-Fives Music, 7 Broomwood Road, SW11 (0171 350 2921). Percussion, musical games and songs for under-2s, 2–4s, and over-4s. Trial lesson available; £2.75 (concs £2).

Languages and Tutorials

Busy Bees, Albercorn Place School, 28 Albercorn Place, NW8 (0171 286 0923). The A-Scheme for over-6s — holiday English, Maths, French, Latin and Spanish; £95 per week.

Computer Courses (0171 585 2067 for details). Alison Townsend runs fun short courses including Child and Parent Typing and using the computer as a tool for learning.

The **Kumon Maths** (centres all over the country; for details phone 0181 343 3307). Kumon maths is most suited to children either more advanced than their class mates or those lagging behind; £15, then £35 per month.

Le Club Français (01962 714036). Courses for children aged 3–11 incorporating games, sports, crafts, cookery and drama. Centres all over London. Ring for details.

Le Club Frère Jacques (0171 354 0589). Clubs in south and west London. Children from 3–11 learn French through games, songs, rhymes and role-playing. All teachers are French. From £56 per 12-week term (half-hour sessions).

Le Club Tricolore (0171 924 4649). In a well-structured but fun club atmosphere children of 5–11 years learn French through songs, raps, games, role-play and activity sheets with qualified language teachers. Venues in Putney, Dulwich, Wimbledon, Hampstead, Chelsea, etc. Ring for details.

Le Petit Ecole (contact Beatrice Paton 0181 876 7596 or Nicole Beaumont 0181 948 6326). Workshops for 3-8 upwards, learning French through games, songs and video; £35 per term (half-hour sessions).

Club Petit Pierrot (0171 828 2129). Learn French through using stories, songs, dance and role-play for two-and-a-half to six-year-olds; £95 per 10-week term (1-hour sessions).

The Tutorial School, The New Learning Centre, 211 Sumatra Road, NW6 (0171 794 0321/5328). Short holiday and after-school courses to help with revision, school entrance exams and homework habits. Ring for details.

Self-defence

Capoiera Workshops, Studio 3a, 22 Highbury Grove, N5 (0171 354 2084). Lessons for 6–12-year-olds in Capoeira, an Afro-Brazilian art form mixing dance, music, and self-defence.; £5 per class, £45 for 10 weeks, £75 for 20 weeks.

Stand Your Ground, Quindo Centre, 2 West Heath Drive, NW11 (0181 455 8698). Quindo anti-bullying self-defence courses, aimed at boosting the confidence of children who encounter the distress of bullying, and teaching them self-defence. Courses £30-£40.

Sometimes you may find yourself in need of a helping hand in London — especially when you're with
small children. If you find yourself in deep water
with no means of escape, refer to this section
for advice.

ACE (Advisory Centre for Education), Unit 1B, Aberdeen Studios, 22-24 Highbury Grove, N5 (0171 354 8321). Advice line open Monday–Friday 2–5pm providing free help and advice for parents, students, governors and others in education.

Artsline, 5 Crowndale Road, NW1 (0171 388 2227). This is an arts advice and information service which gives details of places, events and activities and their accessibility to disabled people.

Childline, Addle Hill Entrance, Faraday Building, Queen Victoria Street, EC4 (Freephone 0800 1111). This is the national 24-hour helpline for kids. You can phone them with any problem and they have a team of experienced councellors and volunteers who offer support and advice.

Childminders, 9 Paddington Street, W1M 3LA (0171 935 2049; 24-hr info 0171 935 9763). Reliable babysitting service which covers Clapham, Battersea and South London. £38 membership, then minimmum £3.15 per hour (weekday evening rate, minimum four hours).

Gingerbread, 16-17 Clerkenwell Close, EC1R 0AA (0171 336 8183). The association for single parent families which will put you in touch with local groups. They also organise after-school and holiday activities for children with a working parent.

Handicapped Adventure Playground Association, Fulham Palace, Bishops Avenue, SW6 (0171 736 4443). Specially designed playgrounds for handicapped children can be used during holidays and on Saturdays by individual families with handicapped children and their siblings. There are also youth clubs, camping trips and holiday playschemes.

MAMA (Meet a Mum Association), 14 Willis Road, Croydon (0181 665 0357). Local groups and one-to-one contacts.

Message Home (Freephone 0500 700 740). If you have run away and want to get a message home without anyone knowing where you are, you can leave a message on this answer phone and it will be passed on.

National Council for One-Parent Families, 255 Kentish Town Road, NW5 2LX (0171 267 1361). Call for advice on all aspects of single-parenting.

National Eczema Society, 163 Eversholt Street, NW1 1BU (0171 388 4097). Practical advice and moral support.

One O'Clock Clubs and Play Centres. These are usually situated in parks and consist of an outdoor play area, with an indoor area for bad weather and special events. Staff on hand but parents or carers must be responsible for their children at all times. Open weekdays (including school holidays) from 1–5pm in summer, noon–4pm in winter. Charge to cover refreshments. Ask your health visitor for information.

Parents At Work, 77 Holloway Rd, N7 (0171 628 3578 on Tues, Wed or Fri 9am-1pm.). An association which offers information on childcare and will put you in touch with local working mother groups.

Parent Line Endway House, The Endway, Hadley, Byfleet, Essex SS7 2AN (01702 559900) to obtain details of regional help. Helpline for parents under stress or in need of advice.

Playgroups. The Pre-School Playgroups Association (PPA), 69 Kings Cross Road, WC1 (0171 833 0991). Playgroups are a good half-way house between home and the more formal atmosphere of nursery school.

Pippa Pop-Ins, 430 Fulham Road, SW6 (0171 385 2457). Children's hotel open day and night, by appointment. Guests aged 2-12 years book in after 4.30pm; £25-£30 per night.

Samaritans (0171 734 2800 – 24-hr helpline). They are there to listen to and offer support for anyone of any age with emotional problems of any kind. Nothing is too trivial and all calls are confidential.

Universal Aunts (0171 386 5900) This organisation deals with any domestic crisis, from providing babysitters, meeting kids from the train, to taking children out for the day.

Emergencies

Dial 999 or 112 for police, fire and ambulance services. The calls are free. There are 24-hour casualty departments at:

Central Middlesex Hospital, Acton Lane, NW10 (0181 965 5733). There is no separate A&E department for children.

Charing Cross Hospital, Fulham Palace Rd, W6 (0181 846 1009). There is no separate A&E department for children.

Chelsea and Westminster Hospital, Fulham Road, SW10 (0181 746 8000). There is a separate A&E department for children.

Greenwich District Hospital, Vanburgh Hill, SE10 (0181 858 8141). There is no separate A&E department for children.

Guy's Hospital, St Thomas Street, SE1 (0171 955 5000) There is a separate A&E department for children.

Hackney and Homerton Hospital, Homerton Row, E9 (0181 919 5555). There is no separate A&E department for children.

Hammersmith Hospital, 150 Du Cane Road, W12 (0181 740 3030). There is no separate A&E department for children.

Lewisham Hospital, Lewisham High Street, SE13 (0181 333 3000). There is a separate A&E department for children.

Medical Express (Private Casualty Centre), 117a Harley Street, W1 (0171 499 1991). Treatment is guaranteed within half an hour but a fee is charged for consultation (from £70) and treatment.

Royal Free Hospital, Pond Street, NW3 (0171 794 0500). There is no separate A&E for children.

St Georges Hospital, Blackshaw Road, SW17 (0181 672 1255). There is a separate A&E department for children.

St Thomas's Hospital, Lambeth Palace Road, SE1 (0171 928 9292). There is a separate A&E department for children.

Whittington Hospital, St Mary's Wing, Highgate Hill, N19 (0171 272 3070). There is no separate A&E department for children.

University College Hospital, Grafton Way, WC1 (0171 387 9300). There is a separate A&E department for children.

For dental emergencies call **Dental Emergency Care** (24hrs) 0181 837 3646. For advice on the phone for any illness or health problem call **Medical Advisory Service Healthline** (0181 994 9874). A list of 24 hour and duty **chemists** can be obtained from your local police station at any time of day or night. **Bliss Chemist** at 5 Marble Arch W1 (0171 723 6116) is open 9am-midnight daily all year

Index

Index

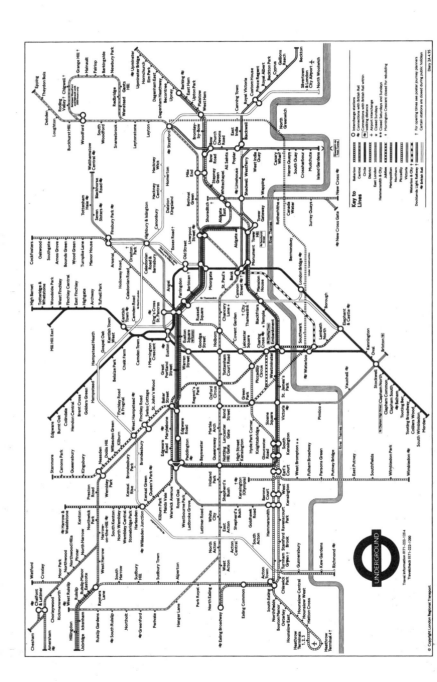